BLACK

BLACK OSCARS

FROM MAMMY TO MINNY, WHAT THE ACADEMY AWARDS TELL US ABOUT AFRICAN AMERICANS

Frederick W. Gooding Jr.

ROWMAN & LITTLEFIELD
Lanham • Boulder • New York • London

Published by Rowman & Littlefield
An imprint of The Rowman & Littlefield Publishing Group, Inc.
4501 Forbes Boulevard, Suite 200, Lanham, Maryland 20706
www.rowman.com

6 Tinworth Street, London, SE11 5AL, United Kingdom

British Library Cataloguing in Publication Information Available

Library of Congress Cataloging-in-Publication Data

Names: Gooding, Frederick W., Jr., author.
Title: Black Oscars : from mammy to minny, what the Academy Awards tell us about
　　African Americans / Frederick Gooding Jr.
Description: Lanham : Rowman & Littlefield, 2020. | Includes bibliographical
　　references and index. | Summary: "Frederick W. Gooding Jr. provides a thorough
　　analysis and overview of black people that were nominated for their Hollywood
　　roles, going decade by decade in highly accessible language. The book shows how
　　the Oscars are a litmus test, ultimately reflecting what degree our society has truly
　　embraced diversity within the hallowed confines of our sacred imaginations."
　　—Provided by publisher.
Identifiers: LCCN 2019050171 (print) | LCCN 2019050172 (ebook) |
　　ISBN 9781538123720 (cloth) | ISBN 9781538123737 (epub)
Subjects: LCSH: Academy Awards (Motion pictures) | African American motion
　　picture actors and actresses. | African Americans in the motion picture industry.
Classification: LCC PN1993.92 .G66 2020 (print) | LCC PN1993.92 (ebook) |
　　DDC 791.43079—dc23
LC record available at https://lccn.loc.gov/2019050171
LC ebook record available at https://lccn.loc.gov/2019050172

♾️™ The paper used in this publication meets the minimum requirements of American
National Standard for Information Sciences—Permanence of Paper for Printed Library
Materials, ANSI/NISO Z39.48-1992.

To my queen, Sharon; my future, Frederick and Saja; and my "road dog," Ms. Puppy—this is the preferred company I keep when watching and enjoying movies. Truly, we have "scene" it all together.

CONTENTS

ACKNOWLEDGMENTS

This work would not be possible without the contributions of others, whether they are luminaries in the field, such as Donald Bogle or Sheila Yvonne, or the humane librarians staffed at the Margaret Herrick Library of the Academy of Motion Picture Arts and Sciences. Additionally, funds from TCU's Research and Creative Activities Fund aided me in spending valuable research time in California. Had I been rushing, I would not have been relaxed enough to strike up pleasant conversation with Herrick Library staff, who facilitated my holding an actual Oscar statuette in my own hands!

Lastly, I wish to acknowledge the families of all the Black Oscar nominees and the Black nominees themselves—it is not easy being in the spotlight, let alone having one's image scrutinized and analyzed. The roles discussed herein are not being criticized inasmuch as they are being critiqued—may we all grow as we go accordingly.

INTRODUCTION

Setting the Stage:
What's So Oscar Worthy?

THERE'S NOTHING LIKE A GOOD MOVIE

At the risk of sounding melodramatic, what force on earth is capable of

transporting us across time and space alike?
tickling our imaginations in a flash of light?
whether midday or in the middle of the night, showing us new worlds that
amaze and delight?

Modern American, mainstream Hollywood movies, of course!

Anyone who has had the pleasure of watching a good movie intrinsically knows how truly transformative an experience it can be. A well-crafted movie can move people to tears, provide ample fodder for inside jokes, change one's behavior or thoughts, and create community.[1] In full recognition of all of these powers and more, once a year, with the fluid faithfulness of a rising tide, our world beckons the possibilities of this shared imagination that harbors our biggest dreams, fuels our wildest imaginations, and nurtures our most far-fetched fantasies. Since we value movies and especially appreciate the good ones, our society collectively reflects upon the *best* that the moviemaking world had to offer us the year prior, as so many of us remain in fascination and veneration of a form of storytelling that continues to captivate and amaze.

With the two words "Envelope, please," nominees (and especially winners) become memorialized as part of the annual internationally televised Academy

Awards show presented by the Academy of Motion Picture Arts and Sciences (AMPAS). And so, our business here: The purpose of this book is to document this star-studded annual event from an African American perspective. Given the immense popularity and influence of Hollywood movies generally and of the Academy Awards specifically, it is equally important to assess both the quantity and quality of African American participation over the years within this shared imaginative space and to analyze whether such imagery reflects our terrestrial reality. Here, we will explore whether the boundless realm of our collective, shared imagination (as produced by Hollywood) is unburdened by the gravity, friction, or inertia of historical racial restrictions. Since the Academy Awards are designed to celebrate the best of what our seemingly endless and possibility-filled movie world has to offer, this will be a space to consider what Academy Award recognition (through nomination or actual win) tells us not just about African Americans but also about the greater America in which they live here in the real world.

NOW SHOWING

Many readers may be familiar with the age-old philosophical adage: "If a tree falls in the forest and no one hears it, does it make a sound?" This thought experiment was designed to question our understanding of perception and experience, which can be extrapolated to the larger concept that an event may not have meaning for us individually if we are unaware of its occurrence. Yet with the high-profile, heavily hyped media extravaganza known as the Academy Awards, no such puzzling intellectual conundrum exists; the Academy is quite vocal in trumpeting its star-studded event. The founders of the Academy Awards envisioned a ceremony that represented more than a modest commendation for good work; this ceremony was conceived as a full-fledged production worthy of public celebration.

Produced annually by AMPAS, this industrywide event, more than three hours long on network television, is now televised in 225 countries.[2] Also affectionately and commonly known as the Oscars, these awards are more than a mere ceremony—they are a phenomenon. More so than the amorphous, loosely organized, multifaceted entities that comprise Hollywood, the Oscars are the high-profile intersection where fantasy, fashion, beauty, romance, high class, and success all collide. The Academy Awards are such a spectacle that they are "generally the most-watched entertainment program of the year, often only second to the [National Football League's] Super Bowl."[3]

Such immense interest in the Academy Awards suggests that viewers and the media are genuinely interested not just in the movies but in all the culture, pomp, and circumstance that surrounds them. Such sustained interest generally helps explain how theme parks like Disney's Hollywood Studios or Universal Studios generate billions annually as movie fans of all types attempt to literally see behind the scenes. Enthusiasm for the Academy Awards is so high that fans line up for hours to catch a glimpse of their favorite celebrities, while those who sagely stay at home can see the televised reports the following day about which movie star's outfit was most elegant. Richard Dyer, who pioneered the study of film stars in the mid-1980s, argues, "Stars matter because they act out aspects of life that matter to us; and performers get to be stars when what they act out matters to enough people."[4] Thus, movies and the attendant movie star system promote collective escapism at its highest level when considering the public's desire to fawn over glamorous celebrity red carpet wardrobe choices in tabloid magazines and on social media.

Unsurprisingly, the Academy Awards are eagerly anticipated in the weeks before the awards, following the public announcement of the nominees, and are heavily discussed and debated in the weeks afterward. Due to the show's ginormous audience, the Academy Awards are able to command an eye-popping $2 to $3 million for thirty-second commercials during the televised broadcast.[5] Hence, the Academy Awards are one area where traditional rules of social justice are relaxed. Fans may be too occupied admiring their favorite stars to notice that all nominees benefit from gift bags that contain nearly $150,000 worth of merchandise. High-priced vendors willingly line up to contribute to these bags because of the high-profile exposure they receive in turn.[6] And it is not just the adjacent vendors who benefit, but the nominees themselves. Merely by being nominated, most actors and actresses find a mere nomination to be career changing, often experiencing an "Oscar bounce," whereby their commanding rates and popularity increase as a direct result of Academy Award exposure.[7]

How did an event built around celebrating movies become even bigger than the movies themselves? Well, it all started in 1927 at the home of one of the premier movie moguls, Louis B. Mayer of Metro-Goldwyn-Mayer Studios (MGM). MGM "was known as the biggest and the best of the major studios,"[8] which suggests that the original idea behind the Academy Awards was far from altruistic. The gathering was not so much a means to exalt the craft of filmmaking as it was an opportunity to shore up a relatively new industry that was unsure of its future—with those leading the charge to self-organize coincidentally standing to profit the most. The genius brainchild that resulted from this intimate dinner meeting of four White males[9] was an annual ceremony to celebrate key contributors within the filmmaking community and that also served as a clever way for the industry to protect itself in the midst of uncertainty surrounding outside censorship and early internal scandal.[10]

The early Academy Awards ceremonies looked remarkably different from the three-hour extravaganzas they have become. There was not nearly as much pomp and circumstance, and in fact the winners of the first awards ceremony, in 1929, were announced as much as three months ahead of time. For subsequent ceremonies, awardees were revealed to the press on the day of the event, but it was not until 1940—when the *Los Angeles Times*, impatient to meet an 11:00 p.m. deadline, printed the results prematurely—that the Academy decided to switch to the still-observed tradition of utilizing envelopes to protect and seal the winners as a complete surprise.[11] No ordinary envelope will suffice; as AMPAS prefers a special type of austere quality, Oscar envelopes are one-eighth inch thick and stamped with gold paper inside, taking several weeks to craft using materials imported from Germany.[12]

However, the Academy Awards are not synonymous with golden-lined envelopes. Likely the most enduring symbol of arguably the most prestigious of all televised award shows, is the Oscar itself. "Oscar" is the nickname given to the gold statuette bestowed upon named winners at the ceremony—with the official name "Academy Award of Merit," a nickname certainly does not hurt. The use of the name Oscar has several stories attached to it, which is not uncommon for a name that has grown to be so famous. According to AMPAS, the Academy Awards ceremony itself was first officially referred to affectionately as "the Oscars" in 1939.[13] As further evidence that the statuette has become an iconic representation of the entire enterprise, the very first image on the AMPAS website (http://www.oscars.org) is a close-up shot of the statuette (stylized in a slick black-and-white video montage).

Weighing eight and a half pounds and measuring thirteen and a half inches in height, the Oscar statuette (as it is called, not statue) represents a crusading knight. Closer inspection reveals a sword clasped in the hands at the middle of the faceless statue. Moreover, the knight is standing on a film reel with five spokes that represent the five original branches of the Academy: producers, directors, actors, technicians, and writers.[14] This simple, elegant design more than fulfills its purpose—the Oscar has become an international symbol of the highest recognition for a popular art form.

RED CARPET TREATMENT

The first iteration of the Academy Awards had a modest twelve categories; there are now twenty-five categories in which one can be nominated for (and win) a competitive Oscar. Since this book focuses upon what the awards say about African Americans and their position in America, the glamor categories—the acting and supporting acting awards—will be given the most attention. African Americans have a long and storied history with film generally and within Hollywood specifically, with many having played crucial and instrumental roles both in front of and behind the camera. However, not only do certain awards command more attention due to their relative significance (e.g., Best Picture as opposed to Best Short Subject), but when most people reflect upon their movie-watching experience, it is the characters' actions from a movie that remain most prominent in mind. In other words, of all the moving parts required to make a motion picture, actors command a disproportionate amount of attention by audiences. In fact, if the others involved in making a film have done their job correctly, then audiences are able to focus exclusively upon the actors without being distracted by the detail that the movie is ultimately not *real*.

In Oscar parlance, references are often made colloquially to the "Big Five" Academy Awards: Best Picture, Best Director, Best Actor, Best Actress, and Best Screenplay. However, in analyzing Academy Awards won by African Americans, the crux of our focus concerns the following four categories: Best Actor, Best Actress, Best Supporting Actor, and Best Supporting Actress. African Americans have indeed won awards in other categories,[15] but this alternate presence has typically been statistically too small to merit more investigation and analysis for patterns over time. For example, in the whole history of the ninety-one years of the Academy Awards, only one Black director has ever claimed the award for Best Picture: Steve McQueen for the 2013 film *12 Years a Slave*.[16] (No Black director has ever won in the category of Best Director.) It must be noted that McQueen is British, not American. While he may be a Black Oscar winner, that he is not an *African American* Oscar winner only speaks to the institutional and structural barriers many African Americans continue to face within their own country when it comes to generating their own images for mainstream society to share.[17]

African Americans are in a unique, poorly leveraged position, since most of their iconography sold to the public is invented, crafted, and created by those with no direct relation to the African American experience. While there is no law forbidding this, we must consider how such imagery and messaging might be different if more African Americans had more agency in their creation. Accordingly, the four acting categories combined make for the largest collective representation of African American images by the Academy, so we will concentrate our energies on the visually dominant acting categories, those Oscar nominations that typically receive the most red carpet treatment.

BUT WHY MEMORIALIZE MOVIES?

Before we get too far afield, a reasonable inquiry possibly posed by our audience might be, "But what exactly is so important about the movies?" The answer is, quite simply, that movies have a documented profound social impact upon society. Consider that "in 1942, recognizing the importance of motion pictures and the need to preserve them as a historical record, the Library [of Congress] began the collection of the films themselves."[18] The Library of Congress justifies such a collection by remarking that the movies "are not selected as the 'best' American films of all time, but rather as works of enduring importance to American culture. They reflect who we are as a people and as a nation."[19]

Psychologists and sociologists differ about the full extent of movies' impact upon society, as it is difficult to draw direct correlations. Yet it is equally difficult to deny that movies capture the imagination, time, and attention of many, in contrast to other forms of media such as magazines or newspapers. One writer reflects that "movies, in the United States at least, become more than stories or pastimes. They function as myths that are an integral part of the process through which we remember history, interpret experience, and prescribe a course for future action."[20]

This sentiment that movies reflect "who we are" and become shared "myths" for remembering societal and historical experiences off-screen is only underscored by the movie studios' original intention to disseminate their packaged images within controlled environments. While movies can indeed be shared in public parks, classrooms, or downtown squares, the original model calls for movies to be released in quiet, darkened public theater spaces on screens that are literally larger than life.[21] This unique environment is especially suited for concentrating the audience's attention on the world portrayed within the visible continuum, or the known events that occur between a movie's opening and closing credits.[22] In fact, when the moviemakers perform their task correctly, viewers can get into a movie and possibly forget—for at least ninety minutes—where their car is parked or even who is seated directly to their left or right inside the theater.[23] To this extent, "film acts out an interaction with a world, which thus becomes a mirror for us to [recognize] *our* interaction with our world."[24]

In recognition of the powerful impact of this unique environment, it is not coincidental that early theaters were hallowed, palatial spaces that reflected the capacity of the austere experience moviegoers could expect. Grand lobbies, sweeping staircases, and ornate designs on the walls and ceilings are just a few features that proud movie theaters boasted. While movies may not accurately convey all aspects of societal life, they often reflect and reinforce existing ideas or trends within mainstream society—even if only aspirational.

When we speak of African Americans, however, we must recognize that for much of Hollywood's early history, these palatial spaces were also racially segregated spaces. Segregated theaters, if they accommodated African Americans at all, allowed African Americans to sit in only the balcony or scheduled separate viewing times when no Whites were in the theater.[25] But one place where all patrons were treated relatively equally was at the box office, where all money was accepted just the same.[26] During Hollywood's early years, movie watching skyrocketed in popularity as leisure time and disposable income increased. Movie watching quickly became an affordable activity that was easily scaled for large audiences several times a day within densely populated metropolitan areas. By 1946, "a weekly average of ninety million Americans—roughly 75 percent of the country's total population—attended the movies."[27]

More than seventy years later, the mainstream movie business remains a significant enterprise indeed, as movies generated $11.9 billion domestically and $41.7 billion in global box office sales in 2018.[28] The lucrative nature of the movie business is even more staggering when factoring in additional revenue streams through multiple on-demand streaming services, soundtracks, licensed merchandise, endorsement deals, and video game spinoffs, to name just a few. Since movies produced in Hollywood are shown in more than 150 countries worldwide, the US film industry provides the majority of movies seen in millions of homes worldwide.[29] Hollywood mainstream movies enjoy unparalleled exposure throughout the nation and the world over.

It follows that with this unparalleled exposure comes the opportunity for unparalleled influence. Given the high-risk investment opportunities mainstream movies present, every film is the result of considerable care and planning—even those deemed bad or commercially unsuccessful. Substantial amounts of time, energy, and thought go into the innumerable decisions made about how a movie's images are portrayed and what feelings they will evoke if properly depicted. Indeed, some films "are invested with extraordinary amounts of cultural capital, remaining in the public consciousness and even entering political discourse."[30] Movies that claim the Best Picture Oscar may certainly qualify in this regard.

As Hollywood mainstream movies reflect and reinforce public sentiment, it is incumbent upon moviegoers today to think critically and analyze not only the images created and distributed by Hollywood but also the images that are most widely circulated, celebrated, and lauded as part of American iconography. Thinking critically about mainstream media offers a creative but revealing lens toward understanding African Americans' political and positional relationship within the United States generally. Specifically analyzing Black Oscars over the years contributes toward this critical inquiry, since those Black images canonized by the Oscars beg for further analysis and understanding, as they reflect and reinforce race relations within mainstream society outside the theater. Many a movie may come and go from the movie theater, but Black Oscar winners (and nominees) are historically here to stay. It is now time to explore the meanings of those images hidden within plain view and see what they say.

Spoiler Alert!
Reading further may result in the revelation
of key plot points for the movies referenced herein.

LIGHTS, CAMERA, ANALYSIS!

MORE THAN MEETS THE EYE

Films can fool us. We can capture images with our eyes but miss any larger symbolism the images suggest. In other words, we can watch a sequence intently and yet unintentionally overlook its significance hidden in plain sight! Race, just like any other observable phenomenon on-screen during the visible continuum, certainly means *something* to both the moviemakers and the audience, but figuring out exactly what that is can be difficult and is subject to speculation. Here, we aim to narrow this space between the intended and interpreted symbology of race using some consistent rubrics for analysis. This important consistency is possible because movies as a medium of study represent unchanging texts: The film *Gone with the Wind* first shown in 1939 is the *exact same film* offered as in-flight entertainment on Delta Airlines in 2019.[1] Thus, viewers today have the opportunity to watch the same unchanging text that moviegoers saw upon its release decades earlier. However, what can change is our analytical approach to what we see. Thus, this book represents throwing down the proverbial gauntlet in order to better organize our difficult dialogues about race at the movies.

While readers are naturally free to argue and debate the findings here, the presumption is that readers will do so *only using evidence available from the fixed visible continuum of the movie as originally made*. In other words, all the analysis contained within this book is based upon observable material in the movies discussed. Returning to our *Gone with the Wind* example, readers may disagree with our bottom-line analysis that Hattie McDaniel's Mammy character played a subjugated role; some may argue that Mammy actually exerted power and control in her own clever, subtle, and subversive way.[2] While we may disagree about the extent to which Mammy exerted power—assuming that she did so—there is no debate that McDaniel played an enslaved Black housemaid (complete with head scarf and apron) whose official character name was "Mammy" (as opposed to Barbara Smith). It is also a fact that the Academy chose to recognize and honor this role during an era in society where racial segregation was deemed the law of the land. What must be determined is what this image meant then and what the continued memorialization of this iconography means now.

Currently, many Black characters fulfill a wide range of roles in mainstream movies much like their White counterparts, albeit at a lower rate, based upon data from the Screen Actors Guild, the predominant union that governs all public appearances of actors for pay in Hollywood.[3] Therefore, if and when Black characters appear on-screen, any disparaging and marginalizing images may have a disproportionately negative impact, especially considering the paucity of prominently featured non-Whites in leading mainstream roles, which are generally reserved for White (male) protagonists.[4] However, Hollywood's modern era operates in an age where blatant displays of discrimination and racism are publicly frowned upon. Such overtly stereotypical images do not appear as frequently as they did in the past, yet many minorities remain marginalized.[5]

Our task here is to explore whether the pattern of marginalization for Blacks in mainstream movies has been remarkably consistent throughout the history of Hollywood and the Academy Awards. While the Academy may not be responsible for racially problematic content appearing within individually nominated movies per se, of interest is whether the Academy has been consistent in awarding *and rewarding* racially problematic images of African Americans. Thus, the aim of this book is to focus on the overall quantity *and quality* of these Black Oscar–nominated character roles, as it is no secret that Hollywood still struggles with finding opportunities to include Black characters. For instance, in a 2019 academic report entitled "Inequality in 1,200 Popular Films: Examining Portrayals of Gender, Race/Ethnicity, LGBTQ & Disability from 2007 to 2018," Stacy L. Smith offers insights such as that one-third of the top one hundred films of 2018 contained no Black females whatsoever, which was an improvement over the fewer than half that included Black females in 2015.[6]

While the number of Black actors generally and Black Oscar nominees specifically has undoubtedly grown, with the decades of 2000–2009 and 2010–2019 scoring twenty-two acting nominations apiece (in contrast to 1940–1949, when there was only one), what remains to be interrogated is the *quality* of such Oscar-worthy performances as a reflection of society's valuation of Blacks.[7] To better explore whether Black actors[8] have been typecast in subjugated positions or have been able to evolve over time, I employ an analytical rubric to assess true Black worth within mainstream spaces. Just as the Oscar statuette's golden knight stands upon five different reels representing the most important aspects of filmmaking, virtually all Black Oscar performances recognized by the Academy—whether through nomination or win—can be analyzed by five distinct characteristics or Black Oscar Angles.

BLACK OSCAR ANGLES

Black Non-American

Why Is It Significant?

This categorization specifies whether the Black image seen on-screen during the movie is indeed an *African American* image. This topic has been debated more vigorously in recent times, with a variety of prominent voices weighing in on the issue, especially in light of several high-profile Black roles going to non–African Americans. For example, *Get Out*, the groundbreaking 2017 "racial horror" movie conceptualized by Jordan Peele, nabbed leading Black British actor Daniel Kaluuya a Best Actor Oscar nomination. In response, fellow Black Oscar nominee Samuel L. Jackson mused on New York radio, "I tend to wonder what that movie would have been with an American brother who really feels that."[9] Jackson's comments opened up debates over whether British actors were more successful landing such roles because they are traditionally classically trained through stage production experience.

Yet the purpose of this category is not to raise questions about the performers as it relates to *craft*, as generally an actor has a job to do and cannot be faulted for taking advantage of an occasion to display their skill. This category is designed instead to raise questions against Hollywood as it relates to *opportunity*, both individually and structurally. Individually, historically documented socioeconomic restraints may heavily preclude many young African American children from even considering a life dedicated to acting, with the necessary lessons and crucial familial support. Structurally, based upon the challenging and at times racially restrictive employment trends in this country, this angle of analysis highlights the limited number of opportunities African Americans specifically have in the United States to showcase their collective image and to tell their stories—most especially those "which are explicitly about America's own turbulent racial history."[10]

What Are We Looking For?

• Black movie stars who claim heritage or citizenship outside the United States.

Crossover

Why Is It Significant?

This designation notes whether the nominee's career originated with acting and exposes how little Hollywood invests in developing classically trained actors rather than taking the easier, less resource-intensive and more marketing friendly approach of utilizing Black entertainers who already have significant name recognition and therefore represent a smaller financial risk at the box office. Thus, not all Black movie *stars* are necessarily Black movie *actors* insofar as Hollywood frequently employs crossover talents already known within mainstream media.

At issue is how—most especially with big-budget movies—Hollywood executives consider the employment of already established Black talent who bring to the theater name recognition as a prudent means of hedging their financial exposure, as "the inclusion of a [well-known] star in a film is often all it takes to lure audiences to the theater, helping to minimize the risk that studios take with their investments."[11] This designation speaks to the perceived bankability of Blacks in Hollywood, insofar as larger financial constraints associated with the high costs of movie production encourage—if not necessarily discrimination—more discriminating eyes in evaluating whether the people employed in the movie are attractive enough to bring paying patrons to the theater. *Spoiler alert:* Those actors deemed most bankable just happen, coincidentally, to be overwhelmingly White.

Similarly, this category raises questions against Hollywood generally as it relates to opportunity. Given the already limited number of roles generated for Black actors by Hollywood overall, it is important to parse out how many of these finite appearances are successfully landed by those who have staked a career in acting *only*. Again, this is not to impugn the litany of Black comedians (e.g., Chris Rock, Chris Tucker, Tiffany Haddish, Kevin Hart), established musical stars (e.g., Common, Queen Latifah, Mos Def), and known athletic personalities (e.g., LeBron James, Jimmy Butler) for seeking diverse outlets to display their artistic talents. No blame or shame will be accorded to these individuals who seek work in any of its forms.

What Are We Looking For?

- Black comedians
- Black musicians
- Black television stars
- Black athletes

Déjà Vu

Why Is It Significant?

This designation speaks to whether a movie's theme is strikingly similar to a previous production; it also is used to indicate a repeat Academy Award nominee. While multiple nominations are great for individual actors, highlighting their accomplished skill in the trade, this category addresses the larger concept of opportunity available for Black actors in Hollywood. Given the limited amount of Black Oscar nominations overall, multiple nominations may quietly obscure how few opportunities exist for African Americans to showcase their talents onscreen. The total number of Black Oscar nominations pales in comparison to the total number of White nominations; this already small number is made even smaller by the total number of individual nominees and the repetitive storylines, thereby exposing just how limited the premier job market truly is.

Repetitive storylines speak to Hollywood's limited imagination when it comes to Black imagery and experience. Hollywood studios become strangely risk averse when it comes to placing Black actors in "unfamiliar" roles or in roles that deviate from or interrupt traditional narratives about Black life and behavior.

What Are We Looking For?

- Black actors with multiple nominations
- Similar, repeated storylines

Gravity of Reality

Why Is It Significant?

As Hollywood has depicted African Americans in years past within a narrow range of what we now call stereotypical roles,[12] this designation looks to analyze to what degree such limitations have been lifted, as many Black characters appear to have a smaller sandbox in which they can play—or exist. In other words, a significant number of Black Oscar nominees appear in para-realistic films (films based upon factual figures, not fantasy) or movies that prominently feature African American characters because they are dealing with themes expressly based around racial identity or race relations. In assessing the quality of Black Oscar–nominated roles, one key question is whether the characters depicted sufficiently rupture stereotypical roles and narratives that typecast most of Black imagery within early American film.

This designation therefore frequently applies to films that feature virtually all-Black casts; while such films allow for typically richer character development in contrast to movies featuring more racially integrated casts, the all-Black world is often another visual cue that the visible continuum suffers from a lack of resources. "Black movies," or movies that prominently feature mostly African American casts, suffer from smaller production budgets and distribution streams.[13] The constrained production budgets can literally hamper the amount of fantasy that can be financed with respect to shooting on location in faraway places, expensive computer-generated imagery (CGI), or the costs associated with building elaborate sets or filming dynamic car chase scenes replete with flaming explosions or staging hundreds of costumed extras. Conversely, many a movie featuring virtually an all-White cast has gone on to achieve blockbuster success with wide distribution (e.g., *Titanic*, *Lord of the Rings*, *Jurassic World*) with all of the aforementioned ingredients in place. In essence, this category analyzes to what degree Black Oscar–nominated characters are grounded by the Gravity of Reality as opposed to their White character counterparts, who are often liberated by the Freedom of Fantasy.

An example of this contrast is seen in the 86th Academy Awards, held in 2014 for 2013 film releases. Lupita Nyong'o received a Best Supporting Actress nomination for her role as Patsey in *12 Years a Slave*. Explaining how an enslaved character's role is directly tied to the concept of struggle is rather unnecessary, but Patsey's struggles were all directly tied to her racial identity. In contrast, the same year, Sandra Bullock received a Best Actress Oscar nod for her gripping performance as Dr. Ryan Stone in the seven-time Oscar-winning movie *Gravity*.[14] Dr. Stone's story—lost in space, trying to make it back to Earth, the only home they know—was certainly about struggle, but in many ways communicated a broader metaphorical and representative struggle for life and existence, something every human can theoretically relate.

What Are We Looking For?

- Films based upon true events
- Films based upon historical figures
- Film plots that expressly deal with racial identity or racial discrimination

Still in the Struggle

Why Is It Significant?

While the previous Gravity of Reality designation addresses a movie's overall thematic content, Still in the Struggle speaks to specific motifs facing Black characters. Due to years of institutional and systemic barriers restricting pursuit of financial freedom (e.g., Jim Crow laws), African Americans are often depicted as being "in the struggle," with their lives somehow constrained by a lack of resources, whether economic or social in nature. In contrast to the Horatio Alger success fantasies brought to life by traditional filmmakers like Frank Capra (e.g., *It's a Wonderful Life, Mr. Deeds Goes to Town*), Black characters often are depicted as quite static in their frustrated economic state, with very little explanation or expectation of transcendence.

Often, such economic angst and frustration directly influences the plot or affects the Black characters' development. Take, for example, powerful dramas such as *Fences* and *If Beale Street Could Talk*, which—although they undoubtedly account for encompassing, riveting, and powerfully strong acting performances—show African Americans in financially compromising positions. Here, the additional qualifier Lack Power within this category refers to those characters—regardless of how individually strong their personalities are—who still lack the institutional and systemic power to fully influence their destinies and are therefore left feeling frustrated or fatalistic as a direct result.

While these works invite viewers to consider the powerfully complex and fragmented emotional nuances of the African American experience, when projected onto the big screen for mainstream consumption, one unfortunate possibility is that many audience members may leave the theater with a still-limited view of African Americans—especially if the viewer lacked historical or personal context in the first place. To wit, "while some films of the 1930s did acknowledge contemporary issues of poverty and unemployment . . . people of color were consistently marginalized as stereotypical servants."[15] Meanwhile, many movies have depicted White characters as lacking resources, but this indigent state is typically more temporal and fluid—and definitely not always in subjugation to a Black authority figure.

Indeed, history is often used to justify the rehashing and redistribution of subjugated Black imagery in contemporary contexts in the name of accuracy. This designation is therefore not created to disparage or detract from the higher literary qualities presented by such emotionally complex and difficult representations; rather, given the more limited spectrum of Black imagery, when studios become myopic, providing depth and breadth only for stories in the struggle, the imbalanced view results in a poverty porn–type experience whereby the "prurient fascination of just how badly behaved the poor have become" essentially becomes fodder for audience entertainment and AMPAS nominations.[16]

Finally, the additional qualifier Scent of Magnolia within this category refers to movies that uphold and support the proverbial magnolia myth of the "nineteenth-century Southern plantation as an idyllic, racially harmonious utopia."[17] To critically analyze whether a movie set within a historically correct time period simply *had* to depict Blacks socially and economically restricted for accuracy purposes, this designation explores how such performances may visually stunt and limit Black imagery to roles that largely perform in such pain.

What Are We Looking For?

- Black characters living in abject poverty
- Black characters in jail
- Black characters who die in the movie

SETTING THE STAGE

Enter Stage Left, the Unholy Trinity

To better appreciate how far Hollywood generally and the Academy Awards specifically have progressed, it is important to start with the first impression Black performers collectively made on-screen, as virtually all early mainstream images were influenced and informed by the Unholy Trinity. The Unholy Trinity is a loosely organized collection of then-contemporary philosophical thoughts and socially fabricated rationales that helped justify the inferior status and improper treatment of African Americans in early America. The three base concepts that comprise the Unholy Trinity—Romantic racialism, femininity, and Negrophobia—are well-worn ideas that I did not personally invent. However, the grouping of all three together as an Unholy Trinity as a lens to view the African American experience is a fairly novel idea. We will now observe whether these original schools of thought evaporated or merely evolved over time.

The Unholy Trinity therefore helps justify, rationalize, and explain why Blacks should be depicted the way they are on-screen. Moreover, these ideas undergird a visual iconography through which information can be "passed quickly and economically to the audience in order to communicate aspects of character or setting."[18] It follows that, much like "the rolling tumbleweed in spaghetti Westerns conveys the harsh and inhospitable landscape the characters inhabit," racially coded iconography can quickly convey space, place, and value of an individual within society.[19] For our purposes, these three core racial narratives can be essentialized as rooted in historical expectations of power and control regarding Black movement and behavior within American society.

To wit, early disparaging racial narratives, although initially trapped within society's collective consciousness primarily through written description (e.g., *The Story of Little Black Sambo*, published in 1899), were subsequently given newfound life through the creation and proliferation of moving images on-screen. In other words, early unflattering African American stereotypes were simply part of the mise-en-scène, or part of the inherent design appearing before the camera, along with the props, lighting, costumes, and spacing on set. Unfortunately, what was commonly accepted as standard representation was based upon misplaced misunderstanding of Black culture and history, which therefore made incorrect and disparaging stereotypes appear to be natural and normal. For example, the 1915 movie *The Birth of a Nation* showed Blacks as "uncouth, intellectually inferior and predators of White women. And this racist narrative was widely accepted as historical fact."[20]

Our task in the following chapters will be to explore how these earlier narratives changed, in either form or substance, over the years. But before analyzing whether any Oscar-worthy Black imagery ultimately challenged or confirmed collective typecasting, we now take time to tease out the three schools of thought that together supported Hollywood's negative but highly influential first impression of Black characters: femininity, Romantic racialism, and Negrophobia.

Femininity

The fictive narrative of femininity stems from the general *anthropomorphizing* of races to genders; the White race was seen as a masculine race due to its ability to build and design, whereas the Black race was seen as feminine, or more docile and better suited for servile positions, whether the individual was male or female.[21] This narrative allowed many a White plantation owner to believe that the enslaved laborers simply had no other lot in life except to serve. Thus, the height of fantasy was for Whites to go to bed guilt-free at night, knowing that the enslaved Blacks who labored tirelessly at their plantations with no pay and plenty of torture did so because they were simply doing what they were naturally best suited to do.

Uncle Tom, the eponymous character from Harriet Beecher Stowe's 1852 megahit *Uncle Tom's Cabin*, embodied this image of an older, nonthreatening, devoutly religious, and fiercely devoted slave who would willingly sacrifice everything for his master.[22] Although considered a sympathizer with the Black cause at the time, Stowe herself directly stated that Blacks were "confessedly more simple, docile, childlike and affectionate, than other races," thereby suggesting a condescending perspective in the vein of femininity informed her work.[23]

Given the political climate of the 1850s, it is no coincidence a nonthreatening Black character molded in femininity instantly took a firm hold within the mainstream consciousness. It similarly is no coincidence that the first Academy Award ever to go to a Black actor was for a character written in the trope of dutiful, servile, and loyal domestic worker: Hattie McDaniel's rendition of Mammy in the 1939 classic *Gone with the Wind*. While *Gone with the Wind* broke several cinematic barriers and is appropriately lauded for being one of the first Best Picture Oscar winners to have a strong female lead (Vivien Leigh), recognizing a strong Black female character with a nomination or Oscar win was improbable—if not impossible—given the standard accepted social norms of racial social hierarchy at the time.

Femininity was also the intellectual fuel for many minstrel shows created and popularized in early American film, as illustrated with the 1927 release *The Jazz Singer*. The fact that the first popular film to ever successfully synchronize a separately recorded audio track with visual images had a plot that specifically dealt with the practice of blackface reflects just how popular it was as a form of entertainment. In the film, Jewish male actor Al Jolson longs to break free of his family's wish that he become a cantor, or religious singer, in favor pursuing his secretly professed love for showtime in blackface. *Spoiler alert*: The young man gets his wish. While some film scholars have attempted to contextualize Jolson's blackface act as a subversive illustration of a Jewish male's identifying with the nadir of his larger social rejection, à la African Americans, the bottom line is that he performed in blackface. Blackface was a particularly inflammatory derivation of minstrelsy, whereby performers used burnt cork or shoe polish to darken their faces and then were free to act out how they thought Black people behaved, complete with exaggerated voice intonations, hand gestures, and facial expressions. Jolson was by no means alone; famous early Hollywood luminaries such as Judy Garland, Mickey Rooney, Betty Grable, and Bing Crosby all "blacked up" at some point in their careers.[24]

Blackface and minstrelsy provided a psychological advantage to Whites who harbored newfound fears about true free market competition in an increasingly urbanized and industrialized society. In other words, by simultaneously emasculating and publicly denigrating Black imagery, Blacks were put "in their place" while even lower-class Whites were elevated above the lowest social station. Accordingly, the exaggerated minstrel "was a persona calculated to produce howls of rage and scornful laughter from working-class audiences,"[25] and blackface "would focus the anger of an emerging working class."[26] Those White workers closest to the bottom of the economic hierarchy famously exploited by turn-of-the-century robber barons were among those who derived the most delight from minstrel shows, with many poor Irish immigrants performing in blackface in the early days of its genre: "Once Blacks were free men, White workers saw them as free to compete with them for limited jobs. They were terrified that Blacks would become their equals or even their betters."[27]

"In 1920, despite the Great Migrations to many Northern cities, where movies were more widely available, 85 percent of Blacks still lived in the South; in 1940, 77 percent. Not until 1960 did 50 percent of African Americans live in the move movie-intensive North." Therefore, strategically speaking, "a White performer could . . . be a Hollywood star, without ever bringing a single Black patron into a theater. In contrast, a Black performer could never hope to be a Hollywood star without appealing to a vast, White-dominated mass audience."[28] Too often, to appear appealing, Black actors had to engage in the humiliating trade of minstrelsy or something quite close to it—even without blackface. These historical facts easily explain how the Black film minstrel actor Stepin Fetchit became a household name and an immensely financially successful star early in his career in the 1940s and 1950s. Fetchit's on-screen antics and bumbling incompetence were deemed humorous by audiences who left the theater self-assured that their positions within society were secure. While most Whites never approached the financial success of the robber barons, minstrelsy provided a reassuring reminder that at least they were not Black.

Romantic Racialism

Unlike femininity, which automatically presumed a lesser societal role for male and female Black bodies, Romantic racialism was an influential nineteenth-century theme that propagated the narrative that Blacks were actually *superior* to Whites—but only within limited, nuanced, and subjugated contexts. In other words, such thinking "projected an image of the Negro that could be construed as flattering or laudatory in the context of some currently accepted ideals of human behavior and sensibility."[29] This concept arose concurrently with emerging eugenicist ideas promoted by Harvard professor Louis Agassiz and others about presumed Anglo-Saxon superiority and the need for a homogeneous White nation.[30] Thus, enslaved Blacks, while generally believed to be incapable of possessing intellectual prowess, were lauded for their (natural) physical stature and hands-on skills—but only in relation to how their production increased profits for the plantation owner. On-screen, especially during Hollywood's early era, Blacks were seen as physically gifted and were also admired for their seemingly innate spiritual ability to sing, dance, and praise "De Lawd"[31] despite their oppressed existence (e.g., *Green Pastures*, *Stormy Weather*).

Under Romantic racialism, a false sense of racial comity developed wherein many Whites were convinced that they actually liked and appreciated Blacks for their work product, but this was not necessarily a deep abiding love or respect for their person.[32] Think of the numerous instances where Whites are seen interacting cordially with "the help" on-screen as evidence that race relations could not have been that bad, without interrogating to what degree the relationship was an unnatural occurrence forced through class and racial—and thereby social—constraints.

One illustrative example of Romantic racialism comes from the 1934 version of *Imitation of Life* whereby the White female protagonist, Miss Bea, unilaterally pilfers her domestic worker's pancake recipe and successfully packages and sells it on the open market. Miss Bea then wants to give her domestic, Aunt Delilah, a whopping 20 percent of the profits so that Delilah can eventually have her own home and car, like any freethinking independent woman would apparently want. *Spoiler alert:* The faithful and dutiful domestic refuses the offer, protesting, "How I gonna take care of you and [Miss Bea's young daughter] Miss Jessie if I ain't here? I'se your cook. And I want to stay your cook." Linguist Lisa J. Green observes that "taken together, Aunt Delilah's submissiveness, her Aunt Jemima smile and her uses of *I'se* and *am* . . . go a long way in convincing viewers that she is content with Miss Bea and in the best place she could possibly be."[33]

Nothing could have likely been more heartwarming and comforting to a majority White audience during the height of Jim Crow segregation than to see a Black domestic maid who loved her job and truly loved the family for which she labored, to the point of sacrificing pecuniary gain for her own Black family. Aunt Delilah's refusal to "get out" or escape her subordinate position was not viewed as an affirmation of her subjugation in society, but rather was likely interpreted by White audiences as an affirmation of the fantasized love and friendliness Blacks and Whites shared for one another on-screen, despite glaring social, political, and economic power imbalances off-screen.

In contemporary society, the sports entertainment industry is currently one of the few industries where, based upon rules of meritocracy, Whites have been forced to acknowledge exceptional Black performances or "superiority." But the premise of Romantic racialism rears its head when a professional superstar athlete like LeBron James, while adored for his prowess on the basketball court, is told to "shut up and dribble" the minute he voices an opinion—especially a political one—publicly.[34] In other words, racial comity can immediately dissipate if Black performers forget to "know their place"—in LeBron's case, the insensitive comment by political pundit Laura Ingraham implied that his relevance should be confined to his talents on the basketball court.

The restraints placed by Romantic racialism upon Black performers must be compared with White actors, who are more frequently viewed as independent individuals and are free to express themselves, publicly and politically, without significant retribution or restriction from future projects. For instance, actors such as Nicole Kidman, Emma Watson, and Anne Hathaway are all listed as United Nations Women's Goodwill Ambassadors on the official UN Women website; all are at liberty to "highlight key issues and draw attention to [the UN's] activities."[35] Kidman is even specifically listed as "Academy Award–winning actor," indicating that even in a global forum, the aura of the Academy Awards is both admired and advertised.

With respect to the film world, early releases such as *Gone with the Wind* (1939) and *Song of the South* (1946) fit perfectly within this prong. For *Song of the South*, James Baskett received an honorary Academy Award for his performance as Uncle Remus, who bears a striking resemblance to Harriet Beecher Stowe's Uncle Tom. Uncle Remus is a deeply spiritual, older, genteel Black male who uses the magical power of song to wash all of his cares away. Let us also recall that the "title" of Uncle has its own pejorative and demeaning history, as "'Uncle' and 'Aunt' were used with older slaves, since blacks were denied the use of courtesy titles in the antebellum South."[36]

Yet Baskett was recognized by the Academy for his rendition of "Zip-a-Dee-Doo-Dah," a cheerful tune presented using the then-innovative technique of live-action characters performing with cartoons on screen.[37] Baskett's Uncle Remus sings this reassuring song to a little White child about how "everything is satisfactual" despite a storyline and background setting both heavily suggesting—though not explicitly stating—that Uncle Remus is an enslaved individual on a plantation. For those who have researched and adequately documented the horrors of enslavement, it is difficult to envision anything romantic about "my o my, what a wonderful day" when forced to work all day in grueling conditions without pay under the constant threat of the whip.

Song of the South features a romanticized version of slavery that, while deemed too racist for Disney to release publicly in the present day, is nonetheless popular and treasured enough that "Zip-a-Dee-Doo-Dah" is included as a song feature on the hit ride Splash Mountain at Disneyland and Walt Disney World.[38] In keeping with the idea that Romantic racialism literally beautifies and sanitizes problematic, dark, and flat-out racist chapters of our shared historical past, half a century after the movie's original release, the "spirit" of Uncle Remus remains alive with the constant replaying of the song "Zip-a-Dee-Doo-Dah"—but with only the cartoon character Br'er Rabbit visible. Riders will find no sign of the enslaved Uncle Remus to distract or remind them about the tiny detail that the song bellows from the throat of a Black man who was considered property.[39]

Thus, while they may indeed be characterized as feel-good movies, films like *Song of the South* and more modern offerings such as *Cross Creek*, *Driving Miss Daisy*, and *Green Book* frequently manifest themes of Romantic racialism where historically complicated and complex race relations are glossed over with the broad brush of friendship. The feel-good display of friendship provides audience members with a false sense of comity or camaraderie among Black characters and the typically more powerful White characters with whom they interact.

Negrophobia

The Negrophobia school of thought developed later in the enslavement era as a preemptive narrative used to justify and defend Whites' use of aggressive displays of force against "threatening" Blacks. Such force was necessary for effective segregation, "to prevent the contamination of the White community while the doomed race reverted to savagery and declined morally, physically, and economically."[40] The only issue here is that such justifications of violence often required great leaps of logic that were ultimately immaterial to the user. Blacks were enslaved and subsequently legally, politically, and economically mistreated, mostly by Whites, against their will. Many Blacks resisted, rebelled, or at least thought about doing so. Many Whites placed themselves in the shoes of the enslaved and thought about the anger and outrage they would feel if they were so oppressed, and many then feared the backlash they might receive from the enslaved if freedom was ever obtained for all, as any rational display of anger by Blacks was instantly interpreted as a direct challenge and threat to the existing White power establishment.

Simultaneously, Whites' violent actions were framed and rationalized as being in response to legitimate fears they harbored of Blacks. Thus, any slight perception of Black anger was—and continues to be—immediately distrusted as dangerous and must be quelled and subdued, and forcefully if need be. In 1991 the Supreme Court of the United States upheld a workers' compensation claim made by a Florida woman who, after being robbed on the job by a Black male, was able to show that she was unable to return to work due to her debilitating fear of *all Black people*.[41] More recently, the concept of Negrophobia resurfaced with the story of a police officer named Amber Guyger, who in August 2018 quickly shot Black male Botham Jean dead in his own apartment; her excuse was that she thought she had entered her own apartment. One of the key issues at trial was whether it was reasonable for her to engage Jean with deadly force upon ascertaining a belief that Jean was an intruder in her apartment. Material to this defense posed by her attorney was that Guyger "so feared for her life that she had no choice but to shoot," especially when Jean was acting so "aggressively, moving toward the officer" in what was an ill-fated attempt to confront what he discerned to be an unwelcome intruder in his own residence.[42]

Negrophobia later expanded from concerns about degenerate contamination to include the unexplained, fiery hate that many Whites openly exhibited toward Blacks. For instance, members of vigilante groups such as the Ku Klux Klan often cited fears of miscegenation, rape, and joblessness for Whites if Blacks were allowed to run amok unchecked, thereby requiring the need to keep the Negro "in his place."[43] This Negrophobia fueled many of our country's extrajudicial lynchings and other terrorist acts of violence against members of the Black community and their allies dating back to the end of the Civil War.

Adding to the visual pleasure of the minstrel audience were numbers and routines that deliberately showcased Blacks as "hypersexualized, with an irresistible attraction to White women."[44] Speaking of the Ku Klux Klan, in modern Hollywood's first ever mainstream film, *The Birth of a Nation*, a White female character, Flora, affected audiences when she preferred suicide rather than submit to the wiles of the Black savage, Gus (played by a White male in blackface). Enraged, the Ku Klux Klan literally rode in on their white horses to "save the day" by movie's end.

In adding up the early philosophical rationales of the Unholy Trinity, it is no secret that, with respect to Negrophobia in early American film, "presentations of African American physical attributes were often grotesque," which helped distance or "other" the Black character from the audience, which then felt less sympathy if the Black character was later punished. In order to emphasize the subhuman existence of Blackness, expressions were exaggerated, with "eyeballs bulged out, feet shuffled due to inherent laziness, and these characters spoke in ungrammatical local dialect."[45] The 1954 film *Carmen Jones*, starring

Dorothy Dandridge, is but one Black Oscar example of an African American woman whose sexuality was depicted as a weapon of destruction—but for her own demise.

RACISM 2.0

No HARM Done?

In analyzing Black movie images set against the backdrop of Racism 1.0, the Unholy Trinity provides the general overarching themes while there are also more specific manifestations of certain image patterns or archetypes. Archetypes focus on racial symbology that has been merely updated. For example, take the food product brand Aunt Jemima. From its founding in 1889—a time when Blacks were routinely exploited—the brand denigrated the Black female image with the depiction of an obese, asexual woman with no other purpose but to cook and serve. After more than a century in business, Aunt Jemima now has an updated, modernized look replete with a perm, pearl earring, and smaller neckline to indicate a loss of weight. However, these changes are superficial rather than sub-stantive in nature since the brand is *still* called Aunt Jemima and *still* generates revenue off of an admittedly racist trope.

"Several classical racial motifs dominated the early period of American film: the faithful servant, the buffoon, the savage. These images glorified the institution of slavery and Southern chivalry, with its attendant myth of white racial purity."[46] Such early images left a strong first impression that has been difficult to change. Thus, the witty wizardry and legendary logic of Sherlock Holmes are completely unnecessary to appreciate that the mother of mainstream movies with respect to innovative film grammar technique is *The Birth of a Nation*, the 1915 film whose content openly glorified the Ku Klux Klan—a domestic terrorism organization that routinely killed, bombed, harassed, and intimidated Blacks—and features African American images (many of which were played by White actors in blackface) in the mold of the Unholy Trinity. The Unholy Trinity sets the stage for the HARM theory—an acronym for "Hollywood's Acting Rule for Minorities"—as many of Hollywood's historically overt and offensive stereotypes have been replaced by a new set of more covert and subtly marginalizing character patterns, which we refer to as *archetypes*.

Just as feminist film critic Molly Haskell identified four themes that largely govern all female interaction in movies (i.e., sacrifice, affliction, choice, competition)—"like grammatical models from which linguistical models are formed,"[47] the HARM theory similarly allows for facile categorization of specific racial patterns based upon the larger sociohistorical narratives espoused in the Unholy Trinity. The HARM theory holds that if and when a minority character (in this discussion, African American) appears in a mainstream movie, that character's image is likely to be compromised or marginalized in some way, shape, or form.[48] The HARM theory thus provides a convenient rubric for analysis that consistently applies to virtually all African American characters.

This analytical pattern has been crafted through years of research and writing about critical race theory and honed and refined by years of teaching professionally at the university level and presenting nationally and internationally. Thus, virtually *all* minority characters fulfill one of six primary archetypes for minority roles in mainstream movies, most especially in movies where both Black and White characters share the same space. When Black characters inhabit a largely insular world, writers are subconsciously able to concentrate on more substantive character development of one Black character relative to another. However, once a Black character is isolated or is squarely within a dominant White world, implicit hierarchical rules emerge. It is the quiet, yet steady maintenance of this archetypal pattern that shows no sign of change, despite extraordinary social changes made outside of Hollywood.

The Angel Figure

What's the Pattern?

This Black character is usually found in a servile position or as a sidekick, serving as a source of spiritual strength, guidance, and support to the central character, who is most often White. Frequently, this character occupies a teacher-type role, imparting insightful perspectives or life lessons despite having less privilege and commanding less screen time relative to the protagonist.

What's Old

This role connects to established patterns of expected Black servility that fall under the femininity prong of the Unholy Trinity. This debasing or deferential behavior is not unlike the limited options Blacks initially faced off-screen within the free market economy and that were accordingly reflected onscreen in film. In the decades following the failed Reconstruction in the South, Black workers could happily find work as domestics or sadly be put to work if ensnared in the ruthless peonage scheme or convict leasing system.[49] Sharecropping was also a common labor option, with few Blacks realistically paying off their debts, which came with usurious interest rates.

Hence, one slim but possible pathway to middle-class living before World War II was by serving as a Pullman car porter, who worked tirelessly to make luxury customers feel comfortable on overnight train trips. Not only did Black porters serve on call at their White customers' beck and call, routinely on twenty-hour shifts, but they ultimately had to make themselves obsequious and mute their masculinity in order to appear less threatening and more worthy of a generous tip.[50] This power dynamic was applauded through the on-screen appearance of Black actors like Fred "Snowflake" Toones, who appeared as a porter in nearly fifty films, and Dudley Dickerson, whose comedy included bug-eyed, scared reactions while also serving mostly as a porter or waiter in most of his films up until the 1950s.[51]

Film historian Donald Bogle, arguably the preeminent pioneer of Black film scholarship, identified five consistent stereotypical patterns of Blacks in early film leading up to the 1990s.[52] Bogle's designations of *Uncle Tom* and *mammy* would fall into this new, broader category as one who serves at the behest of a more important White character on-screen.

What's New

Similar to Aunt Jemima's image upgrade from a bandana-wearing Negro to an African American sporting a pearl earring and a perm, this role has been upgraded from "the help" to being a "best friend." Observe how these Black characters are typically isolated from other minorities in the visible continuum of the movie and usually fade to black once their primary function has been served.

The Background Figure

What's the Pattern?

This is a Black character who is rather inconsequential to the overall storyline and does not perform actions or contribute dialogue that advances the plot in any meaningful way. This character serves as mere window dressing on-screen.

What's Old

This character also speaks to the femininity prong of the Unholy Trinity whereby Blacks—especially within working settings—were expected to stay silent in the background. In accordance with the adage of "being seen and not heard," this went along with the idea that Blacks were childlike. What this meant for Hollywood was a paucity of leading roles for Black actors, with Sidney Poitier supposedly challenging that barrier in the late 1950s.

What's New

While these Black characters appear to play insignificant roles, they are vital to moviemakers in their attempt to illustrate to the audience—through limited screen time and dialogue—that diversity has not been completely overlooked. It is common to see this character early in the movie to help establish setting as part of the movie's larger, abstract mise-en-scène.

The Comic Relief

What's the Pattern?

This Black character appears where culture serves as fodder for most the jokes in which they are involved. Typical traits include a loud voice, improper grammar, intense emotion, and exaggerated motions and expressions in contrast to middle-class norms.

What's Old

It is no secret that a large portion of early Black American film was dedicated to minstrelsy as a means of comic entertainment. This type of character fits under the Romantic racialism prong of the Unholy Trinity, for what gives the symbol additional power is the idea that the self-debasing Black character is happy serving as fodder for humor. Bogle's designation of *coon* would fall into this new, broader category.

What's New

Since this minority character pattern is defined in a comedic context, humor often serves as a protective veil to openly defend the use of such racially themed humor. Then again, when considering the percentages of Blacks involved in the composition of scripts, the greenlighting of productions, or the directing of movie projects, this archetype raises additional questions not only about what is actually funny but also about who has the privilege or authority to define that which is acceptable to burlesque.

The Menace to Society

What's the Pattern?

This Black archetype character is portrayed as possessing a value system that poses a threat to civil "normalcy," through violence (or potential violence) and/or moral corruption.

What's Old

This pattern fits under the Negrophobia prong of the Unholy Trinity. *The Birth of a Nation* immediately comes to mind as helping to establish Hollywood's first impression of Blacks (or White males in blackface) as savage, lustful attackers of White women. Ironically, it was the opposite that historically happened, with White males routinely violating the sexual boundaries of enslaved Black women with impunity.[53] Nevertheless, fears of sexually deviant men were projected upon Black males through numerous ugly political cartoons immediately after the Civil War, coming to life in D. W. Griffith's *The Birth of a Nation*. While "it's just a movie," such irrational fears became pretext for numerous extrajudicial lynchings documented by the Equal Justice Initiative as headed by MacArthur grant recipient Bryan Stevenson.[54] Bogle's designation of *tragic mulatto* would fall into this new, broader category.

What's New

This archetype is significant in that it often blurs the line between perceived and actual criminality by Black characters. These movie characters usually are not fully developed through screen time and dialogue, and therefore the threat they represent to society is often taken for granted as their criminality often appears static and unexplained. If criminality is not at stake, these characters also appear not to "get it"—both in failing to observe common White social rules and in that they are presented as generally stupid or slow and therefore represent threats to White-dominated social norms and mores.

The Physical Wonder

What's the Pattern?

These Black characters are regarded for their physical or sexual prowess, typically at the expense of intellectual or emotional capacities.

What's Old

Nestling under the Romantic racialism prong of the Unholy Trinity, these characters are valued for what they can do rather than for who they are. There has been a premium placed on Black bodies from the very beginning of their time on-stage in the United States. Bogle's designation of *Black buck* would fall into this new, broader category.

What's New

This character pattern is exceedingly complex and dates back to the era of enslavement, during which there was a perverse fascination with Black bodies. While the Physical Wonder may appear to be lauded on-screen, it is important to note to what degree such "respect" is limited to the character's physical ability or whether the character is valued in any other way by leading White characters.

The Utopic Reversal

What's the Pattern?

Typically found occupying high social positions (e.g., police chief, judge, etc.), these characters in actuality are pseudo-authority figures since their power and authority are undercut (either explicitly or implicitly) in relation to other characters on-screen, rendering their authority or position as mostly symbolic in nature.

What's Old

This character pattern connects to the Negrophobia prong of the Unholy Trinity. Historically, the idea that Whites deserved to be in higher positions than Blacks at all times was underscored by the rash of Hate Strikes that occurred in workplaces, wherein Whites simply refused to take orders or directions from any Black managers.[55] While not necessarily promoting or subscribing to overt racism per se, many Hollywood studios naturally were cautious not to offend the sensibilities of the paying public, as portraying equality inside the theater may have been too far a stretch of fantasy in contrast to life outside the theater.

What's New

This character pattern is key to understanding the more subtle and nuanced displays of modern racism. These characters are deceptively alluring, for they give the appearance of racial progressivism on-screen and satisfy potential attacks for noninclusiveness. Yet this character pattern fits within a larger pattern of minority marginalization, since the audience rarely has the opportunity to see these characters actualize or utilize their authority. Thus, in accordance with many whites who complained about the "impudence" of "uppity Blacks" in the immediate aftermath of post–Civil War freedom, tensions raged over free Blacks exercising their rights to purchase and utilize material goods versus "knowing their place" in society. Blacks were *free but not equal*, and many segments of White society went to great lengths to communicate this. What this means is that often Black characters initially appear to be in positions of power, but by movie's end they are put back in their place—which is usually in a subservient position relative to another White character on-screen. Rare is the movie in which a Black character's power over a White character is absolute.

SNEAK PREVIEW: WHAT TO EXPECT

Format

This book employs a simple, user-friendly format that allows readers to filter key pieces of information quickly and efficiently. Every Black Oscar acting nomination is profiled with a focus upon the role itself and what the role says regarding the larger conversation about the space and place of African Americans within society. The nominees are not ranked but are merely listed in chronological order. As of this writing, there have been ninety-one total Academy Awards ceremonies, in which 1,728 actors have been nominated, with 77 total nominations going to African American actors.

Discussions of the nominees are organized according to decade. Further, each decade is framed by a brief introduction to better contextualize the symbology of the Black characters recognized as worthy of an Oscar nomination or win. What may be slightly confusing is that the Academy Awards ceremony is typically held in the spring of the year after the films it recognizes were released. For example, *Gone with the Wind* was released in 1939, but the award ceremony in which the first African American to ever claim an Oscar for acting (Hattie McDaniel, Best Supporting Actress) was held on March 24, 1940. Thus, while the award was technically released in the 1930s, the film is listed under the 1940s because of its award date. Similarly, *Pinky*, the famous race drama about a White woman playing a Black woman passing for White (long story), was released in 1949 but its nominations were issued in 1950.

Finally, each nomination is profiled in four complete parts: (1) Backstory, (2) Black Oscar Angles, (3) the Bottom Line, and (4) Bonus Features. The Backstory provides details concerning the name and date of the movie responsible for the nomination, along with a brief character and movie overview; these overviews vary in length depending upon the historical and social significance of each film. Every Backstory also includes a profile of at least one movie scene to provide context for the second layer, Black Oscar Angles, which allow for analysis of both the quantity and quality of Black imagery (described earlier in this chapter). In the Bottom Line, a final qualitative assessment is offered based upon an examination of the original stereotypes in the Unholy Trinity and any possible patterns or connections to contemporary archetypes in contemplating the value of Black Oscar symbology. Finally, if warranted, additional commentary appears under Bonus Features, which cover a number of miscellaneous topics ranging from the character's specific physical appearance, to concurrent Oscar racial news, to random but relevant supporting anecdotes under the subsection Outtakes. Ultimately, readers should be amply stimulated to learn more so they can ask themselves more incisive questions for critical thinking.

2

EARLY DRAMA BEHIND EARLY BLACK IMAGES (1927–1939)

In looking at the Academy Awards' first decade of existence, by way of preamble, a few notes are in order. For starters, the first decade as defined here is not a traditional ten-year period but rather a thirteen-year period between the founding of AMPAS, in 1927, and 1939. During this time there were only eleven Academy Awards ceremonies, with two taking place in 1930 and with none occurring in 1933. The first Oscars for Best Supporting Actor and Best Supporting Actress were not handed out until 1937. The number of films nominated for Best Picture fluctuated from three to twelve before finally settling upon five in 1945; this was revised upward to up to ten again in 2009.

Furthermore, with respect to Black Oscars, there were neither any nominations nor any wins by Black actors for films released from 1927 and 1939.[1] The obvious barriers of Jim Crow racism made it virtually impossible for an enterprising African American to finance and produce a studio film, let alone act or star in one with any meaningful presence. Thus, our focus in this chapter will be on the development of the movie industry generally, and how AMPAS set the stage for the Black Oscar nominations and wins that would follow.

THE BIRTH OF AN ACADEMY

Have you ever heard of a successful business idea birthed on a cocktail or dinner napkin? Well, the idea of the Oscars was literally birthed at a dinner party, likely over cocktails! In Hollywood, California, where most American mainstream movies are produced, there are currently seven major studios that create the works that entertain audiences worldwide.[2] Netflix, Amazon, Sony Pictures, Paramount Pictures, Walt Disney Studios, Warner Bros., and Universal Pictures essentially comprise the bulk of what is affectionately known as "Tinseltown," the one place on earth where light and magic continue to delight and amaze audiences from around the world. In some circles, Hollywood is also known as the "dream factory."[3]

One of the major studio heads at the time, Louis B. Mayer of MGM, invited several other prominent figures in the burgeoning, mostly silent film industry together to strategize on how to advance the industry. Much like police officers or schoolteachers have unions that support the maintenance of their related job responsibilities and enable them to advocate for better pay and working conditions, these different movie studios also saw that there was strength in numbers and decided to form a nonprofit organization designed to protect the integrity of moviemaking. No one knew then that movies would someday become a staple of just about every living human's life, but we would not have arrived at this point had these visionaries not decided to shore up the movie industry by forming the Academy of Motion Picture Arts and Sciences. Even the last three words— "Arts and Sciences"—are telling, as the word *sciences* connotes an intellectual, observable phenomenon, and although many are entertained by movies, motion pictures were serious business.

AMPAS was formed quickly, and roughly two years later, in 1929, the first Academy Awards ceremony was held at the Hollywood Roosevelt Hotel, with actor Douglas Fairbanks wearing multiple hats as both the inaugural president and inaugural ceremony host. If only Fairbanks could see how the ceremony has changed over time—the first group of awards consisted of only twelve categories and lasted just fifteen minutes![4]

In 1923, before there was the Hollywood we now know, an obscure housing developer erected a large sign to advertise a housing development called Hollywoodland in thirty-foot-high letters. The last four letters were removed in 1949, after the Hollywood Chamber of Commerce took over maintenance and operation of the sign to advertise and bring attention to the general area of commerce just north of the city of Los Angeles.[5] Movie studios first went out west to escape lawsuits by lawyers for Thomas Edison, who held a firm grip on film patents, but also found access to mountains, sea, and flat land along with temperate weather to be ideal for making movies.[6] The first movie studio, the Nestor Company, set up shop in Hollywood in 1911, and others soon followed. By the time the original Hollywoodland sign transformed into just Hollywood, the district had become home to the most powerful film industry on the planet. AMPAS did what it could to help in this regard.

Early studio heads were anxious to ensure that their products were well liked and well distributed, and readily supported the additional exposure their stars and their movies received as the Academy Awards grew in popularity, even though they first occurred during the Great Depression. If anything, the struggles of the Great Depression may have provided an indirect catalyst that made the escapist Hollywood star system all the more tantalizing. The founders of AMPAS recognized that the power and influence of movies was always in question, and that it was best to be aggressive in providing an answer: namely, that the Hollywood movie industry was one to be respected, adulated, and worthy of perpetual patronage.

HOLLYWOOD GAINS INFLUENCE

As industrialization and urbanization swept the nation after the turn of the century, the movie industry only continued to grow. Unlike a traveling acting troupe, where performances might vary slightly from night to night, the exact same movie could be packaged, shipped, and seen by countless people countless times. As entertainment was entering a new dimension of accessibility, major studio heads were quite interested in fortifying their power and position in a field still undergoing organic growth. Along the way, Hollywood had come under fire for its perceived power to influence its devoted patrons. Many psychologists debated the ability of movies to influence viewers through subliminal advertising, whereby a message or image could be flashed across the screen too briefly for the mind to consciously record but long enough to be subconsciously recorded, after which the mind would then consciously react. Infamous market researcher James Vicary conducted arguably one of the most famous such experiments, recording an increase in popcorn sales after subliminal images of popped popcorn kernels appeared on-screen. Yet Vicary's findings were never formally accepted and he later backtracked when he was forced to admit he did not collect enough data.[7]

While Vicary may have been a bit overzealous in promoting a theory he wanted to prove, what we know is that there is indeed a correlation between product placement and sales. For example, when Tom Cruise visits Gene Hackman in the Cayman Islands in the 1993 movie *The Firm*, Hackman suggests that he "grab a Red Stripe" and Cruise opens the fridge for a bottle of the Jamaican-brewed beer. Within a month of the film's release, Red Stripe sales in the United States had increased by more than 50 percent, and just a few weeks later the company's owners sold a majority stake in the brewery for $62 million to Guinness Brewing Worldwide. Similarly, after the hit movie *Night at the Museum* debuted in theaters, the American Museum of Natural History in New York, which served as the movie's setting, experienced a 20 percent boost in attendance.[8] Pizza Hut pizza from *Back to the Future*, Ray Ban sunglasses from *Men in Black*, Ford Explorer SUVs from *Jurassic Park*, or Reese's Pieces from *E.T. the Extra-Terrestrial*, are all products whose sales increased after being depicted or featured in a blockbuster mainstream movie. This correlation has prompted advertisers to be quite explicit and aggressive in courting moviemakers for opportunities to place their products in exchange for funds that can defray the rising costs of production.[9]

Yet it is difficult to conclusively prove the blanket assertion that movies serve as propaganda or that they serve as influential vehicles that can alter social and political thought. The Motion Picture Production Code, also called the Hays Code, was concerned about this relationship, although (just as no concrete links between Hollywood and communism were found in the 1950s during the McCarthyist Red Scare) little was found to officially manipulate society for the worse.[10] The Hays Code specifically forbade "white slavery" and "miscegenation" (sexual relations between two different races). Such policies already inhibited and limited the range of roles that could possibly be made available to Black actors in an era of relatively conservative cinema during which the mere pointing of a gun at the camera in a movie like *The Great Train Robber* was deemed too "violent."[11] Along these lines, article 7 of the Hays Code held that "ministers of religion in their character as ministers of religion should not be used as comic characters or as villains." This aspect of the code suggests sensitivity to a perceived relationship between image and reality—one that was seemingly overlooked when it came to consistent on-screen discrimination of African Americans in early American film.[12]

While the propagandistic effects of film may never be conclusively proven, we do know that major Hollywood studios did indeed forge formal partnerships to create films for the World War II effort: "In the 1940s, US war films not only served the war effort and buckets of money for Hollywood studios, but also had a profound influence on that era's generation and subsequently on their posterity."[13] A Hollywood-created Film Industry War Activities Committee worked closely with the Office of War Information to ensure that fictional films released during the war effort were as "realistic" as possible, as a service to the American people.[14] Hollywood's working relationship with the military continues to this day.[15]

Movie studios often spare no expense in their efforts to make their fantasy tales appear as real as possible. This probably explains why the military actually has an outreach office in Hollywood. The FBI, CIA, Department of Defense, Office of Homeland Security, and NASA also have liaison offices. Hollywood has always relied on the US military for assistance (including access to tanks, aircraft carriers, helicopters, and troops) that would be too expensive to re-create. In return for offering access and equipment, the Pentagon gets to approve scripts to ensure the military is portrayed in a positive light; for example, in the 2005 movie *Stealth*, the film crew was originally denied access to real aircraft carriers since the love story conflicted with the navy's fraternization policy. This rift was eventually resolved in spectacular fashion—since the premise of *Stealth* revolves around a plane that operates on artificial intelligence, producers arranged for a full-scale remote-controlled plane landing for the premiere.[16] Nonetheless, the temporary standoff was a tangible reminder of how seriously some institutions regard their portrayal in movies, even within fictional stories. "These days, there is an unwillingness to criticize individual servicemen and women, which was quite common in the Vietnam era," says Phil Strub, who heads the Pentagon's film liaison office. "Americans are very disinclined to do that now, and we're very glad this attitude tends to pervade all entertainment."[17]

BUT WHAT DOES THIS MEAN FOR BLACKS?

With respect to Black Oscars, all of this background about the influence of movies leads us to an important milestone that took place during this first decade of the Academy Awards: namely, the creation in 1922 of an oversight committee also intent on ensuring the health and vitality of the film industry, originally called the Motion Picture Producers and Distributors of America. Now known as the Motion Picture Association of America (MPAA), it is best known for its ratings system, originally created as a resource to assist parents who were concerned about the quality of film content.[18] Based on the premise that exposure over time to harmful images will have a negative influence upon viewers, the MPAA takes into account profanity, nudity, drug use, violence, and sexual themes in "recommending" a rating of G (General Audience), PG (Parental Guidance Suggested), PG-13 (Parents Strongly Cautioned), R (Restricted) or NC-17 (No Children under 17 Admitted). The adoption of the MPAA rating system in 1968 was an attempt to self-regulate to avoid confusion from different state government regulations. The Comics Code in 1954 and with the Entertainment Software Review Board (for video games) in 1994 are similar examples of self-regulating systems.

While the Negro Actors Guild was similarly formed as a populist effort in 1936 to help "give the [Black] actors status," this effort quickly faded as integration held out the promise of equal inclusion and equal pay within the mainstream.[19] The result is that African Americans have been uniquely dependent upon Hollywood as an institution to create, develop, and promote their collective image with ultimately little leverage in the process. Thus, with respect to Black Oscars nominees, here is the rub: There never has been a consistent metric to rate or judge the harmful effects of repeated exposure to disparaging racial stereotypes about African Americans. In other words, racism was and remains simply part and parcel of how Hollywood does business. This early nexus between any Black image and racism has unfortunately disproportionately influenced the type and quality of early Black on-screen symbology, with later, more modern images not dramatically departing from established, accepted, and largely unquestioned racist patterns of old.

For example, the groundbreaking 1915 movie *The Birth of a Nation* contained a stereotypical smorgasbord of unflattering, historically racist images of African Americans, among them "pickaninnies"—unkempt, uncombed, and uncouth Black children—eating watermelon; heavyset, dark-skinned mammies; White men in blackface who lusted after White women; and images of the domestic vigilante terrorist group Ku Klux Klan literally riding in on horses to "save the day." This movie, shown in the White House and described by President Woodrow Wilson as "writing history with lightning," is still screened today at educational institutions all over the country.[20] Why? The film's director, D. W. Griffith, is considered a pioneer with the way he constructed the film as grammar, meaning that each silent film sequence was connected to another to tell a larger story.

In fact, the fictional movie was so compelling in its presentation that the real-life Ku Klux Klan successfully leveraged it as an effective rallying cry. Initially a regional organization formed by disgruntled Confederate soldiers upon the Civil War's conclusion, Klan members were now nationally energized by seeing their greatest fears of lascivious, savage, bloodthirsty Negroes (as played by Whites in blackface) come to life on-screen.[21] Some Klan chapters went so far as to register new members outside movie theaters screening the movie, while others booked exclusive screenings to "close the deal" on new recruits.[22] Nonetheless, *The Birth of a Nation* still benefits today from multiple and repeated showings, despite the fact that the content is unequivocally objectionable; the film's technical value apparently outweighs its cultural insensitivity. And so, with "heavy hearts," film instructors nationwide continue to recycle these problematic images in perpetuity as they attempt to isolate students' focus upon the other aspects of Griffith's creativity.[23]

Similarly, the first ever talking picture is *The Jazz Singer*, released in 1927. The movie is explicitly and expressly about a White male Jewish cantor who wants to break family tradition and stake his claim in show business as a minstrel singer. This movie was rewarded with an Honorary Academy Award at the first-ever ceremony in 1929 for its pioneering contribution, despite its racially problematic content.[24] Incidentally, the movie was not eligible for Best Picture or other awards, as it was deemed to have a competitive advantage over all the other—silent—films nominated. Thus *The Jazz Singer*, objectionable content aside, is forever an indelible part of both film and Oscar history.

While never nominated for an Oscar, Lincoln Theodore Andrew Monroe Perry—better known by his stage name of Stepin Fetchit—made films popular during the 1930s. Perry played slow, dim-witted characters to the merriment of majority-White audiences, playing the role so successfully that he became the first Black actor to earn a million dollars.[25] Based upon the Romantic racialism and femininity prongs of the Unholy Trinity, Perry's talents were not sought out because he portrayed strong, alpha-male Black characters—akin to the White male heroes revered within Hollywood annals (e.g., Humphrey Bogart, John Wayne, Steve McQueen, Chuck Norris, Arnold Schwarzenegger, Bruce Willis, Daniel Craig, etc.)—but rather because the opposite is what appeased White audiences' sensibilities.

Along similar lines, Bill "Bojangles" Robinson gained acclaim for his tap-dancing routines with White child actor Shirley Temple (who also donned blackface at one point in her young career)—as "it was assumed that this adult-child dance couple was 'safe' and inoffensive in that it did not suggest a romantic relationship between the two."[26] Having started his career distinctly in minstrelsy, Robinson helped break racial barriers on-stage and on-screen, but he would die penniless.

Furthermore, while this book focuses upon Black Oscar nominees and winners, I would be remiss not to mention one of the first African Americans to ever be showcased in a major motion picture: the incomparable Josephine Baker, the vaudeville performer who starred in the 1927 film *Siren of the Tropics* before renouncing her US citizenship in favor of France in 1937, in part due to her frustrations over Jim Crow segregation, and was adamant about not performing before segregated audiences.[27] The aforementioned influential and highly visible Black entertainers do not fall squarely within the realm of Black Oscar territory, but their influences were undoubtedly felt by those who did enter the Black Oscar circle.

ACTING OUT RACISM ON-SCREEN

In telling the story of highly visible African Americans who were nominated for or won Academy Awards for their public participation in a motion picture, readers must not be robbed of the backstory or historical context in order to fully appreciate what the subsequent nominations and wins mean. While the roots of this story can be traced to the immense continent of Africa, the setting for this story's American genesis begins fully enveloped in the shadows of enslavement at the docks of Jamestown, Virginia, in 1619. Yes, before we get to the modern age of red carpet, paparazzi, glitz, and glamour associated with the pageantry, pomp, and circumstance that is the modern Academy Awards, to tell this true story accurately and not awkwardly we must begin with some of our nation's darker chapters. Before we talk about African Americans in Hollywood movies, let alone award-winning ones, we should begin our conversation with African Americans in America.

Understanding the image of African Americans in their initial opening scene is key to understanding how this collective character develops over time. If the African American experience was encapsulated as a movie, the opening scene would certainly qualify under the genre of gritty horror, easily earning a NC-17 MPAA rating. The beginning moments of the African American experience were fraught with horror, mayhem, murder, mutilation, rape, and castigation. Neither were these beginning moments flitting nor fleeting, as the era of enslavement lasted more than two and a half centuries before it was finally outlawed with the passage of the 13th Amendment to the United States Constitution in 1865—not by President Abraham Lincoln's signing of the 1863 Emancipation Proclamation, as some mistakenly believe.

In order to better understand the significance and symbology of the African American image in Hollywood, it is important to understand the first images and where they came from. Not to belabor the issue, but this first impression that Blacks were inferior subhumans naturally fit for enslavement endured for more than 250 years.[28] It is therefore no surprise that early images of African Americans in film reflected this negative first impression of inferiority:[29] "A survey of films released between 1915 and 1920 revealed that during this five-year period, more than 50 percent of Black actors played maids, stable boys, or other servile roles. During the next decade, the number rose to more than 80 percent."[30] With this context in mind, it is hardly a revelation that the first-ever Black Oscar nomination and win would be for the portrayal of a character literally called Mammy, a maid, in an idyllic plantation setting of a nostalgic civilization "gone with the wind."

However, it is vital to point out that enslavement, while certainly evil, was not the purest evil unto itself. It is easy to isolate a white-robed and white-hooded Klansman as the proverbial boogeyman, but it is important to note that the cruelties of enslavement had a supporting cast. In order for slavery to last so long, it had to be justified. Since "a large majority of the owners held only a few slaves,"[31] more dangerous for our purposes were the intellectual scaffoldings erected to help maintain a broader slave society. Many rationales were offered framing slavery as a necessary evil that fundamentally influenced the economic health, growth, and prosperity of the nation.[32] This supporting cast comprises the Unholy Trinity of femininity, Romantic racialism, and Negrophobia (all outlined in more detail in chapter 1). While we have near consensus today that racialized enslavement in the United States was a moral affront to the nation's principles, we must still contend and wrestle with the tensions surrounding the inconsistency or hypocrisy around the fact that several early presidents—including Thomas Jefferson—owned slaves at some point in their lives, all in the name of free enterprise and entrepreneurship.[33] It therefore makes sense that many early Hollywood movies reflected and reinforced older ideas of disparate treatment for Black images on-screen that did not meet ideal White image standards.

WAS THE ACADEMY EVER RACIST?

Traditionally, mainstream movies have been an almost exclusively White domain. It simply is not possible to replace the word *White* in the previous sentence with another racial category in order to obtain a truer statement (e.g., "mainstream movies have been an almost exclusively *Native American* domain"), as the available statistics from the Screen Actors Guild, Writers Guild of America, and the Directors Guild of America would demonstrate otherwise.[34]

Many classic Hollywood movies, from *Miracle on 34th Street* to *Singin' in the Rain*, did not prominently feature any people of color as characters. This is not to say that Hollywood did not feature images of people of color in its early history. As discussed earlier, the first groundbreaking feature-length movie (*The Birth of a Nation*) and the first talking film ever released (*The Jazz Singer*) both featured White actors in blackface. This acting method is now understood as controversial because the White actors who did so were not paying homage to Blacks but rather denigrated what they perceived to be humorous Black mannerisms in the most unflattering of ways. White actors literally painted their faces with burned, blackened cork and painted enlarged "lips" on their face before settling into their minstrel characters. The deliberate disparaging of

Blackness in turn elevated Whiteness. Accordingly, "Whiteness defined citizenship, freedom; Blackness connoted slavery, bondage. Whiteness moved from being just something to be proud of to a legal form of property."[35]

As we reflect in retrospect, we seek to distance ourselves from these darker chapters of our past. Yet, until 1999, the Directors Guild of America's feature film lifetime achievement award was named after *The Birth of a Nation* director D. W. Griffith. Then-president Jack Shea remarked, "There is no question that D. W. Griffith was a brilliant pioneer filmmaker whose innovations as a visionary film artist led the way for generations of directors. However, it is also true that he helped foster intolerable racial stereotypes."[36] Yet, during Hollywood's nascent stages when such movies were regularly made, Blackface was a prominent and highly profitable form of entertainment popularized by mainstream stars such as Fred Astaire, Shirley Temple, Bing Crosby, Spencer Tracy, John Wayne, and many, many others.[37]

In both *The Birth of a Nation* and *The Jazz Singer*, as with many other films throughout the early history of Hollywood, African American characters were openly denigrated by the stereotypical images they literally embodied. While these two films still command considerable attention in contemporary times due to their historical significance, one need not search long in the Hollywood archives to find movies such as *Green Pastures*, which found every conceivable stereotype associated with Blacks and essentially front-loaded them in a black-and-white musical.[38] Again, these movie images merely reflected and reinforced widely popular and shared social narratives about African Americans off-screen in real life. Popular restaurant chains such as Coon Chicken Inn thrived up until the 1950s, only matching the tastes cultivated on the big screen, or vice versa.[39]

The default quality of African American roles in Hollywood mainstream movies was invariably inferior to the roles of White heroes and protagonists. This inferior status was tacitly acknowledged and openly celebrated. Hattie McDaniel was rewarded with a Best Supporting Actress Oscar for her portrayal of a sassy but servile Mammy figure in *Gone with the Wind*, becoming the first minority actor to ever win an Academy Award. While many heralded the award as a sign of progress, it simultaneously represents a reward for prioritizing and sanitizing racial narratives that were far from romantic—especially for those Black domestic workers who had little choice but to accept such denigrating and financially restrictive roles within society outside of the movie theater.

3

OSCAR'S UNEASY BREAKTHROUGH (1940–1949)

KEEPING THE PAST IN THE PRESENT

The years 1940 to 1949 mark the first full decade of Academy Awards ceremonies in the modern format with which many readers and viewers are familiar. For Black Oscar purposes, there is only one competitive nomination and win to speak about for the entire decade: Hattie McDaniel as Best Supporting Actress for her role as Mammy in the 1939 classic *Gone with the Wind*. Even though during this decade James Baskett became the first African American male to receive an Oscar (an honorary award for his Uncle Remus role in the controversial Disney film *Song of the South*), McDaniel's nomination and win will dominate this chapter's attention.

Heeding the good king's advice from *Alice's Adventures in Wonderland*, let us start at the very beginning[1] of the movie for which McDaniel's name was forever inscribed in Hollywood lore. The introduction to the movie is as follows:

> *There was a land of Cavaliers and*
> *cotton fields called the Old South . . .*
> *Here in this patrician world*
> *the age of Chivalry took its last bow . . .*
> *Here was the last ever seen*
> *of Knights and their Ladies Fair,*
> *of Master and of Slave . . .*
> *Look for it only in books, for it*
> *is no more than a dream remembered,*
> *a Civilization gone with the wind.*[2]

The title of this famous movie, borrowed from an 1894 Ernest Dawson poem,[3] comprises the last four words of this introduction, which not only glorifies the patriarchal relationship between White males and White women, but also romanticizes an era of power and control for Whites that was borne about through savage brutality for Blacks. While it may be inconceivable to contemplate blockbuster mainstream movies made in the early 2000s wistfully recalling the wilting and passing of inhumane Nazi regimes sixty years after the Holocaust, this is what indeed happened here for Blacks. The introduction's first four words, "There was a land," frame the almost sorrowful loss of a nostalgic, idyllic era where "Master and of Slave" was the rule. In other words, the key crucial flaw in this Romantic racialist notion of the past comes from the fact that Whites envisioned an era where everything was perfect *that included the physical, emotional, legal, and psychological subjugation of Black bodies.* But here, consistency is key. It is amazing as it is alarming that one of the most profitable movies ever made[4] happens to be one that glamorizes White supremacy at the expense of human subjugation, dominance, and oppression in the form of enslavement.

To many Whites, McDaniel's win signaled a new era of diversity and tolerance; encouragement was in the air, considering the more drastic race relations a few years prior. Even for McDaniel herself, the Oscar win was a point of pride, as she saw it as a stepping-stone for more opportunities in the future. However, Jim Crow segregationist society was fairly entrenched, and after landing a few more Mammy/maid type roles (including in the 1946 movie *Song of the South*), McDaniel finally scored with audiences for her resuscitation of the Mammy figure on the radio show *Beulah*. However, due to a limited job market, "McDaniel . . . played mostly maids in almost thirty films" and was certainly typecast over the course of her career.[5]

Perhaps because she was the daughter of former slaves, McDaniel's victories were viewed and treasured differently, relatively speaking. McDaniel herself stated that "if I had for one moment considered any part of the picture degrading or harmful to my people I would not have appeared therein."[6] Unfortunately, she may have been too close to see clearly. As the daughter of sharecroppers, she was directly affected by the economic evils of racial discrimination. Thus, her personal history may have primed her to the point where it did not take much to persuade her that she was making significant change relative to her original socioeconomic position.

To wit, a twenty-year study conducted by the Graduate School of Business Administration at the University of California, Los Angeles noted that in 1946 the overwhelming majority of Blacks in mainstream commercial advertisements "were depicted in the ads as having laborer or service jobs: maid, waiter, slave, field hand, personal servant, the Aunt Jemima, or the Uncle Tom. The higher status occupations (including police and firemen) shown in the ads constituted three percent of the American Negroes."[7] However, these images were not just limited to media. As further reflection of this popular view of Blacks within the collective White imagination, one of the more popular syndicated radio programs during the early 1940s was *Amos 'n' Andy*, in which two White male actors (Freeman Gosden and Charles Correll) impersonated fictional Black characters from Harlem, New York, because, according to their logic, "blackface could tell funnier stories than whiteface comics."[8]

Gosden and Correll supplied the minstrel fuel for the radio show before Black actors played the imagined caricatures in the shorter-lived television show that ran in the early 1950s. The successful radio show merely capitalized on a popular pastime whereby "glee clubs and civic groups, fraternal organizations and PTA fundraisers, schoolkids and factory workers, prison inmates and volunteer firemen blacked up [in Blackface], banged the tambourine, and traded jokes."[9] To be clear, the healthy appetite for minstrelsy did not surreptitiously vanish overnight: "Putting on an amateur minstrel show remained a popular—if increasingly furtive and guilty—pastime for White Americans into the 1970s."[10]

Outside the imaginary world of radio, television, and film, in everyday life nearly 60 percent of all African American women workers nationwide were employed as private household workers around the time that Hattie McDaniel won her Oscar portraying a servant on the big screen.[11] Notwithstanding these challenges and limitations, McDaniel famously opined that "I'd rather play a maid rather than be one."[12] In making this statement, McDaniel was just being factual, as she really did work as a maid in between acting jobs early in her career.[13] McDaniel also stated the night she won her Oscar that she saw her victory as representative of any woman, regardless of race. While she took the high road to be inclusive in her verbiage, the mere mention of the concept of race in her speech signals concern with the topic. Thus, a blanket criticism of McDaniel suggesting that she played a fool and had no political consciousness would be patently unfair. While in retrospect she may not have had the impact that she was hoping for—she was largely typecast and did not play any roles other than maids—she was aware of the limited roles from which she had to choose.

Conversely, for some Blacks, the win symbolized the rewarding of stereotypical behaviors: Blacks had to be subservient to even get on-screen with whites.[14] While Hollywood movies in the 1930s were still viewed as large, ostentatious productions to be exclusively showing in large movie houses, promoting the possibilities that could exist within the boundless realm, for African Americans they were still largely grounded by the Gravity of Reality. In other words, the roles Blacks took on-screen reflected or reinforced their actual roles within mainstream society, or perhaps even worse, promoted a perverse, inverse fantasy in which Blacks were typically depicted to accentuate a social, economic, and political juxtaposition of Black life in contrast to "normal" or desired White life.

Miriam Petty makes the argument that performers like Hattie McDaniel negotiated a complex space confined by limited exposure and expectations to ultimately "steal the show."[15] Perhaps the full argument is that given the established limitations, McDaniel was able to bring the most amount of nuance to a limited role. The conversation takes on a different character if the debate hovers around whether McDaniel portrayed a character of low position in the hierarchy of power with dignity and respect, but to remain stuck on the idea that McDaniel can display ingenuity only for a maid role is limiting and shortsighted in and of itself. However, there were significant forces working against her. In that time, Black women were known for playing maid or servant roles. *Gone with the Wind* was no different.

THERE WAS A LAND OF CAVALIERS

Gone with the Wind is not the only movie that contributed to this juxtaposition, as many other movies followed suit during this era. In fact, most movies released in the early Hollywood era freely contributed to these routine portrayals of Blacks as "less than"; Black inferiority was normalized and was to be expected. For example, the original 1940 classic animated feature *Fantasia* was rightfully lauded for artfully combining light, color, and sound in dynamic ways, as truly animation was breaking new barriers. What might get lost in all the compliments about the movie's contribution to innovation is that it undoubtedly contained what we now call racist material; under the theory of relativity, it was simply normal at the time.

It is fascinating to hear how many people retreat to the "product of the times" argument, which asserts that esteemed gentlemen like Thomas Jefferson were complex men of their time and that we cannot discount or disregard their intellectual contributions on account of a moral lapse or inconsistency.[16] Essentially, the argument holds that such conduct was not considered racist at that time; we now know better, but should not be hasty in judging people from the past based upon current standards. Changing standards may properly apply to health and building or environmental and safety codes based upon new information. But as then as now, murder was still murder; rape was still rape. Therefore, it follows that racial discrimination was still racial discrimination.

Included in the Walt Disney classic *Fantasia* is a small bit colloquially referred to as the "Sunflower scene." In this scene, a blonde centaur is literally having her black hooves shined by a smaller, diminutive Black centaur with nappy hair in braids, in concert with the traditional pickaninny look, distinguished by a lone sunflower adorned in the pickaninny's hair. "At the time, these stereotypes were not considered racist, but merely a part of the tradition of ethnic humor and cartoon caricature that had been common for decades."[17] In other words, the argument presented here is that the disparaging image is not harmful because it was common. This is patently incorrect. African Americans should not be held hostage to the time-lapse of White collective consciousness to finally admit that past racist imagery was racist. If African Americans must continue to depend upon Whites to determine what is right and wrong, they run the risk of abdicating their innate power and agency to make their own assessments.[18]

On some level, the creators who labored hours, days, and weeks over the hand-drawn animated cells knew that they were creating an image that was inferior to that of another image. In analyzing the brown centaur, one sees that it not only is smaller, which visually communicates lower status, but its face is distinctly less attractive. An open mouth reveals indiscriminate flashings of teeth, suggesting not only inferior hygiene but also a less serious countenance and demeanor. In watching the movie, clearly it is the White, blonde centaur that dominates the viewer's attention. Even if the white centaur was to be the object of our focus and the Black centaur was to be a friend, the question is: What happens to the relationship when she reverts to shining hooves within a service capacity—most especially if the favor is not seen as being returned? Adding to the visual nonchalance is that it is difficult to distinguish or determine whether the brown centaur is a male or a female, where the white female centaur's femininity is indisputable.

This controversial material was again acknowledged when Disney launched its streaming service Disney Plus, thereby raising questions as to what Disney would and would not include as contemporary offerings, eschewing inclusion of the more controversial clips such as those referenced above.[19] All of this to say that at around the same time as maids in antebellum movies glorifying civilizations of "master and slave" were being made, the Black image was facing formalized racial segregation and social marginalization. The clever aspect of this enterprise is that because *Gone with the Wind* is the most financially successful movie of all time, people are free to (indirectly) express their political views through their choice to spend money—or not—to see it. If people want to revisit this civilization gone with the wind, they can. And so the past stays alive in the present, despite its fictional quality.

NO MORE THAN A DREAM REMEMBERED

Also, during the 20th Academy Awards, James Baskett became the first Black male actor to receive an award—or reward—to "ultimately reinforce the vision of an illusory utopia where African Americans are perpetually helpful, passive, and nonthreatening to the privileged whites, who are the only ones to benefit from this way of life."[20] Baskett's "able and heartwarming characterization" of Uncle Remus made popular the Disney hit song "Zip-a-Dee-Doo-Dah."[21] In analyzing the lyrics, the question is: What in the world could make a day born into slavery such a wonderful day? While not explicitly stated, the "ambiguity of the time period of the story suggested that all those happy, singing African Americans might indeed be slaves."[22] And such singing is not necessarily even for the benefit of cheering up the similarly situated, enslaved, or at least socially and economically oppressed and impoverished Black children (although Black children were present in the movie performing cartwheels). Instead, all of the colorful storytelling is designed for a young White male protagonist who is despondent over the separation of his parents.

Disney strategically and cleverly used the motifs and psychology of youth as a means to shepherd in these problematic themes, not only in making a young White male youth the focus of the movie but also in using youth generally as the window with which to introduce these ideas. I recall watching *Song of the South* in the movie theater with my mother and siblings in the early 1980s, when the troubles of adulthood were so far, far away. This memory makes for an extremely nostalgic combination: "The effect of nostalgia generates defenses just as passionately as do the feelings of joy and pleasure. Fans try to protect not only Disney, but their own memories of the past as well. *Song of the South* is itself a nostalgic view of the American South, generating *that* nostalgia for audiences past and present, alongside a different nostalgia for fans today trying to relive their own childhood."[23]

To revisit the thesis that racism is merely relative, what is interesting is that Disney did eventually decide the movie *Song of the South* was essentially too racist to re-release, but the company was not about to let go of something so successful for so long. Nearly half a century after the movie was first released, Disney introduced an amusement park ride based upon the stories that Uncle Remus told in *Song of the South*: the rollercoaster ride Splash Mountain. All evidence of the old, deeply religious Black man was erased in the ride, although Uncle Remus's voice is still used: "The song heard in [Splash Mountain's] finale, 'Zip-a-Dee-Doo-Dah,' has, over the years, become something of a Disney national anthem."[24]

Jason Isaac Mauro writes in one of the more pointed critiques of Splash Mountain that Disney's decision to erase the Tar Baby "acknowledges that they have structured the entire multimillion-dollar ride around a narrative that they regard as fundamentally racist." The Tar Baby "is interpreted by many as a racial slur," partly because of how tar itself was used to police and castigate enslaved persons.[25] Imagineers decided to replace the now-offensive Tar Baby with a pot of honey as the means by which Br'er Rabbit is captured in Uncle Remus's famous stories.[26]

Also during this decade, the US involvement in the World War II both started and stopped. The war did not appear to affect Black Oscar nominations significantly inasmuch as that with an increase of films focused on the war effort, more movies simply featured White characters in glamorized, heroic positions in which diverse roles would not make sense to general audiences at that time— even though American heroes of all types were being formed during the war effort. J. Howard Miller effectively commemorated the infusion of (mostly White) women with the famous "We Can Do It" poster featuring a White female in a working uniform and bandana flexing her muscle. African Americans from the South also took notice of the opportunities the war effort provided and migrated north en masse, landing so many federal jobs that, for a time, in some cities such as Washington, DC, the face of the average federal worker was actually likely to be Black, in stark contrast to the typical image portrayed within movies.[27]

NOMINATION #1, WIN #1—HATTIE McDANIEL

Backstory

Oscar Details

Best Supporting Actress Nomination and Win for Hattie McDaniel as Mammy in *Gone with the Wind* (1939) for the 12th Academy Awards (Ambassador Hotel) on February 29, 1940.

Character and Movie Overview

Hattie McDaniel, the first African American to ever win an Oscar in any category, won for her role in the 1939 film and Best Picture winner (then called Outstanding Production), *Gone with the Wind*. Mammy had a significant amount of screen time and by serving as the faithful hand was indeed loyal and helpful to the fictional O'Hara family, putting the family's needs above her own despite the ravages of war—Civil War, that is.

Have You Scene It?

Likely one of the most memorable scenes for Mammy is when she dispenses advice to Scarlett O'Hara (Vivien Leigh, who also won an Oscar for Best Actress) while helping her dress and fit into her corset. The argument is often advanced here that McDaniel, even within the confines of these subjugated spaces, asserts her character's personality and nuances her performance with a deep, underlying irony that she was actually in possession of more power informally than what was publicly acknowledged. Specifically, one film critic observes that "some of the most time-honored scripts and protocols of southern social life for Scarlett, including rules for getting a husband, are articulated and policed by Mammy.... Mammy is the *rule* model to whom we need to look for a thorough epistemology of the character Scarlett."[28] While this may be true, the overarching visual limitation is that the viewing audience never sees Mammy utilize all of these skills and wits to marry and manipulate rich White men for personal gain and power.

Black Oscar Angles

Crossover

McDaniel started her career as a vaudeville performer, not as a classically trained actor. She led a female minstrel troupe entitled the McDaniel Sisters Company.[29]

Gravity of Reality

This movie heavily invokes themes of race, the premise being that a White woman must figure out how to survive on her plantation during the antebellum period.

Still in the Struggle

The Scent of Magnolia is strong in the air: Whites are wistful and mournful about a time when not only were Blacks impoverished, enslaved, and subjugated, but both Blacks and Whites were happier for it. The movie's enduring legacy is often defended with the argument that the movie is set in a historically correct time period wherein Blacks were undoubtedly subjugated, so perpetually circulating this image is not blameworthy insofar as it is accurate. Racial segregation was still openly observed, not just during the time period in which the movie was set, but also in the present moment in which McDaniel received her Oscar—so much so that only through aggressive campaigning by producer David O. Selznick was she able to obtain entrance to the Academy Awards, where she "was relegated to sitting with her escort at a rear table away from the Caucasian attendees."[30]

To recap, within the fantasy space of the movie world's visible continuum, Mammy was seen in close physical contact cinching the waist of Scarlett O'Hara, doubling as a sassy confidante in a performance lauded and praised enough to merit a Best Supporting Actress nomination. Yet when Hattie McDaniel attempted to attend the Academy Awards ceremony in real life, she was physically segregated from Best Actress winner Leigh—a concession borne about only after heavy haggling from the producer. (In contrast, McDaniel was barred from attending the movie's premiere in Georgia.)[31] The symbolism in this true event is clear: Blacks performed a defined function in movie fantasy, and inhabited an even more limited role off-screen in reality.

Bottom Line

Final Cut

With respect to traditional images of power and control regarding Black females on-screen, this movie character satisfies the Romantic racialism and femininity prongs of the Unholy Trinity generally and satisfies the Angel Figure archetype specifically for rendering aid and assistance to the protagonist, Scarlett O'Hara, while serving as an enslaved domestic maid.

Physical Appearance

A word must be said about Mammy's physical appearance. Part of the reason Mammy was celebrated was not because of who she was, but what she was not: "In many films of the pre-1960 period, the physicality of the Black actress as shadow was used as a contrast to enhance the whiteness (sexuality and beauty) of the leading white actress."[32] Mammy (especially in the widely circulated photo selected from the scene described above) serves as a visual foil to Scarlett O'Hara, the attractive, slim, and determined White female protagonist. Brilliant Black author Ralph Ellison once opined, "Since the beginning of the nation, white Americans have suffered from a deep inner uncertainty as to who they really are. One of the ways that has been used to simplify the answer has been to seize upon the presence of Black Americans and use them as a marker, a symbol of limits, a metaphor for the 'outsider.'"[33]

It is significant to note that Black women have been, and continue to be, subjugated to a standard and measure of judgment that is unfair and unparalleled in scope to any other demographic. Constantly juxtaposed against the standard of Whiteness, Black women have routinely been characterized as "less than." These characterizations stretch back to the era of enslavement, where the Jezebel-type character was said to entrap and corrupt the Christian slave-owning master into having unsanctioned relations outside of marriage (that is, it was the Black female rape victim's fault). In actuality, many Black women were deemed highly attractive by many White men, but a frontstage/backstage dance ensued in which White women were publicly elevated and put upon a pedestal even though Black women were secretly targeted. While it was no secret that not every White woman did or could look like the ideal images of beauty Hollywood movie stars sold to the public, historian David Roediger notes that the psychological wages of Whiteness helped many a White woman compensate for their individual shortcomings when braced by the fact that no matter how far they were individually from the standard, they were undoubtedly closer to it than Black women.[34]

To be clear, White women have been *and continue to be* objectified within Hollywood spaces. The contemporary #MeToo social media campaign highlights the apparently well known but little discussed abuse of White male power to exploit women (socially and/or sexually) and their desire for careers within the creative space. While objectification of White women is unacceptable, in a perverse hierarchy of oppression, Black women were not deemed attractive enough to be objectified in the first place. Thus, in early Hollywood film it is not uncommon to see Black women in stark contrast to White women, who were often made to look attractive, affluent, and affable.

For instance, compare the asexual character and appearance of Hattie McDaniel's Mammy to that of Mae West, Greta Garbo, Betty Grable, or Joan Crawford—all leading ladies making movies around the same time. If anything, these White women were elevated in society for their ability to sell a mostly fabricated but realistic ideal of perfect beauty to be captured and mounted on one's mantlepiece like a prized trophy of conquest. To this extent, most of these leading White women were "considered glamorous beauty queens, which meant that both onscreen and in real life they dressed in designer gowns, wore impeccable hair and makeup, and could be seen frequenting the best and most beautiful homes and nightclubs in America."[35] Close-up shots during the movie, extensive focus on delicacy and daintiness through the White male gaze, and the celebrity culture that emerged off-screen in support of these newly created stars all contributed to the glorification of White womanhood, despite their collective objectification.[36] Accordingly, the overwhelming majority of female images prominently showcased by movie studios featured White women with waiflike, skinny features and long, wispy, and if at all possible, blonde, hair.

Mammy is none of these things.

Mammy is heavyset and dark-skinned, quite brusque in manner and mood and somewhat rough in her speech. With respect to her hair, it is presumably short, but nonetheless always covered in a bandana, providing for a slightly different effect than that of the unifying, propagandistic image of Miller's Rosie the Riveter, also clad in a bandana.[37] If we were to simplify the universe and have all interested movie patrons choose "the fairer" between the two, chances are high that Vivien Leigh would win out over Hattie McDaniel because the Mammy character image does not fit within the mold of what was consistently promoted as "beautiful" or even "the girl next door"—at least not by Hollywood standards. For, "at first sight, the figures of Scarlett and Mammy are opposites: Scarlett is white, rich, young, thin, and beautiful; Mammy is Black, poor, middle aged, and fat and has a big, round face."[38] Thus, for viewers, the moviemakers have created an easy choice: "'Gone with the Wind' defines Scarlett's whiteness in relation to Mammy's Blackness, deeply intertwining the two while privileging whiteness."[39] Even when commenting on McDaniel's landmark win February 29, 1949—a Leap Day that extended Dr. Carter G. Woodson's Black History Month by another precious twenty-four hours—"Metropolitan paper reviewers who covered the [award ceremony] say that her entrance was the big moment of the evening." Notes film scholar Charlene Regester, "The choice of the words 'big moment' would have no significance but for McDaniel's size and the press's preoccupation with her physical appearance."[40]

The Romantic racialist imagery in *Gone with the Wind* was widely received with open arms, stimulating many an imagination that enjoyed Hattie McDaniel's fine portrayal in a medium that would carry on in magical memory even if the era officially concluded in reality. A full year after McDaniel's Oscar win, *Modern Screen* magazine featured a two-page spread on the Oscar winner—not to talk about McDaniel's personal interests or upcoming projects, but instead, adjacent to a sepia-toned picture of Tara, the named mansion from the movie, is a picture of McDaniel in character with the caption "My, my! Here's Scarlett O'Hara's 'Mammy' to tell us how to make her favorite Southern specialties." Underneath the picture of Tara, along with the accompanying caption "Fine foods were traditional on plantations like 'Tara,'" are no fewer than eight different cooking recipes.[41]

What we must now pause to consider is that an inanimate object—a home—is bequeathed the name Tara, contrasting sharply with the dehumanization of a living being—Hattie McDaniel's character—who is simply called "Mammy." Not "Haley, the Mammy" or a first and last name like "Haley Winthrop," who the audience can discern is a mammy from her visible actions on-screen. According to Margaret Mitchell's novel, the male protagonist, Rhett Butler (portrayed by Clark Gable in the film), was a professional gambler, yet in the credits "Rhett Butler" is still listed as opposed to "Gambler Professionale." With Mammy, the character's name is merged with her identity and job function—or, in less delicate terms, her stated use to the White family and her only purpose for being on-screen in the first place.

The author of the *Modern Screen* article easily misleads readers into believing that a slave fantasy character endures by introducing Mammy as a possession of the movie character Scarlett O'Hara. More than half a century after the era of enslavement concluded, the article directly references plantation life with an adulatory portrait of a devoted maid figure who faithfully provides recipes. Here, the line between fantasy (i.e., plantation life) and reality (i.e., Jim Crow segregation) is sufficiently blurred, and the bottom line is the continued structural subjugation of Black female images.

Nearly a decade after her landmark Oscar win, and after most of her on-screen domestic roles had dried up, McDaniel starred in a radio program called *Beulah*; the character was described in 1948 as "the delightful domestic, as

Outside shot of Tara, Scarlett O'Hara's named plantation home from *Gone with the Wind*. MGM/Photofest

played by rotund, rollicking Hattie McDaniel."[42] These references to McDaniel's weight and physical appearance date back to her early appearances on-screen (e.g., "McDaniel, a brown-skinned gal, with a red bandana hanky around her curly black hair, and a large apron over her voluminous hips, appeared on the *Judge Priest* set to play 'Aunt Dilsey'").[43]

Still Popular within Popular Culture

One can conceivably make the argument that due to its historical innovations, *The Birth of a Nation* has some sort of utilitarian value, thereby necessitating its continued circulation and use. But with *Gone with the Wind*, there is no such justification. The data suggest that this movie remains popular only because people appreciate its content or want it to remain popular. It is still possible to attend a litany of tours based around the movie and even to purchase costumes for themed parties centered around *Gone with the Wind*, just as nearly two thousand moviegoers did during opening weekend in Georgia.[44]

It is difficult to describe just how this movie "captured the imagination" of so much of White America. The film's premiere in Atlanta on December 15, 1939, offered "an occasion to recreate 'this pretty world'"—or an excuse to celebrate an ugly past. *Smithsonian* magazine notes that for the premiere, "Women wore hoop skirts, black laced gloves and family heirlooms, and many men donned the Confederate uniforms and swords of their grandfathers and great-grandfathers." One can say that "it's just a movie," but Georgia's governor declared the day a state holiday, and Atlanta's mayor commissioned a three-day festival for the premiere, with Loew's Grand Theater specially outfitted to resemble the O'Hara plantation mansion. "Before the movie began, approximately 300,000 fans lined the [Confederate?] flag-decorated streets to greet the movie's stars. Many of these stargazers also wore period clothes, including elderly women who held fading Confederate [yes, Confederate] banners. A black choir in plantation dress—wide straw hats, cotton shirts and dresses and red bandanas, sang, 'Thank the Lord.'"[45]

Although McDaniel broke the color barrier in life as the first African American attendee at an Academy Awards banquet, the first African American nominee and first winner of an Oscar, the looming specter of discrimination was alive and well at her death. In 1952 her remains were refused interment at Hollywood Memorial Park Cemetery, according to her wishes; the renamed Hollywood Forever Park subsequently installed a pink granite memorial marker in her honor six decades later.[46] But perhaps McDaniel lives on in another manner: She is the only Black Oscar nominee to have a United States Postal Service stamp issued in her honor.[47] Mammy also lives on internationally, as Delta Airlines (based in Atlanta, Georgia, the state in which *Gone with the Wind* was set) as recently as December 2018 still offered the film as an entertainment option on long flights.[48]

Outtakes

- As early as 1944, efforts to create a counternarrative to the overwhelmingly White-dominated Academy Awards began when the Committee for Unity in Motion Pictures, chaired by Caleb Peterson Jr., held the First (and possibly last) Annual Motion Picture Unity Award Assembly. The event was sponsored by the Youth Council for the National Association for the Advancement of Colored People at Second Baptist Church Auditorium in Los Angeles, California, on April 23, 1944.[49]
- As a possible hint to how powerful the reverberations were from McDaniel's Oscar win, upon her death, the Negro Actors Guild (which dissolved in 1982), pledged to remember her accomplishments in perpetuity at its Annual Memorial Services.[50]
- While McDaniel largely defended her actions on-screen—"I do not feel that I have disgraced my race by the roles that I have played"—she also acknowledged room for external criticism by indirectly critiquing Hollywood herself: "I only hope that the producers will give us Negro actors and actresses more roles, even if there will be those who call us Uncle Toms. Which, I am sure that when they so speak, they are doing so, because of their frustrated minds. And so be it."[51]
- As another indication of how pervasive the mammy narrative was during Hollywood's early years, in 1923 the US Senate authorized and approved a national monument in Washington, DC, "in memory of the faithful slave mammies of the South."[52] While the bill died in Congress due to vociferous grassroots opposition, Arlington National Cemetery already featured a mammy figure—complete with tear in her eye—holding up a White baby for a departing rebel at the 1914 Confederate Memorial, not too far from the Tomb of the Unknown Soldier.
- Disney was not one to miss out on the public's fascination or "nostalgia" of mammy figures, employing Aylene Lewis at one point to portray Aunt Jemima. Lewis sang songs and signed autographs for patrons outside the eponymous Aunt Jemima's Pancake House, which operated inside the Disneyland theme park until 1970.[53]

4

NEW ROLES NOT
LEADING ANYWHERE
(1950–1959)

During this decade, several noteworthy events happened nationally and within Hollywood that helped shape the African American image in film. After World War II, cities were no longer the desired location for many growing families, who instead favored the bucolic planned neighborhoods of the suburbs. Thanks to industrialization and urbanization, workers had more leisure time and disposable income, and thus there was always someone who had time to see a movie. With the advent of aggressive suburban growth, movie theaters also morphed in form from palatial edifices in the center of town to the anchors of shopping centers or "drive-in" theaters, which did not exist before the automobile became affordable and more common.

What this meant for media, especially television, is that many shows and movies depicted homogenized portraits of virtually all-White neighborhoods. African Americans still were segregated visually as well as in real life. It was not until 1954 that the Supreme Court finally agreed to effectively put an end to Jim Crow legislation by declaring that the "separate but equal" myth was inherently unconstitutional and that the nation's schools should be desegregated "with all deliberate speed."[1] While the court's decision in *Brown v. Board of Education* signaled progress for a new postwar society, Emmett Till's murder just one year later was a sobering reminder that there was still work to do; the elimination of racial discrimination and its residual effects was neither instantaneous nor institutionalized.

For Black Oscar purposes, the decade began right where the previous one left off—steeped in traditional racial narratives generally, few of which were flattering for African Americans specifically. It must be mentioned that films made during this era, at the zenith of the Western film genre, freely disparaged Native Americans as bloodthirsty, whooping savages.[2] While 1950 was the last year in which all the Best Picture nominees were black-and-white films, the 1949 film *Pinky* was entrenched in old Black and White segregated social barriers and hardly did much to move the needle far from the mammy image dominant in audiences' minds. While *Pinky* featured a White woman (Jeanne Crain) playing a Black woman with fair complexion passing for White (reread that again), the Black Oscar nomination went to Ethel Waters's portrayal of an elderly caretaking Black woman literally wearing a bandana in the same movie. (Later in the decade, in 1957, this blackface/brownface technique would be rewarded when White actor Yul Brynner snagged a Best Actor Oscar for his portrayal as King Mongkut of Siam in *The King and I*.) However, with respect to the stark continuity between the 1939 Oscar-winning Mammy character and the appearance of Waters's character a decade later, the primary difference between the two portrayals was probably that Waters's character had fewer lines of dialogue than McDaniel's Mammy character.

The collective Black male image arguably deviated significantly from the status quo pattern when Sidney Poitier became the first Black male to receive a Best Actor nomination for his role in the 1958 race drama *The Defiant Ones* toward the end of the decade. While chained, his self-confident, younger, and even at times aggressive character differed significantly from the Uncle Tom/ Remus mold. The hope was strong that this Bahamian actor would open new doors that Stepin Fetchit and Bill Bojangles could only have dreamed of walking through. It is clear that Poitier was a pioneer; less clear is whether he also became a new pace setter.

We shall also analyze Black female imagery in discussing Dorothy Dandridge as the first Black woman to receive a Best Actress nomination, for her role as the titular character in the 1954 film *Carmen Jones*. Similar to Poitier's role, Dandridge's role was complicated, and it would be far too sloppy to hastily proclaim it an unqualified failure. Dandridge pushed the collective image of Black women into new territory where it became an image that could be perceived as sexually attractive, in stark contrast to the asexual, caretaking mammy mold to which so many audiences were accustomed. While Dandridge did have sex appeal, it came at a significant cost to both the character she portrayed on-screen and herself personally off-screen.

NOMINATION #2—ETHEL WATERS

Backstory

Oscar Details

Best Supporting Actress Nomination for Ethel Waters as Dicey Johnson in *Pinky* (1949) for the 22nd Academy Awards (RKO Pantages Theater) on March 23, 1950.

Character and Movie Overview

In the movie, Waters plays an impoverished and illiterate grandmother named Dicey Johnson, who has a fair-skinned African American granddaughter (Pinky) who passes for White to fulfill her educational and romantic goals in the North. On-screen, "Waters's character Dicey Johnson reprises an all-too-familiar image in American films, bandana wearing, devoutly religious, and an always-faithful servant"[3] insofar as she is quite passive in her dialogue except when it comes to her prayers. Film historian Edward Mapp notes that "most of Dicey's dialogue is with God, not with the other characters."[4]

Ethel Waters, adorned with bandana, on set of *Pinky*. *Twentieth Century-Fox Film Corporation/Photofest*

Themes of Romantic racialism are strong here, with the idea that race relations are not as fraught and complicated as they appear. Dicey, despite her financial struggles, somehow agrees to work for free for her "friend" and rich elderly White neighbor, Ms. Em. Furthermore, Dicey convinces Pinky to temporarily care for the terminally ill and cantankerous Ms. Em as well while Pinky is in town, which Pinky initially refuses to do, assuming Ms. Em is a bigot like most other Southerners she has encountered. Eventually, the relationship between Ms. Em and Pinky grows to the point that Ms. Em bequeaths her home (and twenty acres) to Pinky, which becomes the subject of a climactic court case toward the movie's conclusion. In her will, Ms. Em specifically gives "to my faithful servant and friend, Dicey Johnson, colored," her clothes.[5] Note how Dicey does not receive the home and acreage despite being a "faithful servant and friend" to Ms. Em over the years.

Have You Scene It?

In the movie's closing scene, we see that Pinky successfully wins her legal battle (despite the fearful admonitions of Black male family friend and con artist Jake Walters) and secures the home and land. Pinky decides to convert the home into a clinic for the needy, and plenty of Black children can be seen on-screen utilizing the dizzying array of services Pinky offers. Dicey is last seen ushering children inside as Pinky rings the bell outside the sign the newly created Ms. Em's Clinic and Nursery School. Dicey is still dressed in a domestic uniform, has no dialogue in closing, and is still seen working despite her granddaughter's newfound largesse. Pinky looks up to the sky as the closing music begins and the audience is left to contemplate her heavenly relationship with Ms. Em, which is arguably more influential and important than that with her still-living grandmother.

Black Oscar Angles

Crossover

Waters started her career as a singer, not as a classically trained actor.

Déjà Vu

This is not the first time a White author has leveraged success from his or her own personal perception of racial tensions. Cid Sumner, a White female author from Mississippi, penned the novel *Quality*, which was later adapted into the film *Pinky*. Similar cases of Oscar-winning adaptations of books by White authors into race drama films include: Fannie Hurst's *Imitation of Life*, Harper Lee's *To Kill a Mockingbird*, William H. Armstrong's *Sounder*, Michael Lewis's *The Blind Side: Evolution of a Game*, and Kathyrn Stockett's *The Help*. Each of these movies garnered at least one Academy Award nomination.

Gravity of Reality

This movie heavily invokes themes of race, the premise being a fair-skinned African American passing for White before reexamining her identity.

Still in the Struggle

Lack Power is manifest here, with Dicey's living conditions and servile condition as a laundress. The crux of the movie's major plot point hinges upon Dicey's rich White employer, Ms. Em, giving significant assets to Dicey's granddaughter, which are contested in open court.

Bottom Line

Final Cut

With respect to traditional images of power and control regarding Black females on-screen, this movie character satisfies the Romantic racialism and femininity prongs of the Unholy Trinity generally and satisfies the Background Figure archetype specifically with her role serving as a supportive domestic grandmother, based upon her limited screen time and nonessential dialogue.

Bonus Features

Outtakes

- Known for her singing career, Waters has three songs entered into the Grammy Hall of Fame: "Am I Blue?" "Stormy Weather," and "Dinah."[6]
- Jeanne Crain's Best Actress nomination for *Pinky* is not the first time that a White woman has received an Academy Award nomination for playing a Black woman on-screen. The other two times were Flora Robson for Best Supporting Actress in *Saratoga Trunk* (1946) and Susan Kohner for Best Supporting Actress in *Imitation of Life* (1959).

- Theater owner W. L. Gelling of Marshall, Texas, was initially charged and convicted of a misdemeanor for showing *Pinky*, as the local Board of Censors deemed its racial material as being "injurious to the public interest." Gelling's conviction was overturned once the First Amendment was extended to movies with the landmark 1952 Supreme Court decision *Joseph Burstyn, Inc. v. Wilson.*[7]
- Waters went on to play dramatically different (and perhaps more dignified) roles in *Member of the Wedding* in 1952 and *The Sound and the Fury* in 1959.

NOMINATION #3—DOROTHY DANDRIDGE

Backstory

Oscar Details

Best Actress Nomination for Dorothy Dandridge as Carmen Jones in *Carmen Jones* (1954) for the 27th Academy Awards (RKO Pantages Theater) on March 30, 1955.

Character and Movie Overview

In the movie, Dandridge plays a tough-talking termagant who appears easy to admire but hard to love. Audience members casually familiar with the opera *Carmen*, upon which this movie is based, are well aware in advance of the movie's tragic ending. Yet such tragedy only underscores the tragic combination of the first "desirable" Black female Best Actress Oscar nominee and her femme fatale role. It would be decades before an African American received a Best Actress nod for an otherwise redeeming role.

Ostensibly, there is nothing wrong with Black women exploring and exploiting their sexuality on-screen. This analysis focuses upon the fact that given the limited amount of racial capital Blacks have within Hollywood (and even less within the Academy Awards), such representations, while individually fair, may have an unfair and disproportionate affect upon the collective image. Thus, as noted in chapter 1, many Whites have shared a poor first impression of Blacks based upon distorted images sold to them from Hollywood's inception. Following the sassy mammy and virtually mute and impotent grandmother, this third-ever Black Oscar nomination of a venomous vixen does very little to alter the narrow-minded narratives of African Americans widely circulated within mainstream circles at that time.

Have You Scene It?

Early in the movie, Carmen gets down and dirty in a physical fistfight with a coworker who reported her as tardy to work one morning. What is significant is that after triumphing over her (darker-skinned) Black female colleague, Carmen strikes a triumphant pose on top of a table while towering over her defeated and humiliated opponent. This pose of Carmen in a black blouse and bright red skirt with both bent arms defiantly on her hips is the signature picture used on most advertisements for the movie.

This brawn and bravura displayed by Dandridge's character was of little ultimate consequence, however. In her last scene in the film, Carmen is strangled to death, offering little resistance to the two hands gripped upon her neck by Joe (portrayed by famed calypso singer Harry Belafonte).

Black Oscar Angles

Crossover

Dandridge started her career as a nightclub performer, not as a classically trained actor. Dandridge initially achieved fame as a singer on the Chitlin Circuit

Dorothy Dandridge and Harry Belafonte in *Carmen Jones. Twentieth Century-Fox Film Corporation/Photofest*

as part of the Wonder Children and subsequently in nightclubs nationwide as part of the Dandridge Sisters.[8]

Déjà Vu

The 1954 movie *Carmen Jones* was adapted from a 1943 Broadway musical of the same name; the Broadway musical was adapted from the nineteenth-century French opera *Carmen*.

Gravity of Reality

This movie, based around race and racial identity, easily qualifies as a race drama. Despite the operatic numbers performed throughout the movie musical, which may be traditionally associated with White culture, the cast is virtually all Black and qualifies as an insular universal film. The film's characters are not steeped in poverty, although money is a factor in Carmen's switching allegiance from Joe to the boxer Husky Miller, and the lack of resources became a point of tension between Joe and Carmen later in the movie when they escaped to Chicago in search of better prospects for their relationship.

Bottom Line

Final Cut

With respect to traditional images of power and control regarding Black females on-screen, this movie character satisfies the Negrophobia prong of the Unholy Trinity generally and satisfies the Physical Wonder archetype specifically with her role serving as a dangerous object of desire among multiple possessive males. The final analysis is that while this movie breaks the pattern of servile Black women, it is at a great cost with respect to the character's becoming objectified as a target of both desire and male violence. Thus, this character embodies the Physical Wonder archetype in that her body and sexuality remain the central features of Carmen Jones's appeal.

Bonus Features

Where Colorism and Sex Appeal Intersect

It must be mentioned that while the movie *Carmen Jones* has a virtually all-Black cast, Dandridge's character Carmen Jones—as the third Black Oscar nominee and the first ever for Best Actress—is significant in how it departs from the mold set by Hattie McDaniel and Ethel Waters. Both McDaniel and Waters were not cast for their sex appeal, as defined through the White gaze at that time as slim, trim, and White skinned. Both women were darker skinned and heavier in phenotype. Dandridge was one of the first Black female actors to be glamorized for her appearance (as if this is a milestone), but still inhabited a difficult space.

When film historian Donald Bogle coined the term *tragic mulatto*, he likely had Dorothy Dandridge in mind. Objectified for her appearance, Dandridge in no uncertain terms was still quite clear that she was not White, having discovered on one occasion that the Hotel Last Frontier drained the entire swimming pool the day after Dandridge, having been told of its segregated status, deliberately dipped her toe in the pool in defiance.[9] Dandridge "shared several characteristics as aspiring actresses in Hollywood of the 1940s and early 1950s—young, sexy, beautiful, light-complexioned, nightclub singers turned actresses, exploited by the industry for their beauty and sexual appeal, and subjected to essentially the same kinds of racial discrimination in the society at large that other Blacks faced."[10]

It is no coincidence that Dandridge, along with mainstream successes Diahann Carroll and Lena Horne, had a complexion that visually appeared to be closer to the White beauty standard. In fact, Dandridge's skin color was altered as a fungible marketing tool both on-screen and in marketing materials based upon the intended audience: "When producers cast her as an African American, they darkened her skin, but when they cast her in the role of a native West Indian or Polynesian, they lightened her skin color to make her acceptable to White audiences."[11]

However, Carmen's sexuality was framed as an infectious disease that destroyed everything in its path, including Carmen herself. Despite this drawback, within the larger framework of Black domesticity, many critics found Dandridge's performance (and nomination) as groundbreaking for the time. Bogle notes that Dandridge "called a lie to the assumption that the movie goddess could only be some fair-haired White beauty. She had proved that Black women could be cast as something other than giggling maids or hefty nurturers without lives of their own."[12]

In becoming an object of desire, Dandridge was indeed objectified in ways beyond her control. In the press coverage leading up to the 27th Academy Awards, *Time* magazine "published a review that described her body in detail and emphasized its availability. The reviewer praised her 'bee-stung lips,' 'white-sheathed hips,' 'warm brown eyes [that] singled out two or three lucky males for what appeared to be special invitations,' and 'long, discreetly undulating body.'"[13] Such lurid descriptions hearken back to the era of enslavement, when Black women were publicly shamed for their looks and beauty but were privately prized for the looks and beauty—and unenforceable sexual rights of refusal. In other words, part of Dandridge's appeal was exploiting her sexuality in ways that covertly spoke to this taboo, without elevating her status to that of White women, as she never achieved fame in death, unlike her contemporary Marilyn Monroe.[14] This is but one Black Oscar example of an African American woman whose sexuality was depicted as a weapon of destruction—but for her own demise.

Outtakes

- Dandridge did her own stunts (including boarding and disembarking from a moving train), which speaks to the confusing nature of her being simultaneously idolized and taken for granted.[15]
- "Dandridge was forced to play jungle goddesses and an array of Tragic Mulattoes who died for their 'sin' of miscegenation."[16]
- Speaking of tragic deaths, Dandridge died nearly a decade later, in 1965, under questionable circumstances (possible suicide via drug overdose), her life fraught with living between the blurred lines of the on-screen and off-screen reality of a career anchored in taboo White male desire.

NOMINATION #4—SIDNEY POITIER

Backstory

Oscar Details

Best Actor Nomination for Sidney Poitier as Noah Cullen in *The Defiant Ones* (1958) for the 31st Academy Awards (Pantages Theater) on April 6, 1959.

Character and Movie Overview

In the movie, Poitier plays a criminal named Noah Cullen who sees an opportunity to escape when jail transportation breaks down. The only issue is that he is bound by a metal chain to a White criminal, a poor Southerner named John "Joker" Jackson (Tony Curtis).

Have You Scene It?

The movie's climactic scene culminates with Cullen on a train with the opportunity to escape would-be captors. Joker is on the ground, wounded, and is laboring to jump on the train. Rather than preserve his own interest, Cullen jumps off the train to be with his friend. As proof of his caretaking instinct, Cullen props up the injured Joker, takes out a cigarette, lights it, and gives it to his friend to further comfort him. Before accepting the cigarette, Joker observes, "You gonna make someone a fine old lady one day," as an affirmation of Cullen's capacity to care and love. This movie ends with Cullen holding Joker in his arms under a tree and singing a W. C. Handy song entitled "Long Gone" a capella, in possible defiance of his ominous circumstances as the pursuing sheriff arrives and knowingly reholsters his weapon. Some scholars have referenced this pose as similar to striking a Pietà pose.[17] It is unknown whether Joker will survive his injuries after the visible continuum, but we know for sure that Cullen will be captured.

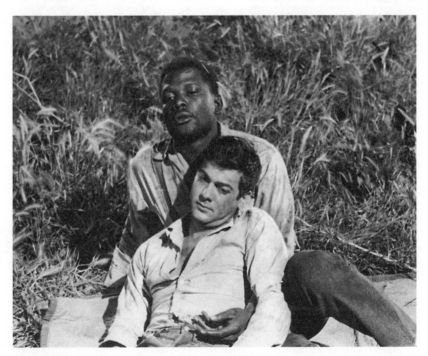

Sidney Poitier and Tony Curtis strike the Pietà pose in *The Defiant Ones*. *United Artists/Photofest*

This scene can be read in one of two ways: either the Black male was so self-less or dedicated to the principle of friendship that he sacrificed his personal agenda in the name of altruism, or the Black male was so selfless or dedicated to the principle of White superiority that he sacrificed his personal agenda in the name of "knowing his place."

Black Oscar Angles

Black Non-American

Sidney Poitier was raised in the Bahamas, born to two Bahamian parents.

Déjà Vu

Poitier personally accounts for more than one Black Oscar nomination, making him a repeat contender.

Gravity of Reality

This movie is based around race. The tagline describes the characters' plight: "They couldn't like each other less. They couldn't need each other more."[18] Director Stanley Kramer created a niche for himself "specializing" in race dramas such as *In the Heat of the Night*. As such, the movie provides classic lines such as, "You can't go lynching me—I'm a White man!"

Bottom Line

Final Cut

With respect to traditional images of power and control regarding Black males on-screen, this movie character satisfies the Romantic racialism and femininity prongs of the Unholy Trinity generally and satisfies the Angel Figure archetype specifically with his role serving as a "natural enemy" who sacrifices his own personal freedom for his newfound White friend. Ultimately, this movie negotiates yet upholds the pattern for nonthreatening Black men.

Bonus Features

Revolutionary, Yet Reassuring

While this movie appears to challenge the status quo, in many ways it only upholds it. After all, Poitier's roles were cleverly calculated to appeal to two different audiences without offending either: "[Poitier's] characters were non-confrontational black men with whom white viewers could sympathize, while black viewers could appreciate that his characters were markedly different from past stereotypes."[19] Themes of Romantic racialism are strong, with idea that race relations are not as fraught and complicated as they appear. Femininity is also present in that Cullen is muted sexually. While a White woman takes the two escapees in and helps to free them from their chains, it is Joker and the White woman who have relations, prompting the White woman to mislead Cullen with false directions. As Joker has also grown affectionate toward Cullen by this point, he angrily departs in search of his friend, but not before the White woman's son shoots and injures Joker.

Any concerns of a threatening Black man were neutralized and abated when, during the movie's climactic scene, Cullen purposely gives up an opportunity to escape clean, as a wounded Joker is unable to jump aboard a moving train. Cullen's decision to sacrifice his personal gain to help Joker also classifies the character as an Angel Figure. Cullen's act creates a false sense of comity[20] and assures Whites that race relations are better than they are. Although the men are chained together as they look to escape, the film suggests a sincere bond of friendship emerges naturally within a short period of time.

Consider Cullen's genteel nature not only in jumping off the train and sacrificing his own freedom, but in comforting his friend by physically (and tenderly) holding his injured companion's head while singing to him in the face of impending police presence and punishment. Then compare Cullen's display of masculinity to the rough, rugged, and above-reproach styles of characters portrayed by White male contemporaries such as Charlton Heston, Clint Eastwood, or Charles Bronson. Further, compare Cullen's masculinity to the hypermasculine displays that helped sell hundreds of millions of dollars of movie tickets in the 1980s, 1990s, and beyond, whether led either by buff, muscular, and artillery-aggressive presences typified by Sylvester Stallone (*Rocky*, *Rambo*) and Arnold Schwarzenegger (*Commando*, *Predator*, *Terminator*), or inspired by approachable Everymen as personified by Harrison Ford's Dr. Indiana Jones in *Raiders of the Lost Ark* or Bruce Willis's earnest police detective John McClane in *Die Hard*. With apologies to Robert Townsend of *Meteor Man*, Carl Weathers of *Action Jackson*, Damon Wayans of *Blankman*, Michael Jai White of *Spawn*, and Will Smith of *Hancock*, Black male displays of masculinity have not quite measured up in size, scale, and sheer force to White males on-screen. In contrast to historical narratives, where Black males had to be mindful of "knowing their place," White males have consistently acted out characters genuinely justified in "taking the law into their own hands" to effectuate solutions to which we all implicitly agree (e.g., Liam Neeson in *Taken*, Matt Damon in *Bourne Identity*, Steven Seagal in *Above the Law*, Jean-Claude Van Damme in *Bloodsport*, Chuck Norris in *The Delta Force*, Michael Douglas in *Falling Down*, and John Cena in *The Marine*).

Some readers by now have no doubt reflexively thought of the hit movie *Black Panther*, produced by Marvel Comics, as a counter to the argument that little room exists for Black males to assert their masculinity and presence on-screen. While indeed encouraging, there are few to no scenes of the Black Panther protagonist exerting his will—physically or intellectually—over White males in the entire movie.

Outtakes

- Poitier became the first Black actor to receive a Best Actor nomination in a film in which he is the only Black male to appear.[21]
- The Black-White male Pietà pose was re-created in *Lethal Weapon 2*.[22]
- *The Defiant Ones* clearly caught the attention of the Academy Awards, claiming Best Picture, Best Director, and Best Original Screenplay wins.
- According to Pixar's John Lasseter, the relationship in *Toy Story* (1995) between Woody and Buzz Lightyear was modeled after Joker and Cullen.[23]

5

SIDNEY IN THE SIXTIES
(1960–1969)

The 1960s will likely go on record as one of the most politically and socially turbulent decades in US history. From the Cuban Missile Crisis to the March on Washington to the making and fulfilling of a promise to put man on the moon to several high-profile assassinations with racial tensions and riots at an all-time high, change was in the air—or hair, if we also include the hippie movement along with the student, antiwar, women's rights, and gay rights protests that all gained momentum during this time period. Essentially, the country exploded with numerous confrontations and challenges to power, and Hollywood reflected this energy with several films highlighting race relations.

During this decade, Hollywood made many movies reflecting shifting sensitivities and changing social winds. Most significant is the 1963 film *Lilies of the Field* (for which Sidney Poitier won Best Actor), which covered new ground depicting Black males interacting with White females—although it did not open the floodgates to similar depictions. Other movies released during this decade, such as *In the Heat of the Night* and *Guess Who's Coming to Dinner* (both 1967 releases starring Sidney Poitier), achieved critical success, strongly suggesting that Hollywood was cultivating an appetite for movies that directly engaged contemporary race-related themes rather than pretending they did not exist. Poitier almost single-handedly challenged decades of unwritten rules for Blacks in film with "the slap heard around the world" in *In the Heat of the Night* and with an interracial kiss (albeit brief) in *Guess Who's Coming to Dinner*.[1]

Earlier in the decade, White actor Natalie Wood received an Oscar nod for her role as a young Puerto Rican woman living in New York in the 1961 classic *West Side Story*, while Latina actor Rita Moreno won Best Supporting Actress for her role in the same movie. In 1963 Gregory Peck won Best Actor for playing the benevolent White Southern lawyer who defended a disabled Black male in *To Kill A Mockingbird* (but as Bryan Stevenson points out in his compelling read *Just Mercy*, while an entire cottage industry emerged around the legend of fictional character Atticus Finch in the author's hometown of Monroeville, Alabama, Finch was actually unsuccessful in beating the dubious rape charge), and later leveraged that Oscar win to launch him to the presidency of the Academy, as many viewers were fond of the folksy, morally sound, patriarchal hero.

To Kill a Mockingbird was also rewarded with Best Picture and Best Director Oscar wins, which indicated a growing appetite for such movies—but only when the stories were told through the eyes of White protagonists. Along these same lines, in 1963 Elizabeth Taylor starred in *Cleopatra*, a movie that featured a White female actor playing the role of an ancient Egyptian queen (White actors Vivien Leigh and Claudette Colbert played Cleopatra in other productions). As proof that progress hardly follows a linear path, it was only two years after Poitier's historic Best Actor win that Laurence Olivier received an Oscar nomination for playing a character in blackface in the 1965 movie *Othello*.

It is important to note that between the release dates of these notable social problem films, many celebrated the unofficial end to the Jim Crow era and legalized segregation with the passage of the 1964 Civil Rights Act. One angle to watch out for is how suddenly or gradually Hollywood movies altered the quality of Black images produced in the aftermath of this high-water mark. The same year the civil rights movement began, the movie industry significantly developed with the opening of the Universal Studios Hollywood theme park, built mostly around the concept and theme of moviemaking and visual iconography as an amusement unto itself. The theme park is still open, with locations nationwide and around the world, and grossed $5.7 billion in 2018.[2]

Another movie that reportedly addressed the topic of race head-on during this decade was *Planet of the Apes* in 1968. As a social problem film with science-fiction flair, the movie made several subtle and not-so-subtle references to the concept of discrimination—seen, of course, through the eyes of White male protagonist Charlton Heston—and has spawned several sequels in the half century since its release. When Heston's character finds himself in a role reversal scenario where he is a visibly identifiable minority negotiating a world where power is concentrated in the hands of creatures unlike him, he attempts to escape at all costs. One wonders how the civil rights movement might have been different if more Americans empathized with the efforts of Southern Blacks' to escape subjugation the same way audiences sympathized with Heston's attempt to escape his captors at movie's end.

NOMINATION #5—JUANITA MOORE

Backstory

Oscar Details

Best Supporting Actress Nomination for Juanita Moore as Annie Johnson in *Imitation of Life* (1959) for the 32nd Academy Awards (RKO Pantages Theater) on April 4, 1960.

Character and Movie Overview

In the movie, Moore plays a domestic named Annie Johnson who works for a White family that has a child roughly the same age as her own mixed-race daughter. The movie centers around the daughter's identity issues both inside and outside her home.

Johnson's relationship with the widowed White matriarch Lora Meredith (Lana Turner) begins accidentally when Lora loses track of her child at the beach and Annie finds the child and subsequently successfully persuades Lora to let her stay and maintain the home so that Lora can be free to pursue her acting career. Racial comity is at play as Lora and Annie are framed as being friends when in actuality Annie is a domestic handling all housekeeping and childrearing duties for both children. Themes of Romantic racialism and "know your place" are strong as Annie never confronts nor challenges the White matriarch, nor does she visually challenge her employer in terms of appearance.

Annie fulfills the more traditional Black domestic mold celebrated by the Academy with Hattie McDaniel's and Ethel Waters's roles and does not pose a competitive threat to the matriarch (as it may have if her appearance were styled in the mold of Dorothy Dandridge). However, like Dandridge's *Carmen Jones* character, Annie dies on-screen, likely due to a broken heart from rejection by her daughter.

Have You Scene It?

After Annie tracks down her daughter, Sarah Jane, performing at what Annie considers to be a morally questionable nightclub, her embarrassed daughter

Juanita Moore as Annie Johnson gives a forlorn look in *Imitation of Life*. *Universal Pictures/Photofest*

repeatedly begs Annie to leave. Sarah Jane even lies to her interrupting roommate, telling her that Annie is a former nanny of hers. Yet Annie's patient presence reminds Sarah Jane that she is not fully White and cannot fully access the accoutrements afforded those who identify as White, including its romantic possibilities. Boiling over to the point of frustration, Sarah Jane weeps exasperatedly, "I just want to be White!"

Black Oscar Angles

Gravity of Reality

This movie heavily invokes themes of race, the premise being that the protagonist attempts to pass for White despite having Black heritage.

Still in the Struggle

Annie Johnson reflects Lack Power as a servant or domestic with limited resources to offer her child a better life free of psychological angst over her identity.

Bottom Line

Final Cut

With respect to traditional images of power and control regarding Black females on-screen, this movie character satisfies the Romantic racialism prong of the Unholy Trinity generally and satisfies the Angel Figure archetype specifically with her role serving as a dedicated domestic maid with a self-sacrificing nature.

Bonus Features

Same, but Different

As this movie was a remake of a 1934 film bearing the same title, director Douglas Sirk and screenwriters Eleanore Griffin and Allan Scott purposefully deviated from the original story line involving the Black maid's exploited pancake recipe, as they felt that such a story would not be accepted during the civil rights movement amid milestones such as the *Brown* decision and the Montgomery bus boycott. In this altered story, Annie's employer, Lora, becomes a Broadway star with her own talents, with Annie still assisting her by serving as a nanny for Lora's child.[3] While these alterations certainly suggest a heightened sensitivity to the changing times, at the same time the image of an asexual Black woman serving as a caretaker for an attractive, independently rich White woman hearkens back to similar power and control dynamics praised and applauded in *Gone with the Wind.* This "innovation" represents a negotiation rather than a negation of existing racial narratives.

Outtakes

- *Ben Hur* won eleven Academy Awards this same year.
- Jewish actor Susanna "Susan" Kohner received a Best Actress Oscar nomination for playing Annie Johnson's mixed-race daughter. In actuality, Kohner is Jewish with an original surname of Weitz, having joined several other actors who changed their names in an attempt to mitigate discrimination (e.g., Kirk Douglas, Winona Ryder, Woody Allen). It is ironic that someone sensitive to her own personal identity saw no problem representing someone else's identity.
- Fredi Washington from the original 1934 *Imitation of Life*, one of the founding members of the Negro Actors Guild, "consistently challenged Black performers who projected Blacks as rural idiots or urban coons."[4]

- Sarah Jane was also the victim of domestic violence when her enraged White boyfriend discovered her mixed-race identity, suggesting that being Black was crime enough even if one's appearance was more ambiguous (as the character was portrayed by a White woman).

NOMINATION #6, WIN #2—SIDNEY POITIER

Backstory

Oscar Details

Best Actor Nomination and Win for Sidney Poitier as Homer Smith in *Lilies of the Field* (1963) for the 36th Academy Awards (Santa Monica Civic Auditorium) on April 13, 1964.

Character and Movie Overview

In the movie, Poitier plays Homer Smith, a single male and former GI who stops at an Arizona farm looking for water for his car. It is unclear where Smith is headed or from where he is coming. While at the farm, he strikes up an unlikely relationship with a group of White European nuns who speak limited English but share faith in God. This sanctimonious connection forms the bedrock of their relationship—a religious relationship—with Smith.

Have You Scene It?

One of the film's most poignant scenes comes when Smith conducts a cross-cultural and religious exchange by teaching the nuns to sing the Baptist-styled hymn "Amen." This feel-good racial comity is repeated when, at the movie's conclusion, Smith leads the group of nuns in happily singing in a call-and-response fashion while merrily completing their chores. Ironically, Smith uses their blind engagement in the song as a soft ruse to slip away under the cover of darkness rather than formally terminating the relationship.

Black Oscar Angles

Black Non-American

Sidney Poitier was raised in the Bahamas, born to two Bahamian parents.

Déjà Vu

Poitier personally accounts for more than one Black Oscar nomination, making him a repeat contender.

Gravity of Reality

The movie is based around race, although race relations are supposed to take a back seat to other identities that can bind people (e.g., religion, good works). Critical reviews of the film clearly indicate that the racial overtones were not overlooked.

Still in the Struggle

Lack Power is manifest here with Smith's highly stylized servant condition—his servitude is masked by larger religious principles of being a servant unto good works, but he nonetheless works for the nuns without any compensation or direct tangible benefit for himself. This selflessness is reminiscent of the characteristics extolled by Uncle Remus in *Song of the South* and Uncle Tom in *Uncle Tom's Cabin*—the only difference is that the Black male image was updated with a younger face and build, but was equally religious, nonvirile, and unthreatening.

Bottom Line

Final Cut

With respect to traditional images of power and control regarding Black males on-screen, this movie character satisfies the Romantic racialism and femininity prongs of the Unholy Trinity generally and satisfies the Angel Figure and Physical Wonder archetypes specifically, with his role serving as an itinerant handyman who agrees to perform free labor for White nuns he has never met before. The asexual Smith might as well be a saint given his willingness to give to the nuns for seemingly so little in return.

Poitier's moderated masculinity fits perfectly under the femininity prong, as "Poitier became the nation's first black movie star by embodying a soft-spoken, honorable, and self-assured masculinity."[5] Anything more than this would have surely upset the expectations placed upon Black males to "know their place," both inside and outside the theater. Consider briefly (skipping forward a few decades) how Poitier's portrayal of "accepted Black masculinity" contrasts sharply with the heavily criticized bravura and bravado of Black males displayed within the burgeoning genre of hip-hop, particularly as it started to cross into the mainstream in the late 1980s and early 1990s.

Bonus Features

Saint Misbehavin'

Themes of Romantic racialism are strong, with the idea that race relations are not as fraught and complicated as they appear. Femininity is also present in that Smith is muted sexually (and sleeps outside) and does not pose any romantic threat to the equally sexually muted nuns. Smith's decision to stay and help the nuns, initially with minor repairs and eventually to the completion of a full-fledged chapel—without any monetary compensation—classifies the character as an Angel Figure. The nuns interpret Smith's appearance and apparent skills as a gift from God to fulfill their purpose, not his. In fact, the movie's title comes from a bible verse Mother Maria Marthe (Lilia Skala) quotes to Smith: "Consider the lilies of the field, how they grow; they toil not, neither do they spin" (Matt. 6:28), meaning that Smith should be humble and grateful to be of service.

Sidney Poitier and Lilia Skala as Homer Smith and Mother Marthe wrestling with principalities from *Lilies of the Field*. *United Artists/Photofest*

Hollywood has a long and established history, dating back to the minstrel era, of calling into question Black intelligence; this tradition, while altered in form, continues in substance with Smith losing verbal arguments to Mother Maria. Not only do these scenes morally obligate him to complete increasingly greater tasks without pay, but they also suggest that an Eastern European immigrant (also a victim of persecution, but for religious reasons) with limited English holds a firmer command not only of language but also of logic, as Smith cannot joust effectively with Mother Maria. Smith appears to regain the upper hand only when he tricks her into saying "thank you," as she ironically had overlooked the least of these right under her nose.

Outtakes

- Poitier was the first Black actor ever to win a Best Actor award.
- The same year, *Cleopatra*, a story of the queen of Egypt (which is located in Africa), garnered nine Oscar nominations, winning four.
- Harry Belafonte, the Caribbean singer whose character killed Carmen Jones in *Carmen Jones*, turned down the Homer Smith role, saying that character was a "nonperson."[6]

NOMINATION #7—BEAH RICHARDS

Backstory

Oscar Details

Best Supporting Actress Nomination for Beah Richards as Mrs. Mary Prentice in *Guess Who's Coming to Dinner* (1967) for the 40th Academy Awards (Santa Monica Auditorium) on April 10, 1968.

Character and Movie Overview

In the movie, Richards plays the mother of a son (Dr. John Prentice, played by Sidney Poitier) who wishes to marry a White socialite named Joey. Joey invites John's parents to her home so that all the parents can meet. John's Black father is made to appear the most obstinate of the four elders in opposing the interracial union. However, Joey's father, Matt Drayton (Spencer Tracy), is also initially hesitant to embrace the interracial union because he does "not want to be pressured into a snap decision about such a momentous life choice."[7] When Mrs. Prentice and Drayton have a private conversation outside, Drayton corrects Mrs. Prentice, saying that he is not upset over the union; "it's just a very difficult problem."

Have You Scene It?

Richards's character contrasts starkly with Tillie, the family's Black domestic worker who appears quite protective of the White child she helped raise. Tillie physically confronts an embarrassed and half-nude John, displaying the fierce protective instinct audiences may recognize from Mammy in *The Birth of a Nation*, chasing away would-be Black attackers.

With respect to Tillie's abrasive countenance, James Baldwin observes, "In *Birth of a Nation*, the loyal ni**er maid informs the ni**er congressman that she don't like ni**ers who set themselves up above their station. When our Black wonder doctor [in *Guess Who's Coming to Dinner*] hits San Francisco, some fifty-odd years later, he encounters exactly the same maid, who tells him exactly the same thing."[8]

Black Oscar Angles

Gravity of Reality

This movie is explicitly based around race; during dialogue between John and his father, Mr. Prentice directly alludes to contextual history off-screen, saying, "Have you thought what people would say about you? Why, in sixteen or seventeen states you'd be breaking the law!" This refers to anti-miscegenation policies that outlawed the marriage of interracial couples; the US Supreme Court rendered these policies illegal with the 1967 *Loving v. Virginia* decision.

Still in the Struggle

Black poverty is likely purposely avoided in a strategic decision to keep the audience focused on the best-case scenario. Poitier's Ivy League–educated medical doctor and professor jet-setting to Switzerland is more appealing to a majority-White audience, who would likely value higher education and the economic ability to travel. In other words, with such an unusual and exceptional pedigree, John, under the auspices of respectability politics, would be more apt to be accepted.[9] To be Black and poor (e.g., *Native Son*) would be doubly detestable. Part of the tension between John and his father comes from Mr. Prentice's working-class background and mind-set, having been a mail carrier for years.

Bottom Line

Final Cut

With respect to traditional images of power and control regarding Black females on-screen, this movie character satisfies the femininity prong of the Unholy Trinity generally and satisfies the Angel Figure archetype specifically with her role serving as a supportive mother who agrees to follow the lead of the White male patriarch. The final analysis is that this movie upholds established patterns of muted Black women, and Richards's character qualifies as a Background Figure for her limited screen time and dialogue.

Bonus Features

The Last Word

While Richards likely earned her nomination for her measured attempts to reason with Drayton in arguing for the parents to consider the feelings of the children involved, to be clear, the movie revolves around White male patriarchy. It might be somewhat surprising that Richards received an Oscar nod despite her severely limited time on-screen as "the film revolves around the crisis of the White patriarch who is forced to give his blessing to a union to which he objects."[10] In fact, the movie concludes with Drayton providing a definitive monologue to all in attendance in his home. This dynamic has since been recycled: "Drayton's speech is one that is often repeated in the history of American film: it is the speech of the White liberal messiah coming to the rescue. The same strategy is used thirty years after *Guess Who's Coming to Dinner* in the climax of Spielberg's film *Amistad* (1997) when John Quincy Adams takes a stand and spells it out in a long speech before the Supreme Court."[11]

Drayton's power, patriarchy, and authority are punctuated with the last line spoken in the movie: In breaking the emotional silence after his climactic and conciliatory speech, Drayton abruptly barks in the direction of his Black domestic, "Well, Tillie, when the *hell* are we going to get some dinner?"

Outtakes

- Interracial marriage was illegal in seventeen states when the movie was filmed; the Supreme Court's *Loving v. Virginia* decision, released in December 1967, made the movie's content legal in all fifty states. "In the 1960 census, the last before the film was made, Black-White couples constituted only one tenth of 1 percent of married couples in the United States."[12]

- Originally scheduled for April 8, 1968, the Academy Awards were postponed for two days due to the assassination of Dr. Martin Luther King Jr.
- Another race drama, *In the Heat of the Night* (also starring Sidney Poitier), won Best Picture that year.
- *Guess Who's Coming to Dinner* was heavy on the mind of Oscar voters that year, garnering ten total nominations and winning two (Best Actress and Best Writing).
- John and Joey appear to engage in an interracial kiss; however, it is only through the White male gaze of the cab driver's rearview mirror.

6

THE BLAXPLOITATION EFFECT (1970–1979)

During the 1970s, calls for more Black self-sufficiency were raised, along with questions about how to manifest and display Black power. While this decade saw an explosion of quickly produced and cheaply made movies called blaxploitation films, these movies frequently glamorized pimps in a frustrated attempt to assert masculinity (and therefore Black power) on-screen, turning a myopic eye to misogynistic messages communicated about the worth of the female body. Critics claimed that such exaggerated, disparaging images were more refined versions of minstrel iconography, likely contributing to the acceptance of these movies as cult classics in certain circles while being widely panned in most others. Films like *Car Wash* and *Cooley High* are therefore culturally significant, but were not Oscar worthy. Such contestable themes reappeared in contemporary movies such as *Hustle & Flow*.

An increase in images did not directly correspond with an increase of Black nominations—in fact, Blacks received no nominations for six of the ten years in this decade. Yet the 1970s saw two public social justice protests on the Academy's main stage—first with George C. Scott in 1971 (*Patton*) and then with Marlon Brando in 1974 (*Godfather*). The nonlinear path to racial reconciliation reared its head with the 1975 movie *Mandingo*, although the 1978 classic hit *Star Wars* featured the disembodied voice of Black Oscar nominee James Earl Jones as Darth Vader, Dark Lord of the Sith.

While 1972 was a watershed year, with three African Americans receiving nominations in one year for the first time ever, there were no Black Oscar wins for the entire decade.

NOMINATION #8—RUPERT CROSSE

Backstory

Oscar Details

Best Supporting Actor Nomination for Rupert Crosse as Ned McCaslin in *The Reivers* (1969) for the 42nd Academy Awards (Dorothy Chandler Pavilion) on April 7, 1970.

Character and Movie Overview

In the movie, Crosse plays Ned, a thief who steals away and joins Steve Mc-Queen (as Boon Hoggenbeck) for a wild, cross-country ride in search of adventure. Themes of Romantic racialism are present with the idyllic relationship struck between Ned and Boon.

Ned provides help to his White friends by figuring out that a racehorse, which coincidentally happens to be the color black, is motivated to run by sardines. This key discovery helps their young companion win a race in exchange for the opportunity to win back a car they stole in the first place. Ned is truly supportive, with sparse dialogue and no love interest; his last scene on-screen is marked by his silent, approving presence in the background while Boon's dialogue with the young Lucius (Mitch Vogel) reveals the movie's final gag.

Have You Scene It?

When the three main characters pull up to a brothel, Boon attempts to explain to the young, innocent Lucius that a "friend" wrote to him before they both enter. Curiously, Ned exits the car at Boon's command and agrees to meet both Boon and Lucius again at eight o'clock the next morning rather than enter the brothel to satisfy whatever curiosities or romantic needs he might have as a presumably sexually active single adult male. In this way, the interracial taboo—Hollywood's third rail of Black male and White female sexual intimacy—was conveniently avoided with Ned smiling and waving goodbye to allow the White males time and space to enter the brothel and conduct their business.

Black Oscar Angles

Still in the Struggle

Lack Power is manifest here, with Ned's muted presence essentially mimicking servant conditions for young Lucius.

Bottom Line

Final Cut

With respect to traditional images of power and control regarding Black males on-screen, this movie character satisfies the Romantic racialism prong of the Unholy Trinity generally and satisfies the Angel Figure and Comic Relief archetypes specifically, with his role serving as a faithful, useful best friend who is always ready to help. The final analysis is that this movie upholds established patterns of non-threatening Black men as an Angel Figure for rendering help and aid to the White protagonist and also as Comic Relief for the humorous flair with which he does so.

Bonus Features

Outtakes

- McQueen originally objected to Crosse's casting due to concerns that at six-foot-five, Crosse would take away attention from his main character. This concern seems unfounded when considering the characters' total screen time and lines delivered; however, it was likely affirmed when Crosse received an Oscar nomination and McQueen did not.
- *Reivers* comes from Scottish word for thief.
- The first time an African American male actor received a Best Supporting Actor nomination occurred for a film in which he literally takes a back seat to a young White male.

NOMINATION #9—JAMES EARL JONES

Backstory

Oscar Details

Best Actor Nomination for James Earl Jones as Jack Jefferson in *The Great White Hope* (1970) for the 43rd Academy Awards (Dorothy Chandler Pavilion) on April 15, 1971.

Character and Movie Overview

Jones plays boxer Jack Jefferson in this movie based upon the true story of Jack Johnson. Jack seems invincible in the ring against his White male opponents, but he is susceptible to seduction by a White woman. The taboo of Black male and White female sexual relations speaks clearly to Hollywood's third rail.

James Earl Jones and Jane Alexander in promotional key art for *The Great White Hope*. *20th Century Fox/Photofest*

Have You Scene It?

While the movie does show the interracial couple in bed (but not in the act), another scene that could easily escape attention involves Jack's decision to partake in a rendition of *Uncle Tom's Cabin* as a way to make a living outside of the ring. While Jack feels humiliated and takes off his wig, the Topsy character is also in the background, complete with a "pickaninny" wig, played by a Black male. The movie's climactic scene culminates with Jefferson *not* being intimate with his White wife; even though the movie brought attention to the intolerance surrounding the interracial relationship, it also chose not to "cross the line."

Black Oscar Angles

Déjà Vu

This is not the first time a White author has leveraged success from or her own personal perception of racial tensions. Howard Sackler's 1967 play *The Great*

White Hope was adapted into the film of the same name. Similar cases of Oscar-winning adaptations of books into race-drama films include: Cid Sumner's *Quality* (which was adapted into the film *Pinky*), Fannie Hurst's *Imitation of Life*, Harper Lee's *To Kill a Mockingbird*, William H. Armstrong's *Sounder*, Michael Lewis's *The Blind Side: Evolution of a Game*, and Kathyrn Stockett's, *The Help*. We also see Black boxers specifically as Oscar nominees in *Ali* and *Hurricane*.

Gravity of Reality

This roman à clef of a movie is based heavily upon the true story of heavyweight champion Jack Johnson and the controversy surrounding his first marriage to a White woman, Etta Terry Duryea.

Bottom Line

Final Cut

With respect to traditional images of power and control regarding Black males on-screen, this movie character satisfies the Negrophobia prong of the Unholy Trinity generally and satisfies the Physical Wonder and Utopic Reversal archetypes specifically, with his role serving as a physical specimen who would dare be heavyweight champion of the world (and lover of White women). The final analysis is that this movie upholds established patterns of threatening Black men as the Physical Wonder archetype for his supreme boxing ability and for Utopic Reversal archetype, as this is less a story about his ascension to power as it is about his fall from it.

Bonus Features

Outtakes

- This movie is based upon the true story of heavyweight boxer Jack Johnson, who defeated Tommy Burns on December 26, 1908, to become the undisputed world champion of boxing.
- With respect to the power of an image, actual film footage of Johnson's fight was censored simply because a "Black champion could not be abided."[1] Footage taken of his successful 1910 rematch with Jim Jeffries was banned and subject to censorship: "The films had to be suppressed, many Whites argued overtly, in order to prevent Black empowerment."[2]

- Jones did not benefit from any substantial Oscar bounce, or significant increase in high-profile Hollywood roles as a result of the nomination, but he did revive a successful Broadway career and later became truly famous for providing the disembodied voice for *Star Wars*'s Darth Vader—one of Hollywood's iconic villains of all time, covered in all black from head to toe.

NOMINATION #10—PAUL WINFIELD

Backstory

Oscar Details

Best Actor Nomination for Paul Winfield as Nathan Lee Morgan in *Sounder* (1972) for the 45th Academy Awards (Dorothy Chandler Pavilion) on March 27, 1973.

Character and Movie Overview

In the movie, Winfield plays Nathan Morgan, a beleaguered father constrained by economic fate who attempts to lift his family up in the midst of the Great Depression. Nathan goes so far as to steal a ham for his hungry but loving family and ends up doing a year in jail. Along the way to jail, Nathan apparently is injured trying to save the family dog, Sounder, from an indiscriminate shotgun blast the sheriff aimed at the barking and agitated dog.

Have You Scene It?

It is quite fascinating that Winfield received this nomination given that his character features prominently only in the first and last twenty minutes of the film. Upon Nathan's return, he has a noticeable limp from the shotgun blast he attempted to avert. The movie concludes by affirming that Louisiana sharecropping is nothing to envy, with the actual protagonist, David (Kevin Hooks) saying, as he makes his decision to get an education instead, "You know something Daddy, I'ma miss this ol' raggedy place, but I sure ain't gonna worry about it!"

Black Oscar Angles

Gravity of Reality

This movie heavily invokes themes of race, the premise being that the family has a difficult life as poor Black sharecroppers in the Depression-stricken South.

Still in the Struggle

The Scent of Magnolia is strong in this story of a Louisiana sharecropper struggling to support his family during the Great Depression. In virtually every scene, the Black characters depicted are wearing torn and tattered clothing that is visibly stained with mud or sweat.

Bottom Line

Final Cut

With respect to traditional images of power and control regarding Black males on-screen, this movie character satisfies the femininity prong of the Unholy Trinity generally; given its largely insular-universe status, no clean archetype pattern emerges. The final analysis is that while this movie upholds established patterns of nonthreatening Black men, given its largely insular-universe status with limited contact between Black and White worlds, no clean archetype pattern emerges.

Bonus Features

Outtakes

- As further proof that the Scent of Magnolia was still strong with Hollywood, the same year *Sounder* was released in theaters, *Uncle Remus and His Tales of Brer Rabbit*, the Disney Sunday comic strip first distributed by King Features Syndicated in 1945, finally concluded its run on December 31, 1972.[3]

NOMINATION #11—DIANA ROSS

Backstory

Oscar Details

Best Actress Nomination for Diana Ross as Billie Holiday in *Lady Sings the Blues* (1972) for the 45th Academy Awards (Dorothy Chandler Pavilion) on March 27, 1973.

Character and Movie Overview

In the movie, Ross plays famous singer Billie Holiday, showcasing her life and her struggle for success.

Diana Ross as Billie Holiday in *Lady Sings the Blues*. *NBC/Photofest*

Have You Scene It?

The movie concludes with Holiday's triumphant performance at New York's Carnegie Hall, but the performance is cropped and paired with sobering newspaper clippings of "Holiday Appeal Denied Cabaret License" (due to drug conviction) and "Billie Holiday Dead at 44." These final clippings appear to seal her fate as a tragic figure in the face of intermittent and ephemeral mainstream approval. After all, if rich Whites gave her approval at Carnegie Hall, then surely she must be worthy of a cabaret license.

Black Oscar Angles

Crossover

Ross started her career as a singer, not as a classically trained actor.

Gravity of Reality

This movie is a para-realistic film based upon a factual figure.

Still in the Struggle

Billie Holiday presents as a talented but tragic figure who endured rape and prostitution but could not defeat drugs.

Bottom Line

Final Cut

With respect to traditional images of power and control regarding Black females on-screen, this movie character satisfies the Romantic racialism prong of the Unholy Trinity generally and satisfies the Physical Wonder archetype specifically with her role serving as a talented yet troubled singer. The final analysis is that this movie fits established patterns of non-free Black women and embodies the Physical Wonder archetype in that her singing talent remains the central feature of Holiday's appeal.

Bonus Features

Outtakes

• This true story is based upon Holiday's autobiography of the same name.

NOMINATION #12—CICELY TYSON

Backstory

Oscar Details

Best Actress Nomination for Cicely Tyson as Rebecca Morgan in *Sounder* (1972) for the 45th Academy Awards (Dorothy Chandler Pavilion) on March 27, 1973.

Character and Movie Overview

In the movie, Tyson plays a supportive wife and mother of a sharecropping family that essentially has only love to see itself through hard times during the Great Depression.

Have You Scene It?

Tyson's first scene on-screen features her fetching water from the well first thing in the morning, with a significant-sized sweat stain on her back. This is hardly a glamorous image of femininity and contrasts starkly with images of White women in movies set during the same time period.

Black Oscar Angles

Gravity of Reality

This movie heavily invokes themes of race, the premise being that the family has a difficult life as poor Black family sharecroppers in the Depression-stricken South.

Still in the Struggle

The Scent of Magnolia is strong in this story of a Louisiana sharecropper struggling to support his family during the Great Depression. In virtually every scene, the Black characters depicted are wearing torn and tattered clothing that is visibly stained with mud or sweat.

Bottom Line

Final Cut

With respect to traditional images of power and control regarding Black females on-screen, this movie character satisfies the femininity prong of the Unholy Trinity generally; given its largely insular-universe status, no clean archetype pattern emerges. The final analysis is that while this movie fits established patterns of muted Black women, given its largely insular-universe status with limited contact between Black and White worlds, no clean archetype pattern emerges.

Bonus Features

Outtakes

- Two of the three Black nominations for the 45th Academy Awards came from the same movie.
- Tyson is the first classically trained Black female actor to receive a nomination in the forty-three-year history of the Academy Awards. She later received an Academy Honorary Award in 2018.[4]

NOMINATION #13—DIAHANN CARROLL

Backstory

Oscar Details

Best Actress Nomination for Diahann Carroll as Claudine Price in *Claudine* (1974) for the 47th Academy Awards (Dorothy Chandler Pavilion) on April 8, 1975.

Fellow Best Acting Oscar nominees Diahann Carroll and James Earl Jones in *Claudine*. *20th Century Fox/Photofest*

Character and Movie Overview

In the movie, Carroll plays a poor single mother on welfare. Claudine has six children, and due to the restrictions of welfare she cannot work or have a partner with income in her home; this will reduce the amount she can receive, which is still insufficient to support her growing family. Somehow, Claudine and Roop (James Earl Jones) kindle a relationship that grows into love despite Roop's own financial troubles.

Have You Scene It?

The movie's climactic scene culminates with Claudine and Roop's marriage ceremony, which is interrupted when her eldest son is arrested for being part of a political protest. Perhaps as an attempt to show the indefatigable nature of the human spirit—similar to when Poitier broke out in song at the conclusion of *The Defiant Ones*—amid the chaos and pandemonium in the crowded city street, the family fights to be united in the departing police wagon and appear happy and triumphant as energetic music plays in the background.

Viewers are left wondering what will happen once the music stops. It perhaps would have been equally as interesting to see the family celebrate after winning the lottery and putting an end to their never-ending financial woes.

Black Oscar Angles

Crossover

Carroll started her career as a singer, not as a classically trained actor.

Gravity of Reality

The movie is based around race and the intersecting themes of poverty and welfare.

Still in the Struggle

This movie is the urbanized Northern version of *Sounder* in that it highlights that once many African Americans moved north in the Great Migration, so did their seemingly intractable financial woes.

Bottom Line

Final Cut

With respect to traditional images of power and control regarding Black females on-screen, this movie character satisfies the Romantic racialism prong of the Unholy Trinity generally; given its largely insular-universe status, no clean archetype pattern emerges. While this movie fits established patterns of beleaguered Black women, given its largely insular-universe status with limited contact between Black and White worlds, no clean archetype pattern emerges.

Bonus Features

Outtakes

- Carroll also appeared in racially significant movies *Carmen Jones* (1954) and *Porgy and Bess* (1959).

7

THE COLOR PURPLE THROUGH THE BLUEST EYE (1980–1989)

Controversy exists, perhaps, because all is not black and white. This is precisely what happened with Alice Walker's *The Color Purple*, the subject of controversy over its symbolic iconography. On one hand, it was groundbreaking to have a space where the intimate and intricately complex lives of African Americans were shared with larger audiences. On the other hand, the possibility exists that notwithstanding the historical weight of unflattering Black imagery amassed in Hollywood, movie patrons lacking exposure and education about the African American experience may simply distill such imagery down to Blacks trapped in this painful performativity space, as envisioned by a White male director. It can safely be said that the debate over who gets to create such iconography and what it means still endures.[1]

The Color Purple received an eye-popping eleven Oscar nominations but failed to win in a single category, despite benefitting from star talent in Danny Glover, Whoopi Goldberg, Oprah Winfrey, and director Steven Spielberg. In addition to the controversy over who tells whose stories, one fair criticism was that the movie did not flesh out what the book *The Color Purple* treated more tenderly with more detail: namely, a complex lesbian relationship that "was reduced to several chaste kisses in the movie" and an intricate commentary that "black men abuse black women as part of a 'chain of oppression' that stems in the first place from White brutality."[2] With difficult visual iconography of brusque and brutal Black men perpetrating physical and psychological abuse upon Black women, many viewers may have unwittingly underscored the

Negrophobic narratives in their minds that moviemakers may have been trying to address and confront. However, it is not one filmmaker's fault that such iconography exists in the first place; given the history and continued momentum of racially problematic patterns of the past, it will take many more movies to overcome this inertia of insufficient understanding.

Black director Robert Townsend sought to burlesque the poor quality of Black images in mainstream media, but his independent 1987 masterpiece *Hollywood Shuffle* was simply seen by too few viewers due to limited distribution networks.[3] Additionally, a slew of dance craze movies captured the essence of a bubbling and burgeoning hip-hop movement, but the hit comedy *Coming to America* likely took Hollywood by surprise with the enormity of its success. Famed comedian Eddie Murphy finally hit pay dirt with his rendition of Prince Akeem, and although the movie's success helped launch the groundbreaking late-night talk show career of Arsenio Hall—who played Akeem's best friend and confidant, Semmi—*Coming to America* failed to nab any Oscar nominations.

Yet *Coming to America*'s crossover success—it appealed to Black and White audiences alike—indicated that comedy was now a safe and neutral meeting ground for the mainstream infusion of African Americans. In developing the successful model employed in *The Defiant Ones*, the 1980s also saw a spate of buddy cop films that paired White and Black males who, while not shackled together with wrought-iron chains, were connected by a case they had to share. *Beverly Hills Cop* (Eddie Murphy) and the *Lethal Weapon* (Danny Glover) series furthered this safe trend. *Action Jackson*, featuring the solitary Black male protagonist Carl Weathers (who played Apollo Creed in the original *Rocky* series), did not fare nearly as well at the box office. Other movies featuring solitary White males did better, but the "buddy system" was a clever way to hedge bets when a Black *male* was playing a prominent role.

Not to skip ahead, but regarding the national outrage in the #OscarsSoWhite campaign of the 2010s, part of the frustration concerned the sluggish responses by the Academy in making changes. In contrast, consider how, when race is not involved, the winds of change appear to blow more swiftly. For example, the lack of recognition for Christopher Tucker's makeup work on *The Elephant Man* (1980) prompted the creation of the Academy Award for Best Makeup *the following year*.[4] While perhaps anecdotal, the Academy's immediate solution and policy change demonstrates that it can indeed move swiftly upon issues it deems important. This reaction time must be borne in mind as we analyze the seemingly malingering condition of marginalized Black images in Hollywood film.

Underscoring how movies reflect and reinforce mainstream society, notice the proliferation of 1980s movies such as *Gung Ho*, *Shogun*, and *Rising Sun*, which happened to coincide with rising fears that Japanese cars and technology would prove themselves superior to American brands (which they did). Even the flair of former Hollywood actor Ronald Reagan's economic policies as president were reflected when Michael Douglas won an Oscar for his villainous role as Gordon Gecko, who famously declared in *Wall Street*, "Greed is good!" (The 1981 award ceremony was postponed a day due to the assassination attempt on Reagan's life; the only other time this happened was in observation of Dr. Martin Luther King's murder in 1968.)

But the topic of race was still captivating audiences—with the caveat that it was best mediated (and marketed) through the White male gaze. For instance, the 1988 movie *Mississippi Burning*, loosely based upon the sad but true story of an interracial triad of freedom fighters who were brutally murdered, received seven total nominations. However, many critics questioned whether such film portrayals were hurtful as they glossed over complex racial tensions while prioritizing White participation (in this case, focusing the story on FBI agents portrayed by Gene Hackman and Willem Dafoe) to better attract viewers. Accordingly, in a review for *Time* magazine entitled "Just Another Mississippi Whitewash," Jack E. White described *Mississippi Burning* as a "cinematic lynching of the truth."[5] At the very least, in the 1980s, only a couple of decades removed from the civil rights movement, the embers from fiery tensions regarding true American race relations were still smoldering. During this decade, the list of African American nominees grew, but still only one win was achieved, ending a drought spanning nearly two decades.

NOMINATION #14—HOWARD E. ROLLINS JR.

Backstory

Oscar Details

Best Supporting Actor Nomination for Howard E. Rollins Jr. as Coalhouse Walker Jr. in *Ragtime* (1981) for the 54th Academy Awards (Dorothy Chandler Pavilion) on March 29, 1982.

Character and Movie Overview

In the movie, Rollins plays a ragtime pianist who becomes quite keyed up over the vandalization of his brand-new Ford Model T automobile after he refused to "pay the toll" in front of the Emerald Isle firehouse. Coalhouse, while very proud of his vehicle, appears to hit the wrong notes with jealous working-class Whites who refuse to give him any respect. Conflict stemming from Coalhouse's car eventually leads to the destruction of all that he knows.

Have You Scene It?

After the indirectly related death of Sarah, the mother of his child, Coalhouse and several other sympathizers seek revenge by killing several of the racist firemen. What is curious is that they specifically asked that the racist firehouse chief be turned over for justice and that Coalhouse's new car be returned to him "in its original condition," as if he were fixated upon material objects.

Coalhouse's last scene on screen features him weeping after a failed hostage scenario, pleading, "God, tell me what to do." When Coalhouse exits the building with his hands up, the police commissioner nonetheless orders his sniper to fire upon him, killing him dead on the spot—a move that may have violated

Howard E. Rollins Jr. as Coalhouse Walker Jr. in *Ragtime*. Coalhouse is seated in the car that literally drives him to his ultimate dead end. *Paramount Pictures/Photofest*

common protocol with unarmed individuals who willingly surrender. Thus, while the audience may sympathize with Coalhouse's vigilante attempts to reclaim justice for himself within the visible continuum, he was not successful and his political threat was abated.

Black Oscar Angles

Gravity of Reality

This movie is based around race; much of the movie's tension emanates from the bigoted treatment Coalhouse receives from the working-class Irish firefighters who vandalized his car after refusing to let him pass. It is no secret that before the Irish became White,[6] racial tensions were highest with those closest to the bottom of the economic ladder.

Bottom Line

Final Cut

With respect to traditional images of power and control regarding Black males on-screen, this movie character satisfies the Negrophobia prong of the Unholy Trinity generally and satisfies the Menace to Society archetype specifically with his role serving as a failed revolutionary in attempting to right the scales of racial justice on his own terms—a failed attempt for which he pays with his life.

Bonus Features

Outtakes

- The movie is based upon the book by White male author E. L. Doctorow.

NOMINATION #15, WIN #3—LOUIS GOSSETT JR.

Backstory

Oscar Details

Best Supporting Actor Nomination and Win for Louis Gossett Jr. as Gunnery Sergeant Emil Foley in *An Officer and a Gentleman* (1982) for the 55th Academy Awards (Dorothy Chandler Pavilion) on April 11, 1983.

Character and Movie Overview

In the movie, Gossett plays a hard-core, no-nonsense drill sergeant. Foley immediately marks an imposing, intimidating presence. Foley clearly presents as a Menace to Society, the type of angry Black man who normally would be formally or informally punished for such brash and boorish behavior (including homophobic references); yet, as a drill sergeant doing "whatever means necessary, fair and unfair" to weed out the noncommitted on behalf and benefit of the security of the United States, such behavior is justified and in fact rewarded with the Oscar.

Have You Scene It?

Throughout the movie, Foley maintains an ongoing narrative about how prospective candidates can quit at any time. He references this theme during his first scene on-screen. During the brutal one-on-one "training" that devolved into bloody fisticuffs for both Foley and candidate Mayo, Foley intones before limping away, "You can quit now, Mayo, if you want to." But alas—the spirit of White heroism cannot be suppressed for long. During a pivotal scene later in the movie, when Mayo (Richard Gere) is enduring one of the most difficult tests he has faced as Foley taunts him about his father's alcoholic past, Foley demands Mayo's "DOR" or Drop on Request. Mayo not only refuses but yells at Foley, "Don't you quit on me! I've got nowhere else to go." Here, the emotional fulcrum of power has now swung back to its rightful place—back to the side of a White male. For the rest of the movie, it is Foley (and the viewing audience) who must marvel at the resolve of the eventually successful White male candidate who will not quit.

Black Oscar Angles

Déjà Vu

Similar to *Jerry Maguire*, this movie revolves around an amorous White couple and not the prominently featured Black male actor. This movie is also similar to another Black Oscar–nominated movie, *A Soldier's Story*, in that it appears to defy traditional Black image patterns insofar as the Black character is housed or protected within the larger institutional structure of the US military.

Bottom Line

Final Cut

With respect to traditional images of power and control regarding Black males on-screen, this movie character satisfies the Negrophobia prong of the Unholy Trinity generally and satisfies the Angel Figure and Menace to Society archetypes specifically, with his role serving as a no-nonsense drill sergeant who actually helps the White male protagonist achieve his goal. Utopic Reversal may also be considered here, as Foley's tough-love approach with the White male protagonist turns out not to be the ominous barrier to success it initially to be—in other words, the Black male is not as powerful as he threatens to be in that he is impotent to make the White male hero quit.

Bonus Features

Fall in Line

Something must be said about how Mayo not only triumphs over adversity generally, but specifically triumphs over the more localized Black face of torment. Foley as an adversary is quite mean, but he is not mean enough to get our

Louis Gossett Jr. and Richard Gere getting down and dirty in *An Officer and a Gentleman. Paramount Pictures/Photofest*

protagonist to quit. At the end of the movie, the officer candidates earn the rank of ensign. Per tradition, each new officer receives his or her first salute from the instructor, and in turn, each officer hands Foley a silver dollar. When Mayo hands Foley his coin, the Marine places it in his right pocket instead of his left. This act symbolizes respect for Mayo as an exceptional candidate.

Outtakes

- This character is protected by the cloak of the military and therefore tests normal bounds of "acceptable" Black behavior; Foley engages in activity that routinely results in death for Black males in civilian life.
- Foley's character was originally written for a White actor, which may help explain the unusually strong depiction of an African American male.[7]
- Gossett struggled with depression and alcoholism after his win, primarily due to disillusionment over his failed Oscar bounce.[8]

NOMINATION #16—ALFRE WOODARD

Backstory

Oscar Details

Best Supporting Actress Nomination for Alfre Woodard as Beatrice "Geechee" in *Cross Creek* (1983) for the 55th Academy Awards (Dorothy Chandler Pavilion) on April 11, 1983.

Character and Movie Overview

In the movie, Woodard plays a poor Black woman who offers her services to a struggling White female author who left her husband in New York in search of new life as an orange grove owner in Florida. Themes of Romantic racialism are present, as this friendship is based upon an employer-servant model.

Have You Scene It?

Geechee confronts the White female protagonist, Marjorie, after Geechee initially decides to leave the orange grove with her husband. Geechee is confused about what to do. Marjorie says she does not want Geechee to leave, to which Geechee retorts, "How am I supposed to know that? It's easy to get somebody

Alfre Woodard, adorned with bandana, with Mary Steenburgen in *Cross Creek*.
Universal Pictures/Photofest

for cooking and sweeping." Marjorie then responds, taking a line out of the racial comity playbook, "I think of you as a friend." Geechee relents and decides to stay with her White female friend. Geechee is largely in servant mode, while Marjorie successfully manages her estate, publishes her book, and falls in love, almost as if she were in a Hollywood movie. However, the idea that Whites have kinship relationships with individuals they employ in subjugated power roles is indeed the stuff of Tinseltown fantasy.

Black Oscar Angles

Gravity of Reality

This movie heavily invokes themes of race when a White female author absconds her urban New York environment and transitions to a rural Floridian orange grove—with the help of locals, of course.

Still in the Struggle

Not only was Geechee fairly indigent, but she also struggled with domestic issues, including a husband returning from prison who refused to work and chose to drink and gamble instead.

Bottom Line

Final Cut

With respect to traditional images of power and control regarding Black females on-screen, this movie character satisfies the Romantic racialism and femininity prongs of the Unholy Trinity generally and satisfies the Angel Figure archetype specifically with her role serving as an indigent domestic maid whom the White female protagonist also considers to be her best friend. The final analysis is that this movie fits established patterns of servile Black women for her dedicated loyalty and service to her White female employer; Geechee ultimately chooses to be with her White "friend" rather than stay with her abusive Black husband.

Bonus Features

Outtakes

- The same year, Joe I. Tompkins became the first African American to be nominated in Best Costume Design.
- In other Oscar racial news, the Best Supporting Actress winner this year was unique. Linda Hunt, a four-foot-nine White female, won the award for her role as Billy Kwan—a male Chinese Australian photographer—in Peter Weir's *The Year of Living Dangerously*, making her the first actor to win an Oscar for playing a character of the opposite sex.

NOMINATION #17—ADOLPH CAESAR

Backstory

Oscar Details

Best Supporting Actor Nomination for Adolph Caesar as Sergeant Vernon Waters in *A Soldier's Story* (1984) for the 57th Academy Awards (Dorothy Chandler Pavilion) on March 25, 1985.

Character and Movie Overview

In the movie, Caesar plays a complicated sergeant who has racial pride, but appears to do and say things in conflict with that identity. It must be noted that

Waters has not only rank and power, but a lighter complexion than most of the Black soldiers he commands (and coaches as part of the Negro league baseball team). The idea of colorism may have been deliberately used as a plot device to explain the conflict and apparent episodes of self-hate exhibited by Waters in the film.

Perhaps because he is shrouded and protected by something more powerful—the US military—Waters is not watered down and fully emasculated, unlike other Black male Oscar nominees and winners.

Have You Scene It?

The movie's climactic scene culminates with Waters standing up to his superiors, utilizing the premise in the military that all are equal according to rank: "Anything you don't wanna do, the colored troops will do for you." While this speaks to an unfortunate reality, Waters is not having any of it. He erupts: "The reasons for orders by any superior officer is none of y'all's business. You obey them! This country is at war! And you ni**ers are soldiers! Nothing else!"

Adolph Caesar as Sergeant Vernon Waters, caught between ranks, race, and revenge in *A Soldier's Story*. *Columbia Pictures/Photofest*

Black Oscar Angles

Déjà Vu

This movie is also similar to *An Officer and a Gentleman*, another Black Oscar–nominated movie, in that it appears to defy the traditional Black pattern insofar as the Black character is housed or protected within the larger institutional structure of the US military.

Gravity of Reality

While *A Solider's Story* is largely an insular-universal movie, it is very much based upon the effects and limitations of racism and segregation within the military ranks during the Jim Crow era.

Still in the Struggle

This Black character dies during the course of the movie.

Bottom Line

Final Cut

With respect to traditional images of power and control regarding Black males on-screen, this movie character satisfies the Negrophobia prong of the Unholy Trinity generally and satisfies the Menace to Society archetype specifically with his role serving as an antagonistic army sergeant. Given its largely insular-universe status with limited contact between Black and White worlds, no clean archetype pattern emerges.

Bonus Features

Outtakes

- This film, directed by Norman Jewison, was adapted by Charles Fuller from his Pulitzer Prize–winning Off-Broadway production *A Soldier's Play*.

NOMINATION #18—WHOOPI GOLDBERG

Backstory

Oscar Details

Best Actress Nomination for Whoopi Goldberg as Celie Harris Johnson in *The Color Purple* (1985) for the 58th Academy Awards (Dorothy Chandler Pavilion) on March 24, 1986.

Character and Movie Overview

In the movie, Goldberg plays a shy, timid, but resourceful Black woman who fights for her own dignity and respect in the face of oppressive forces of racism and chauvinism. Celie is so scarred from her own domestic abuse that at one point in the movie, in a moment of fleeting jealousy, she advises Harpo to utilize the misguided tool of domestic violence as a way to exert power and control inside the household against Sofia. Only after she is confronted with this fact by Sofia does Celie open up about the abuse she has been enduring.

Have You Scene It?

One scene that shows the taut emotional trauma Celie endures comes when it was time for her to shave Mister. The scene is interspliced with footage of an African rite and facial marking ritual, complete with drums, singing, and shouting. Shug catches Celie in time, ironically remarking that the razor looks dull. Mister gets up from his rocking chair and huffs, "Damn women!"

Black Oscar Angles

Crossover

Goldberg started her career as a comedian, not as a classically trained actor.

Déjà Vu

Goldberg personally accounts for more than one Black Oscar nomination, making her a repeat contender.

Gravity of Reality

This movie heavily invokes themes of race.

Still in the Struggle

Poverty and powerlessness are running themes in this movie.

Bottom Line

Final Cut

With respect to traditional images of power and control regarding Black females on-screen, this movie character satisfies the femininity prong of the Unholy Trinity generally; given its largely insular-universe status, no clean archetype pattern emerges. The final analysis is that while this movie fits established patterns of afflicted Black women on-screen, given its largely insular-universe status with limited contact between Black and White worlds, no clean archetype pattern emerges.

Outtakes

- All three Black female Oscar nominations for the 58th Academy Awards came from the same movie, although none of *The Color Purple*'s eleven nominations resulted in a win.
- *Out of Africa*—which many critics panned as an intrinsically insensitive, if not racist, movie—won Best Picture that year.[9]
- Unlike other Black Oscar nominations before 1986, this is a movie adapted from a novel authored by an African American female. Controversy ensued, however, because the movie was brought to life by White director Steven Spielberg.

NOMINATION #19—MARGARET AVERY

Backstory

Oscar Details

Best Supporting Actress Nomination for Margaret Avery as Shug Avery in *The Color Purple* (1985) for the 58th Academy Awards (Dorothy Chandler Pavilion) on March 24, 1986.

Character and Movie Overview

In the movie, Avery plays the mistress of Celie's husband, Mister, and a talented jazz singer with style. This character courted controversy rather than acclaim for being in a mainstream movie that introduced a lesbian relationship, which was not common at the time.

Have You Scene It?

The relationship between Shug and Celie is confirmed on-screen when the two kiss in Shug's bedroom one evening while bonding. Shug is grateful to Celie for helping her nurse back to health, but the relationship grows.

Black Oscar Angles

Gravity of Reality

This movie heavily invokes themes of race.

Still in the Struggle

Poverty and powerlessness are running themes in this movie.

Bottom Line

Final Cut

With respect to traditional images of power and control regarding Black females on-screen, this movie character satisfies the femininity prong of the Unholy Trinity generally; given its largely insular-universe status, no clean archetype pattern emerges. The final analysis is that while this movie fits established patterns of afflicted Black women, given its largely insular-universe status with limited contact between Black and White worlds, no clean archetype pattern emerges.

Bonus Features

Outtakes

- All three Black Oscar nominations for the 58th Academy Awards came from the same movie.

NOMINATION #20—OPRAH WINFREY

Backstory

Oscar Details

Best Supporting Actress Nomination for Oprah Winfrey as Sofia Johnson in *The Color Purple* (1985) for the 58th Academy Awards (Dorothy Chandler Pavilion) on March 24, 1986.

Character and Movie Overview

In the movie, Winfrey plays a strong-minded and determined woman who ultimately pays the price for her own strength.

Have You Scene It?

The character's climactic scene culminates with a traumatic sequence in which Sofia is publicly confronted by a White woman who falsely compliments Sofia's children and then asks whether Sofia would be willing to work for her. Sofia, being the strong-minded individual she is, replies, "Hell

Oprah Winfrey and Whoopi Goldberg in *The Color Purple*. *Warner Bros./Photofest*

no"—although rather quietly at first. As this exchange occurs publicly down-town, nearby Whites witness and take affront to such impudence, causing the White woman's husband to come to her defense. He asks Sofia to repeat her statement, cutting her off with a brutal display of battery by slapping Sofia in the face. Sofia responds by punching the man back—presumptively in self-defense—and covers her face with her hands before a mob of White men descends upon her and punishes Sofia savagely—in the name of chivalry for the White woman, of course.

Earlier in the movie, Sofia says, "All my life, I've had to fight." Not only does this underscore the problematic theme of dysfunctional familial relations among African Americans (see *What's Love Got to Do with It*), but it also shows that strong African Americans are ultimately no match for the system (see *Sounder*). Sofia emerges from jail many years later as a broken individual with a clouded eye, suggesting that while she was strong, she was not strong enough to with-stand the pressures of jail.

Black Oscar Angles

Crossover

Winfrey started her career as a television broadcaster and talk show host, not as a classically trained actor.

Gravity of Reality

This movie heavily invokes themes of race.

Still in the Struggle

Poverty and powerlessness are running themes in this movie.

Bottom Line

Final Cut

With respect to traditional images of power and control regarding Black females on-screen, this movie character satisfies the Negrophobia prong of the Unholy Trinity generally; given its largely insular-universe status, no clean archetype pattern emerges. The final analysis is that this movie fits established patterns of afflicted Black women.

Bonus Features

Outtakes

- All three Black Oscar nominations for the 58th Academy Awards came from the same movie.

NOMINATION #21—DEXTER GORDON

Backstory

Oscar Details

Best Actor Nomination for Dexter Gordon as Dale Turner in *Round Midnight* (1986) for the 59th Academy Awards (Dorothy Chandler Pavilion) on March 30, 1987.

Character and Movie Overview

In the movie, Gordon plays a gifted trumpet player who struggles with drugs and alcohol, despite his talent.

Have You Scene It?

Dale moves to Paris as a way to reestablish his life and career and befriends Francis, who agrees to take Dale in. Francis attempts to help and provide advice for Dale, who says, "Don't cry for me." Despondent, Francis pleads with Dale, telling him, "You are killing yourself." Dale responds, "I'll stop." When Francis points out that he has never stopped before, Dale responds that he has never promised anyone before. This scene exemplifies the seemingly never-ending cycle of addiction and hopelessness that can cloud even the brightest of musical stars.

Black Oscar Angles

Crossover

Gordon started his career as a musician, not as a classically trained actor. He was an accomplished tenor saxophonist in real life.

Déjà Vu

Similar to *Lady Sings the Blues* and *Great White Hope*, in this movie a Black entertainment talent cannot leverage his talent to fully escape the demons of drug addiction.

Gravity of Reality

This movie is inherently based around race and identity; according to the movie trailer: "This motion picture is inspired by and dedicated to legendary jazz artists Bud Powell and Lester Young."

Still in the Struggle

Black family dysfunction is on full display here.

Bottom Line

Final Cut

With respect to traditional images of power and control regarding Black males on-screen, this movie character satisfies the Romantic racialism prong of the Unholy Trinity generally and satisfies the Physical Wonder archetype specifically with his role serving as a talented but troubled jazz musician and given the movie's focus primarily upon the musical talents his body can produce. The final analysis is that this movie fits established patterns of troubled Black men.

NOMINATION #22—MORGAN FREEMAN

Backstory

Oscar Details

Best Supporting Actor Nomination for Morgan Freeman as Leo "Fast Black" Smalls Jr. in *Street Smart* (1987) for the 60th Academy Awards (Shrine Auditorium) on April 11, 1988.

Character and Movie Overview

In the movie, Freeman plays a routine police suspect and pimp whose stable includes White women. Apparently, Fast Black is so good at his job that when a reporter (Christopher Reeve) fabricates a fantastical story about a pimp, Fast Black believes the story is about him.

Have You Scene It?

Later in the movie, Punchy (Kathy Baker), one of Fast Black's White prostitutes, informs him, "I'm thinking I'd like to do something else for a while." In the unbearably long scene that follows, Fast Black physically assaults Punchy, pinning her up against the wall by gripping her neck while berating her for her lagging "sales."

After Punchy departs from Fast Black's presence, a Black woman (Anna Maria Hosford) casually saunters up beside him and comments, "She's gonna keep on making trouble," as if physical battery used as a means to coerce Punchy to sell her body for a man's personal profit was not problematic in the least.

Black Oscar Angles

Déjà Vu

Freeman personally accounts for 6.4 percent of all Black Oscar nominations, with five.

Gravity of Reality

This movie heavily invokes themes of race, sexuality, and identity with Fast Black's antics as a menacing pimp.

Bottom Line

Final Cut

With respect to traditional images of power and control regarding Black males on-screen, this movie character satisfies the Negrophobia prong of the Unholy Trinity generally and satisfies the Menace to Society archetype specifically with his role serving as an intimidating and conniving pimp—most especially and perhaps most unfortunately of White women. The final analysis is that this movie fits established patterns of threatening Black men.

Promotional key art for *Street Smart*. Morgan Freeman's menacing character is portrayed as an armed threat, while a centrally placed White female image suggests heroic tension for the White male protagonist who must save her. *Cannon Group/Photofest*

Bonus Features

Hollywood's Third Rail

Notice how Hollywood's third rail prohibiting heavy sexual contact between a Black male and a White female goes conveniently untouched. While Fast Black commands Punchy to seduce White male actor Christopher Reeve (although it turns into much more), there is no hint of sensuality or sexuality shared between a Black male and White female, even though theoretically the Black man is indeed operating to manipulate the White woman's sexuality.

Outtakes

- Said the *Washington Post* of Freeman's performance in 1987: "The most convincing acting comes from Freeman as the vicious pimp Fast Black. The role is hardly a triumph over racial stereotypes, but the veteran actor gives his character an indelibly ugly and disturbing edge, making quite real the mix of paternalism and sudden sadism that pimps use to keep their victims on a short leash."[10]

NOMINATION #23—DENZEL WASHINGTON

Backstory

Oscar Details

Best Supporting Actor Nomination for Denzel Washington as Steve Biko in *Cry Freedom* (1987) for the 60th Academy Awards (Dorothy Chandler Pavilion) on April 11, 1988.

Character and Movie Overview

In the movie, Washington plays human rights activist Steve Biko, who died while attempting to bring an end to apartheid in South Africa. While Biko provides moving prose throughout the movie, he dies from traumatic brain injuries. The focus of the movie then shifts to the initially skeptical White reporter's successful fight for asylum for himself and his family upon finally arriving in London.

Have You Scene It?

Biko addresses a large crowd at a soccer match, employing a bit of understated humor when he observes, "This is the largest illegal gathering I have ever seen!" in reference to draconian apartheid policies that forbade Blacks from gathering in groups to effectively mount political resistance. Biko then proceeds to deliver an encouraging speech about a hopeful South Africa—for Blacks and Whites. The irony is that Biko is surrounded by a crowd comprising extras from South Africa—in a movie directed by a British director (Sir Richard Attenborough) and starring an American actor portraying a South African icon in South Africa.

Black Oscar Angles

Déjà Vu

Washington personally accounts for 10.3 percent of all Black Oscar nominations, with eight.

Gravity of Reality

This movie heavily invokes themes of race given the protagonist's struggle against the race-based system of legal oppression called apartheid.

Still in the Struggle

Per the above, apartheid qualifies as struggle.

Bottom Line

Final Cut

With respect to traditional images of power and control regarding Black males on-screen, this movie character satisfies the Negrophobia prong of the Unholy Trinity generally; given its largely insular-universe status with limited contact between Black and White worlds, no clean archetype pattern emerges. The final analysis is that this movie fits established patterns of what society calls problematic Black men.

Bonus Features

Outtakes

- The movie's director, Sir Richard Attenborough, smuggled one hundred South African actors out of the country to test for the movie, but none were "right for the part." There is no word on the fate of these individuals after the failed script reading and whether they had to return to apartheid or not.[11]

8

THE DENZEL EFFECT (1990–1999)

Thank "De Lawd"[1] for Denzel! The most nominated Black Oscar actor ever, Denzel Washington accounts for 10.3 percent of all Black Oscar nominations, with eight total nominations and two wins. Furthermore, Washington's popularity and celebrity largely grew on account of strategic decision making early in his career, as he was incredibly sensitive to African American female fans about who he was intimate with on-screen.[2] It was during this decade that he and Morgan Freeman become the first African Americans since Sidney Poitier to receive multiple Oscar nominations.

While Washington's accomplishments are to be celebrated with plenty of fanfare, the repeat nominations speak to larger structural issues regarding who has access to opportunities to hone their craft and build their acting careers. Given the sheer representative numbers that Denzel Washington, Octavia Spencer, Viola Davis, and Morgan Freeman have in total nominations and wins, it would be prudent to advise these four individuals to take separate modes of transportation, for if they ever ended up in the same car accident, Hollywood would have an even bigger problem—it would lose the actors responsible for *one-fourth* of all Black Oscar nominations throughout the course of the Academy's ninety-year history, just between four people.

Also adding to the spectrum of Black imagery during this decade were new filmmakers John Singleton (*Boyz n the Hood*) and Spike Lee (*Do the Right Thing, Mo' Betta Blues, Jungle Fever*), cult classics from Mario Van Peebles (*New Jack City*), and independent offerings like *Straight Out of Brooklyn* by Matty Rich. Wesley Snipes, having gained his initial exposure in Spike Lee films (or joints), branched off with his own Black vampire series entitled *Blade*. But none of these innovations garnered Oscar buzz. *Boyz n the Hood*'s Singleton became the first African American to be nominated for Best Director and the youngest nominee in that category, but lost the prize that year to Jonathan Demme for *Silence of the Lambs*.

Other significant films dealing directly with race this decade include *American History X* (1998) and *Amistad* (1997), both of which received Oscar nominations. However, both movies reignited debates about the prioritization of social problem race films as told through the eyes of White male protagonists, in this case Edward Norton and Anthony Hopkins, respectively.

But who can forget the titanic that was *Titanic*? Kate Winslet and Leonardo DiCaprio combined forces at the direction of James Cameron to make one of the most successful movies of all time. While nary an African American soul can be spotted even milling in the background—insert the historically accurate defense here—the movie's blockbuster status is a sobering reminder that Hollywood success is not dependent upon diverse images. The White-dominated movie was deemed to be a universal love story for all, despite its exclusive focus upon Whites. Yet many of the African American directors listed earlier did not see nearly as much financial success because their themes and movies did not have "crossover appeal"—in other words, not enough imagery that included Whites. Meanwhile, the dearth of Blacks in *Titanic* did not sink the movie's chances of scoring big at the box office.

NOMINATION #24—MORGAN FREEMAN

Backstory

Oscar Details

Best Actor Nomination for Morgan Freeman as Hoke Colburn in *Driving Miss Daisy* (1989) for the 62nd Academy Awards (Dorothy Chandler Pavilion) on March 26, 1990.

Character and Movie Overview

In the movie, Freeman plays a dutiful, obedient, and wise chauffeur for an erudite elderly socialite. Not only can Hoke drive, he can apparently find his way around the kitchen as well; he assumes cooking duties after the Black female maid passes away.

The movie chronicles this relationship over time, but let's be clear: The movie revolves around Miss Daisy's character and her relationship with her son. At one point, Miss Daisy recoils in shock and horror when a Jewish synagogue is bombed. Miss Daisy, who is Jewish, naturally feels the pain associated with a hateful statement. Yet the emotional crux hinges around Miss Daisy's state of mind, not Freeman's, even though he is also the product of a layered existence by serving as the subjugated Black male driver of a wealthy White woman, albeit one who identifies with those targeted by hate crimes.

Have You Scene It?

After the passing of many years, Hoke goes to visit Miss Daisy, who is starting to show early signs of dementia. During this tender moment between two elderly souls, Miss Daisy takes a page out of the racial comity playbook and informs Hoke, "You're my best friend." Hoke almost immediately rebuffs Miss Daisy, as if her faltering mind state has her oversharing information that may not be true. Miss Daisy insists upon it, leaving audiences with a false sense of closeness. This is an example of racial comity at its best; their friendship did not compel her to change the fundamental power and economic dynamics of the relationship.

If Miss Daisy thought so much about Hoke, the movie could have just as easily turned into a romance, just like the screwball comedies of old, released largely during the Depression and focusing upon unlikely romantic pairings that transcended established class lines (e.g., *It Happened One Night* and *Bringing Up Baby*). But alas, Hollywood's third rail, the informal policy prohibiting sexual contact between a Black male and a White female (and especially an A-list actress), would likely frown upon this arrangement.

Black Oscar Angles

Déjà Vu

Freeman personally accounts for 6.4 percent of all Black Oscar nominations, with five.

Gravity of Reality

This movie heavily invokes themes of race, given the movie's focus upon an unlikely friendship between a wealthy White woman and her Black male chauffeur.

Still in the Struggle

Racial violence is part of the story.

Bottom Line

Final Cut

With respect to traditional images of power and control regarding Black males on-screen, this movie character satisfies the Romantic racialism and femininity prongs of the Unholy Trinity generally and satisfies the Angel Figure archetype specifically with his role serving as an older, genteel, and loyal chauffeur. The final analysis is that this movie fits established patterns of servile Black men for his dedication to serving his employer.

Bonus Features

Happily Ever After

The movie ends with Miss Daisy's son (Dan Aykroyd) turning the tables and driving Hoke to see Miss Daisy. The final scene is that of Hoke feeding his

Morgan Freeman and Jessica Tandy getting along just fine with the back seat between them in *Driving Miss Daisy. Warner Bros./Photofest*

"friend" Miss Daisy forkful helpings of Thanksgiving pie with a White female hooded pilgrim in the foreground.

White Anchor

Notice that the emotional crux of the movie is the bombing of the Jewish synagogue. Of course, such an act is undoubtedly horrific and objectionable, but at issue here is that the Black man's pain is not enough for the audience—the writers included the bombing to better build a bridge of empathy with the audience and between the two characters. Studies show that Whites believe Blacks are able to handle more pain as a denial of their humanity.[3] Additionally, centering pain around a White character increases the chances that the movie will succeed—as this strategy was arguably employed for Oscar-winning films *The Blind Side* and *The Help*.

Outtakes

- Jessica Tandy won Best Actress for her role as Daisy Werthan in *Driving Miss Daisy*.
- *Driving Miss Daisy* won Best Picture that year over Spike Lee's race drama *Do the Right Thing*.

NOMINATION #25, WIN #4—DENZEL WASHINGTON

Backstory

Oscar Details

Best Supporting Actor Nomination and Win for Denzel Washington as Private Silas Trip in *Glory* (1989) for the 62nd Academy Awards (Dorothy Chandler Pavilion) on March 26, 1990.

Character and Movie Overview

In the movie, Washington plays an embittered formerly enslaved who joins the Union Army ranks in order to obtain his freedom under the uniquely African American citizen-soldier model. The movie is told through the White male gaze of Colonel Shaw (Matthew Broderick), "whose voiceover narration in the form of letters home controls the narrative, and the Black characters remain secondary."[4]

Denzel Washington as Private Silas Trip in *Glory*. Trip appears to contemplate the citizen-soldier model whereby Blacks risked their lives to fully manifest the rights they were already born with as American citizens. *TriStar Pictures/Photofest*

Have You Scene It?

The movie's climactic scene likely involves Shaw deciding to publicly punish Trip for deserting camp. In actuality, Trip was trying to find shoes for his under-resourced Black colleagues. As Shaw was not privy to this information at the time, the scene culminates with Trip being stripped half-naked and whipped. In what likely sealed the Oscar win for Washington, Trip does not emote as he absorbs the pain, but a lone tear rolls down his cheek as he maintains eye contact with Shaw. Shaw, as a White male still worthy of audience sympathy and support, of course, expresses remorse and regret in retrospect. However, with respect to the visible continuum, the proverbial bell has already been rung—the visual iconography of a Black male being punished and whipped is nonetheless seen and recorded. Such an event could have been alluded to in conversation the next day, but the moviemakers thought this scene was evidently important enough to create and include for viewing.

Black Oscar Angles

Déjà Vu

This whipping scene is reminiscent of the punishment scene involving Black Oscar winner Lupita Nyong'o in *12 Years a Slave* (2013).

Gravity of Reality

This movie heavily invokes themes of race as it is based upon a true historical account of the 54th Regiment, one of the first Union Army units to exclusively use Black soldiers under the citizen-soldier model, whereby valor is proven with a price paid in blood—a price that was discounted at a three-fifths rate when it was time to count personage for voting purposes according to the US Constitution.

Still in the Struggle

This movie qualifies, given the fact that the main characters were fighting against slavery.

Bottom Line

Final Cut

With respect to traditional images of power and control regarding Black males on-screen, this movie character satisfies the Romantic racialism and

Negrophobia prongs of the Unholy Trinity generally and satisfies the Menace to Society archetype specifically with his role serving as a formerly rebellious soldier who eventually gets back in line. The final analysis is that this movie fits established patterns of nonthreatening Black men, given his initially rebellious spirit that was distrusted and punished. Thus, "by the end of the film, Trip has bonded with the regiment and is loyal to the colonel."[5]

Bonus Features

Happily Ever After

However gripping, Trip's final scene on-screen comes after the failed uphill charge, with soldiers throwing dead bodies into a mass grave and Trip falling down upon the chest of Broderick's White savior character almost as if to symbolically signify that the Black male and his White male friend will be forever bonded in the afterlife through the chains of racial comity.

Outtakes

- Washington is the only Black actor with multiple nominations in multiple categories.
- As reflective of the restrictions placed upon early Black soldiers, one film scholar notes that "there are no autonomous Blacks in this film, only Blacks who are led by Whites."[6]

NOMINATION #26, WIN #5—WHOOPI GOLDBERG

Backstory

Oscar Details

Best Supporting Actress Nomination and Win for Whoopi Goldberg as Oda Mae Brown in *Ghost* (1990) for the 63rd Academy Awards (Shrine Auditorium) on March 25, 1991.

Character and Movie Overview

In the movie, Goldberg plays a charlatan psychic who, although she is surprised by her ability to communicate with Sam (Patrick Swayze), nonetheless has the ability to speak with the dead. This Romantic racialist trait comes in useful when she reconnects the mournful Molly (Demi Moore) with her husband after a fatal mugging. Whoopi literally becomes the conduit by which the White couple is able to verify their love when she allows Sam to occupy her body so Sam and Molly can enjoy a slow dance.

Have You Scene It?

In the movie's final scene, Molly is able to hear Sam on her own now that the villain has been vanquished (thereby eliminating the need for Oda Mae). Cue the music as a bright heavenly light streams through, illuminating Sam with a celestial glow as he and Molly share one last kiss. The takeaway with this nomination and win is that Blacks are rewarded to the extent that they can both facilitate and entertain White fantasies.

Black Oscar Angles

Crossover

Goldberg started her career as a comedian, not as a classically trained actor.

Déjà vu

Goldberg personally accounts for more than one Black Oscar nomination, making her a repeat contender.

Bottom Line

Final Cut

With respect to traditional images of power and control regarding Black females on-screen, this movie character satisfies the Romantic racialism and femininity prongs of the Unholy Trinity generally and satisfies both the Angel Figure and Comic Relief archetypes for her ability to help the main White characters with a touch of humor. Although her sexuality is muted, she literally becomes a conduit by which the central White couple is able to communicate their love. The final analysis is that this movie fits established patterns of helpful Black women, given her role serving as a savant who facilitates an otherworldly connection between a White couple.

Whoopi Goldberg holds Demi Moore in *Ghost* in a manner reminiscent of the Pietà pose. *Paramount/Photofest*

Bonus Features

Sound Familiar?

Like Hattie McDaniel's role in *Gone with the Wind*, for which she was heaped with praise for making the most out of her limited appearances, effectively becoming a scene stealer, praise for Whoopi Goldberg's Oda Mae character is in a similar vein.

Outtakes

- For his role as Kicking Bird in Best Picture and Best Director winner *Dances with Wolves*, First Nations Canadian actor Graham Greene received a Best Supporting Actor nomination that same year.
- In this movie, problematic racial narratives are on display, with Latino male character Willie Lopez for portraying a Menace to Society archetype as the individual directly responsible for killing Sam.

NOMINATION #27—DENZEL WASHINGTON

Backstory

Oscar Details

Best Actor Nomination for Denzel Washington as Malcolm X in *Malcolm X* (1992) for the 65th Academy Awards (Dorothy Chandler Pavilion) on March 29, 1993.

Character and Movie Overview

In the movie, Washington plays a loquacious, fierce human rights advocate from the 1950s and 1960s.

Have You Scene It?

One interesting scene chronicles Malcolm's early love life before he became reformed in prison. The scene features Malcolm with his White girlfriend, Sophia, in a bedroom with jazz softly playing in the background. Malcolm is shirtless and Sophia is shown wearing only a full-piece lingerie, suggesting that sexual relations are imminent. Malcolm asks that Sophia kiss his leg, then his foot, before commanding her to feed him. He then sarcastically remarks, "I wish your mother and father could see you now." Still, even with a Black male director, Hollywood's third rail remains untouched, as Malcolm Little is not seen on-screen making love to a White woman—even though his love with a White woman is framed as more interesting and involved than love with any other Black woman within the visible continuum.

Black Oscar Angles

Déjà Vu

Washington personally accounts for 10.3 percent of all Black Oscar nominations, with eight.

Gravity of Reality

This movie not only heavily invokes themes of race, it is also based upon the life of a real historical figure.

Still in the Struggle

The agitation against institutional and systemic racial oppression qualifies as struggle.

Bottom Line

Final Cut

With respect to traditional images of power and control regarding Black males on-screen, this movie character satisfies the Negrophobia prong of the Unholy Trinity generally and satisfies the Menace to Society archetype specifically with his role serving as antiracism advocate. As this movie is based upon a true story and given its largely insular-universe status with limited contact between Black and White worlds, no clean archetype pattern emerges.

Bonus Features

Outtakes

- Spike Lee was $5 million over budget and had to seek funding from Black celebrities in order to complete filming the project.[7]

NOMINATION #28—JAYE DAVIDSON

Backstory

Oscar Details

Best Supporting Actor Nomination for Jaye Davidson as Dil in *The Crying Game* (1992) for the 65th Academy Awards (Dorothy Chandler Pavilion) on March 29, 1993.

Character and Movie Overview

In the movie, Davidson plays a transgender person who is the subject of the protagonist's advances. Fergus (Stephen Rea) is a member of the IRA who, while kidnapping Dil's boyfriend, Jody (Forest Whitaker), to leverage the successful release of IRA hostages, falls in love with Dil.

Jaye Davidson in *The Crying Game*. *Miramax/Photofest*

Have You Scene It?

The movie's climactic scene culminates with Fergus discovering the true sexual identity of Dil, with Dil exposing themselves and Fergus becoming sick to the point of vomiting.

Black Oscar Angles

Black Non-American

Davidson is an American-born British actor.

Crossover

Davidson's career origin was not in acting; this is their first role.

Still in the Struggle

Davidson's character struggled with identity and had to deal with people's reactions.

Bottom Line

Final Cut

With respect to traditional images of power and control regarding Black people on-screen, this movie character satisfies the femininity prong of the Unholy Trinity generally and satisfies the Physical Wonder archetype specifically with the character's sexuality serving as a plot twist for the audience. The final analysis is that this movie fits established patterns of nonthreatening Black people; given its largely insular-universe status with limited contact between Black and White worlds, no clean archetype pattern emerges.

Bonus Features

Outtakes

- *The Crying Game* also won Best Screenplay that year.

NOMINATION #29—LAURENCE FISHBURNE

Backstory

Oscar Details

Best Actor Nomination for Laurence Fishburne as Ike Turner in *What's Love Got to Do with It* (1993) for the 66th Academy Awards (Dorothy Chandler Pavilion) on March 21, 1994.

Character and Movie Overview

In the movie, Fishburne plays a flagrant domestic abuser. Ike Turner's debasement and debauchery almost derailed a successful musical career for Tina Turner, but unlike Billie Holiday in *Lady Sings the Blues*, in this movie Tina was able to conquer her demons.

Have You Scene It?

The movie ends with Tina triumphantly on-stage singing her hit track "What's Love Got to Do with It?" and Ike walking away into the night. His maladaptive presence is confirmed when these words flash on-screen: "Ike Turner was later arrested on drug-related charges. He was convicted and served time in a California State Prison."

Black Oscar Angles

Déjà Vu

This movie is quite reminiscent of the Black Oscar–nominated movie *The Color Purple*, with an abusive male domineering his love interest.

Gravity of Reality

The film is based upon the life of a factual figure.

Still in the Struggle

Black performativity of pain is both manifold and manifest in this movie.

Bottom Line

Final Cut

With respect to traditional images of power and control regarding Black males on-screen, this movie character satisfies the Negrophobia prong of the Unholy Trinity generally and satisfies the Menace to Society archetype specifically with his role serving as an abusive husband. The final analysis is that this movie fits established patterns of threatening Black men.

Bonus Features

Outtakes

- Fishburne's nod coupled with Angela Bassett's was the first time in Academy history that two Black actors were nominated in the Best Actor and Best Actress categories. Both nominations were from the same movie.

NOMINATION #30—ANGELA BASSETT

Backstory

Oscar Details

Best Actress Nomination for Angela Bassett as Tina Turner in *What's Love Got to Do with It* (1993) for the 66th Academy Awards (Dorothy Chandler Pavilion) on March 21, 1994.

Character and Movie Overview

In the movie, Basset plays a talented but troubled singer who fights against the cyclical demons of domestic violence.

Have You Scene It?

The movie's final scene melts into actual footage of the real Tina Turner on-stage with text detailing her subsequent triumph and musical success: "Tina has become one of the world's top recording artists. Her tours continue to break concert attendance records worldwide."

Black Oscar Angles

Gravity of Reality

The film is based upon the life of a factual figure.

Still in the Struggle

Black performativity of pain is both manifold and manifest in this movie.

Bottom Line

Final Cut

With respect to traditional images of power and control regarding Black females on-screen, this movie character satisfies the Romantic racialism prong of the Unholy Trinity generally and satisfies the Physical Wonder archetype specifically with her role serving as a talented but troubled musical artist. The final analysis is that this movie fits established patterns of embattled Black women, although her singing talent remained the central features of the movie.

Bonus Features

Outtakes

- In many ways, the themes of this movie resonate as similar to those in the Black Oscar–nominated *Lady Sings the Blues* (1972).

NOMINATION #31—MORGAN FREEMAN

Backstory

Oscar Details

Best Actor Nomination for Morgan Freeman as Eli Boyd "Red" Redding in *The Shawshank Redemption* (1994) for the 67th Academy Awards (Shrine Auditorium) on March 27, 1995.

Character and Movie Overview

In the movie, Freeman plays a convict and savvy smuggler who is literally instrumental in acquiring the tools his friend Andy (Tim Robbins) uses for escape. However, the movie's final scenes culminate with Red finally obtaining parole after forty years.

Have You Scene It?

Andy meticulously orchestrates specific plans for Red to join him upon his successful escape from prison. Red has a voiceover while on the bus, wistful and hopeful that in breaking parole, he can still join his friend. While Red indeed breaks this mental barrier for a Hollywood ending, it nonetheless pales in comparison to the bravura required for Andy to break free in the first place. All Red has to do is follow instructions, and even that causes him trepidation. Red apparently has no one else to visit outside of the prison walls.

Black Oscar Angles

Déjà Vu

Freeman personally accounts for 6.4 percent of all Black Oscar nominations, with five.

Bottom Line

Final Cut

With respect to traditional images of power and control regarding Black males on-screen, this movie character satisfies the Romantic racialism and femininity prongs of the Unholy Trinity generally and satisfies the Angel Figure archetype specifically with his role serving as an older, genteel, and loyal friend of the White male protagonist. The final analysis is that this movie fits established patterns of nonthreatening and useful Black men, as Freeman's character rendered critical aid and assistance to the White protagonist.

Bonus Features

Plasticity of White Criminality

As a subtle indictment of how intelligence is portrayed on-screen, Andy not only utilizes his wits to successfully skim money from prison accounts, but he also plans and executes a complicated and extenuated escape. Above all, Andy finally obtains complete comeuppance by revealing the corrupt accounting practices of the prison warden, who declined to listen to evidence of his innocence. This speaks to the plasticity of White criminality only in the sense that the audience knows why Andy is in jail and thus is morally free to cheer his release.

Unlike Tim Robbins's character, the audience does not learn the details about why Red is in jail. This lack of contextualization prevents the audience from connecting with Red in the same way they empathize with Andy, since there is context (or evidence of innocence) provided within the visible continuum so that the audience roots for his "rightful" escape from jail. This dynamic contrasts sharply from *The Green Mile*, where even when the audience is apprised of John Coffey's innocence, he nonetheless dies in front of the audience's eyes.

Outtakes

- While not explicitly stated, it is implied that race may have been a factor in Red's repeated parole denials.

NOMINATION #32—SAMUEL L. JACKSON

Backstory

Oscar Details

Best Supporting Actor Nomination for Samuel L. Jackson as Jules Winnfield in *Pulp Fiction* (1994) for the 67th Academy Awards (Shrine Auditorium) on March 27, 1995.

Character and Movie Overview

In the movie, Jackson plays a Jheri-curled, Bible-quoting hitman for Marsellus Wallace, a menacing Black male drug lord.

Have You Scene It?

The movie's climactic scene culminates with Marcellus (Ving Rhames) being sodomized, with dramatic saxophone music in the background. The emasculation of a powerful Black male figure was complete in this scene—such presumed power could not go unchallenged. After all, earlier in the movie, Marsellus's power was famously intimated through Winnfield—a no-nonsense hit man who had no problem violently protecting Marsellus's tough reputation. To wit, in a key scene involving Oscar-nominee Jackson, Winnfield and Vincent (John Travolta) retrieve a briefcase belonging to Marsellus from a double-crossing Brett (Franke Whaley), while Winnfield ritualistically recites the Bible verse Ezekiel 25:177 before executing the hapless Brett—after interrogating him intimidatingly: "What does Marcellus Wallace look like?"

Black Oscar Angles

Déjà Vu

Jackson personally accounts for more than one Black Oscar nomination, making him a repeat contender.

Still in the Struggle

This character's indigent status is implied if crime is deemed to be the principal source of his income.

Bottom Line

Final Cut

With respect to traditional images of power and control regarding Black males on-screen, this movie character satisfies the Negrophobia prong of the Unholy Trinity generally and satisfies the Menace to Society archetype specifically with his role serving as a gun-toting, Bible-quoting hired hit man. The Final Analysis is that this movie fits established patterns of threatening Black men in that he poses a violent threat to others, despite his prodigious knowledge of the Bible.

Bonus Features

Flip the Script

Winnfield makes no protest when his partner "accidentally" fatally shoots an African American male in the backseat. The death becomes comic relief, as the two now have a dilemma about cleaning the car. They go to the home of Jimmie (Quentin Tarantino), who complains about the situation, derisively stating sarcastically at least four different times that he is not a charity performing "dead ni**er storage."

Winnfield, despite his bold and bellowing recitations of scripture before executing others, appears unusually reserved in the presence of such insults.

Outtakes

- Director Quentin Tarantino makes a cameo in his directorial debut; his character has a Black female spouse.
- *Forrest Gump* won Best Picture that year; the film featured a Black character whose Black image and iconography was leveraged into a nationwide restaurant chain entitled *Bubba Gump Shrimp*.

NOMINATION #33, WIN #6—CUBA GOODING JR.

Backstory

Oscar Details

Best Supporting Actor Nomination and Win for Cuba Gooding Jr. as Rod Tidwell in *Jerry Maguire* (1996) for the 69th Academy Awards (Shrine Auditorium) on March 24, 1997.

Character and Movie Overview

In the movie, Gooding plays an energetic and vivacious football player who wants to maximize both his contract potential and his actual playing time through his reluctant agent, Jerry Maguire.

Have You Scene It?

One memorable scene comes when Rod is still making his case about how Jerry should advocate for his financial needs. While the conversation starts in the locker room, the camera pans out to reveal that the whole time the two have been in conversation, Rod has been completely naked, as the camera pans out and shows a rearview shot of Jerry in the background and Rod in the foreground, buttocks notwithstanding. Rod then delivers the famous line, "We ain't fighting, we're finally talking!"

Black Oscar Angles

Gravity of Reality

This movie is based around race; the relationship between Rod and Jerry is framed around cultural differences.

Still in the Struggle

Constant references are made to race and resources (and the lack thereof) by Rod and his family.

Fellow Best Supporting Oscar winners Cuba Gooding Jr. and Regina King in *Jerry Maguire*. *TriStar Pictures/Photofest*

Bottom Line

Final Cut

With respect to traditional images of power and control regarding Black males on-screen, this movie character satisfies the Negrophobia prong of the Unholy Trinity generally and satisfies the Physical Wonder archetype specifically with his role serving as an amped football player seeking greater pecuniary gain. The final analysis is that this movie fits established patterns of entertaining Black men in that his football talent remains the central feature of Rod's appeal to Jerry. Additionally, Comic Relief and Menace to Society also qualify in that much of Rod's "antics," while socially threatening and disruptive to normal White middle-class mores, are nonetheless framed as humorous.

Bonus Features

Out of Bounds

Scenes like the one just described coupled with that of Rod's spouse (played by subsequent Black Oscar winner Regina King: "Please remove your d*ck from my a**?") along with "Show me the money!" feature lines that fuel the narrative Black players are self-centered, egotistical lushes who prioritize immediate financial gain. In actuality, the argument is quite sound considering the average length of a professional football player's career is only four years; the fact that these players can see their entire playing careers abruptly end, means that seeking security is quite sound and prudent. It is not as if any *Fortune* 500 CEO has refused a salary amount in excess of their accounted needs—people are always receptive to additional capital as security for their future within a capitalistic economy. But even though Jerry directly financially benefits from Rod's exerting all of his physical energies, Rod is made to look like the money-grubber.

White Anchor

The film is appropriately titled *Jerry Maguire*, as it is indeed about the White male protagonist and his love life (one of Hollywood's most famous love lines is "You had me at 'Hello.'"). Other examples of this are *Reivers*, *An Officer and a Gentleman*, and *Ghost*.

Outtakes

- Gooding beat out fellow nominee James Woods, of the para-realistic race drama *Ghosts of Mississippi*, to win the Oscar.

NOMINATION #34—MARIANNE JEAN-BAPTISTE

Backstory

Oscar Details

Best Supporting Actress Nomination for Marianne Jean-Baptiste as Hortense Cumberbatch in *Secrets & Lies* (1996) for the 69th Academy Awards (Shrine Auditorium) on March 24, 1997.

Character and Movie Overview

In the movie, Jean-Baptiste plays a financially successful optometrist who was adopted and wishes to trace her roots. The twist is that she discovers that her birth mother is a dysfunctional White woman. While Hortense is framed as the driver of the plot, the movie is unabashedly about the other White relationships that eventually surface as more important.

Have You Scene It?

The movie's climactic scene culminates with the whole family coming to terms with its past. Hortense asks quietly, "Was my father a nice man?" Her mother replies, "Don't break my heart." Hortense then rises and goes to hug her mother.

Marianne Jean-Baptiste wrestles and reconciles with identity in *Secrets & Lies*. *October Films/Photofest*

The movie's final scene features Hortense visiting her half-sister and gaining her good graces despite the fact that she occupies a higher class and standing.

While there is nothing wrong with Hortense going down the economic ladder to mix and mingle with her family, Whites over the years of hierarchical structuring of society have made it abundantly clear that poor Blacks and rich Whites were not to mix. When the tables are turned, however, the dysfunctional Whites are of interest and deserving of empathy from the audience.

Black Oscar Angles

Black Non-American

Jean-Baptiste is a British-born actor.

Gravity of Reality

This movie heavily invokes themes of race, given Hortense's attempt to interrogate her adopted childhood roots, which led her to the surprising discovery that her birth mother was a White woman.

Bottom Line

Final Cut

With respect to traditional images of power and control regarding Black females on-screen, this movie character satisfies the Romantic racialism and femininity prongs of the Unholy Trinity generally and satisfies the Angel Figure archetype specifically with her role serving as an understanding daughter who helps her family stay together. The final analysis is that this movie fits established patterns of helpful Black women, given her focus on forgiveness and helping her family.

Bonus Features

Outtakes

- Although the writers endowed Hortense with higher class status (she is a well-educated Black middle-class optometrist in London), it is the White working-class characters who dominate the screen time and the audience's attention. An arguably similar dynamic occurs in the hit television series *This Is Us*, which debuted on NBC in 2016, in which the Black male is more successful than his White twin siblings.

9

NEW CENTURY,
NEW BEGINNING?
(2000–2009)

In considering the exploitation of Black images in early American film and fast-forwarding to movies made after the twentieth century, it is patently clear that the quantity of minority images has evolved, with more than half of all Black Oscar nominees and roughly three-quarters of all winners coming in the twenty-first century. In the seventy-three ceremonies that occurred in the twentieth century, there were only five Black acting winners total; this number was achieved in the third ceremony, in 1930, for Whites. In other words, it took seventy-three years for Black actors to achieve what White actors had done in three. Thus, the *quality* of this evolution remains the billion-dollar question.

Despite Hattie McDaniel's breakthrough victory in 1939, more than six decades passed before another female minority actor won an Academy Award, when Halle Berry claimed the Best Actress prize in 2002 for her role in *Monster's Ball*—a role that some may argue was not that much more flattering than McDaniel's with respect to traditional racial imagery seen on-screen.[1] After a considerable lull in consistent minority presence at the Academy Awards, diversity was center stage in 2002, as Denzel Washington also claimed Best Actor honors for his uncharacteristically villainous role in *Training Day* and Sidney Poitier received an Academy Honorary Award—an acknowledgment, perhaps, of his many breakthrough roles during his career (e.g., *Lilies of the Field, In the Heat of the Night, Guess Who's Coming to Dinner*).

In considering other non-White individuals who garnered Oscar attention, in 2001 Benicio Del Toro broke a four-decade drought at the Academy Awards for Latinx actors when he won the award for Best Supporting Actor for his role in *Traffic* (although in the movie, sex with a Black male was "used to show the depths of depravity to which White female characters have fallen (because of their drug habits)").[2] In 2005, Black actors Morgan Freeman and Jamie Foxx claimed Oscars for Best Supporting Actor and Best Actor in *Million Dollar Baby* and *Ray*, respectively, the first time in Hollywood history that two minority males claimed both prestigious awards. In 2006, Ang Lee became the very first Asian director to claim honors for Best Director with his work in *Brokeback Mountain*. In 2007, not only were 40 percent of the nominees minority actors,[3] but Black singer Jennifer Hudson won Best Supporting Actress honors for her role in *Dreamgirls*, while Black actor Forest Whitaker claimed Best Actor honors for his leading role in *The Last King of Scotland*. In response, members of the mainstream media stated that the 2007 Oscars represented "something of a watershed moment for people of color, a veritable field day for diversity and internationalism."[4]

By way of quick example, let us briefly analyze how the HARM theory operated during the blockbuster summer of 2008 when applied to one of Hollywood's most hallowed characters: the superhero (recall that this is before *Black Panther* was released in 2018). The summer is the special season reserved for the superhero, when Hollywood makes its annual offering of movies driven by alpha-male characters faced with the overwhelming task of saving the city/ planet/universe from imminent peril. Such movies are typically led by White males, and a quick look at the blockbuster summer of 2008 confirms as much, with movies like *Batman: The Dark Knight* (Christian Bale), *The Incredible Hulk* (Edward Norton), and *Iron Man* (Robert Downey Jr.). The only comparable superhero movie in 2008 without a White male lead was *Hancock*, starring Will Smith.

We should not gloss over the detail that *Hancock* was a pioneering big-budget mainstream movie featuring a minority protagonist *in the year 2008*—which evidences that pre-*Hancock*, virtually all of Hollywood's superheroes (which in turn become *our* superheroes) were dominated by White characters. There is nothing racist about this fact, but it certainly underscores how a hierarchy of power is *racialized* when it comes to conditioning audiences to accept likeable characters tasked with the responsibility of helping larger communities. Nevertheless, when we apply the HARM theory to the character Hancock, we find that he pales in comparison to his White male counterparts in terms of of romantic interest development; definable character arc; compelling dilemma of global magnitude; understanding, harnessing, and controlling his superpowers, and so on. The lack of intimacy between Will Smith and Charlize Theron in *Hancock* is particularly telling—not merely because they were scripted to be married spouses but because if there were ever a minority lead that a Hollywood studio would feel safe risking an onscreen kiss with a White female lead, it would be the bankable Will Smith. If Smith was not allowed to do so, then the odds are less favorable for a lesser-known minority male actor to lock lips with a prominent White female lead in a mainstream movie anytime soon.

In analyzing Smith's role in *Hancock*, the point is not to vilify Smith for his portrayal or condemn the movie for departing from more traditional heroic conventions adopted in the other three examples. Rather, the point is to question to what degree the resulting images of Smith (as disheveled, unkempt, unshaven, foulmouthed, and drunk), despite any lighthearted intentions harbored during their production, will help or hurt in terms of the overarching marginalization and emasculation suffered by so many minority male characters in Hollywood's extensive history. Given the global distribution and box office success of *Hancock*, one must also consider the quasi-ambassadorial role that *Hancock* assumes for international moviegoers who, while enjoying the comedic appeal of the movie, have yet to visit the United States (and in many cases never will), possibly forming a stronger impression of Black males in particular than many moviegoers would realize or care to admit. At the end of the day, *Hancock* only further suggests that even in the current era, there is a difference with respect to depicting minority images when compared to the dignity and respect commonly attributed to their White male counterparts.

Even still, women are subjugated and suppressed relative to White males in this decade. However, relative to other non-Whites, White women celebrated Oscar breakthroughs that may not be as plausible for Black women.[5] For instance, Sofia Coppola won Best Original Screenplay for *Lost in Translation* (2003) and Kathyrn Bigelow was the first female director to ever claim the Best Director Oscar for *The Hurt Locker* (2008). Both of these are compelling films deserving of high-quality praise, but with respect to access to resources, social capital, and key contacts, it must be noted that Coppola is the daughter of Francis Ford Coppola and Bigelow is the former spouse of James Cameron. Both Francis Ford Coppola and James Cameron are not just movie directors but extraordinarily successful and influential White male directors whose financial, technical, and artistic successes reverberate throughout the industry. Without diminishing the artistic quality or talent of Sofia Coppola or Kathryn Bigelow, it simply does not hurt to have close personal relationships with White males of this ilk when seeking a place for one's talents within a closed and cutthroat industry. Few Black women can lay claim to these kinds of relationships.

Even when Black women are publicly adorned with the enhanced social capital that Oscar nominations can bring, change can still be difficult. Best Actress

Oscar winner Halle Berry discovered that neither she nor anyone was immune from the swampy morass of blurred race relations the year after her landmark win in 2002, when Best Actor winner Adrien Brody, without warning or permission, swept her up in a relatively impassioned, mouth-to-mouth kiss during his acceptance speech, gripping her neck while her husband at the time—musician Eric Benét—watched in shock, much like the rest of the international television audience.[6] As of this writing, Lisa Churgin of the Academy's Film Editors Branch can still be seen on YouTube describing the scene as a "Favorite Oscar® Moment." It is unknown what, if any, effect that the #MeToo movement against unwanted and unprofessional sexual harassment (whether in public or private) has had on the Academy's position of this publicly documented, unplanned and nonconsensual sexual contact.

NOMINATION #35—DENZEL WASHINGTON

Backstory

Oscar Details

Best Actor Nomination for Denzel Washington as Rubin Carter in *The Hurricane* (1999) for the 72nd Academy Awards (Shrine Auditorium) on March 26, 2000.

Character and Movie Overview

In the movie, Washington plays a frustrated former boxer who was jailed for a crime he did not commit. A young Black male being fostered by a Canadian family persuades his family to get involved, and it is the White couple that demonstrates understanding and forgiveness—even though it was bad, racist Whites who put Carter in jail and kept him there. This is one of several Black Oscar–nominated movies (e.g., *The Great White Hope*, *Ali*) where we understand Blacks through their bodies.

Have You Scene It?

The movie's climactic scene culminates with the judge reading the terms of Carter's successful appeal and securing his release from jail. Part of the rationale articulated by the judge was that Carter's "conviction was predicated upon an appeal to racism rather than reason."

Black Oscar Angles

Déjà Vu

Washington personally accounts for 10.3 percent of all Black Oscar nominations, with eight.

Gravity of Reality

This is a para-realistic film based upon the life of a factual figure.

Still in the Struggle

The movie's entire plot is predicated upon racial struggle.

Bottom Line

Final Cut

With respect to traditional images of power and control regarding Black males on-screen, this movie character satisfies the Negrophobia prong of the Unholy Trinity generally and satisfies the Menace to Society and Physical Wonder archetypes, given the focus on the boxing talents of his body and upon the fear behind the thoughts his mind could produce. The final analysis is that this movie fits established patterns of frustrated Black men, with his role serving as a wrongly imprisoned boxer and social advocate.

Bonus Features

Outtakes

- The movie was adapted from Carter's autobiography, *The Sixteenth Round: From Number 1 Contender to 45472.*

NOMINATION #36—MICHAEL CLARKE DUNCAN

Backstory

Oscar Details

Best Supporting Actor Nomination for Michael Clarke Duncan as John Coffey in *The Green Mile* (1999) for the 72nd Academy Awards (Shrine Auditorium) on March 26, 2000.

Character & Movie Overview

In the movie, Duncan plays a larger-than-life, barefoot Black male in overalls who has a special gift to heal everyone—everyone but himself, that is: "We can legitimately ask why, in *The Green Mile*, John Coffey is never seen working his miracles for fellow African Americans, only for Whites."[7]

Have You Scene It?

When John first arrives, he is the epitome of every White male's nightmare: a large, hulking figure of muscle, complete with bald head and stoic expression. He was supposed to be eight feet in height. But this fear quickly dissipates once he opens his mouth and stutters his name and when it is revealed that he is afraid of the dark.

What John's mouth is good for is the releasing of negative toxins from the people he heals, in the form of swarming insects. Paul Edgecomb (Tom Hanks)

Michael Clarke Duncan as John Coffey recalls traditional narratives about Blacks' propensity to heal Whites in *The Green Mile*. *Warner Bros./Photofest*

is seen "later coyly telling Coffey that his missus was pleased by his cure, 'several times.'"[8] Given that Edgecomb suffered from a urinary tract infection earlier in the movie, the obvious implication is that Edgecomb's sex life had dramatically improved. Taking another page out of the racial comity playbook, the movie depicts Paul as innocent of any moral culpability, as he even considered helping John escape his fate of being electrocuted for a crime he did not commit, rather than legally having the system free him.[9] As a result, Hanks must literally live with the bittersweet curse of enjoying a prolonged life, but one now burdened with guilt and remorse over his memory of John and his failure to help him escape a wrongful execution.

Black Oscar Angles

Gravity of Reality

This movie is based around race. It is implied that John's conviction was influenced by race, as he was found with the blood of two White girls on his hands. Had they been Black women, perhaps the public reaction would have been different.

Still in the Struggle

The Scent of Magnolia is detectable in this example of a contemporary movie that jumps in time to a historically correct time period in which Blacks were undoubtedly subjugated. Additionally, this movie character dies in the film.

Bottom Line

Final Cut

With respect to traditional images of power and control regarding Black males on-screen, this movie character satisfies the Romantic racialism and femininity prongs of the Unholy Trinity generally and satisfies the Angel Figure and Physical Wonder archetypes specifically with his role serving as an otherworldly, literally larger-than-life figure who uses his special powers for the benefit of the White characters. The final analysis is that this movie fits established patterns of useful Black men, given the focus on the special ability of his body to heal the White characters in the movie, but not himself.

Bonus Features

Black in the Hat

In *The Cat in the Hat*, a 1957 classic children's story book authored by Dr. Seuss (Theodore Geisel), a mother leaves two children at home with strict instructions about keeping the house in order in her absence and a talking cat magically appears, proceeding to make the house a mess, to the children's initial chagrin. One possible interpretation of this story is that the cat and his attempt to get the children to "have some fun," is a revolutionary impulse against authority that governs people by rules, especially in the physical absence of such authority, which underscores the travesty of individuals in society agreeing to restrict and self-regulate themselves.[10]

This is relevant to our discussion because, as a movie made in the "modern era" near the turn of the twenty-first century, themes of emasculation in *The Green Mile* are present, but simply more subtle. At the beginning of the movie, John is framed and depicted as a hulking, indomitable, physical specimen and a threat, replete with bulging biceps barely contained inside his overalls. All of this raw, physical power, on a rudimentary level, suggests power and the potential to control the White men around him. But just like in the book *The Cat in the Hat*, all of the chaos the visiting cat caused and all of the potential problems the children would face upon their mother's return are magically made to go away with the cat's magical machine that nicely and neatly puts everything in its proper place right before the mother enters.

Suffice to say that all the potential problems a physically imposing Black male could have upon society are dissipated the moment he opens his mouth and stutters out his name. The Black male's initially imposing power only becomes less so as the movie progresses, as he confesses his fear of the dark and more so when the White males "figure it out" and start to systematically exploit John's gifts for their own personal gain. John's full emasculation is made complete with his torturous death on-screen, which, akin to the magical machine in *The Cat in the Hat*, by end of the visible continuum puts everything back in its place with respect to power and control along traditional and historical racial lines.

Outtakes

- Duncan's nomination was his first, but his image portrayal was not new: "Rooted in (18th c.) assumptions about Blacks' inferiority, these depictions of African Americans showed them as childlike, easily fooled, and satisfied by simple, almost bestial pleasures. . . . They were afraid of the dark, intolerant of cold weather, and unable to learn higher-level skills."[11]

NOMINATION #37—WILL SMITH

Backstory

Oscar Details

Best Actor Nomination for Will Smith as Muhammad Ali in *Ali* (2001) for the 74th Academy Awards (Kodak Theater) on March 24, 2002.

Character and Movie Overview

In the movie, Smith plays a gregarious, loquacious, and politically daring heavyweight champion boxer at the height of his career.

Have You Scene It?

In one scene early in the movie, Ali asks a Black male youth to hold up his hand and says that he can hit it faster than the youth can count to three. The youth dutifully counts to three and Ali seemingly does not move. After an expectant pause, he asks the youth, "Did you feel that?" suggesting that Ali moves so fast, he can't be detected with the naked eye.

Black Oscar Angles

Crossover

Smith started his career as a rap musician before turning his attention to television sitcom acting; he did not start his career as a classically trained actor.

Déjà Vu

Smith personally accounts for more than one Black Oscar nomination, making him a repeat contender.

Gravity of Reality

This movie heavily invokes themes of race; it is also a film based upon the life of a factual figure.

Bottom Line

Final Cut

With respect to traditional images of power and control regarding Black males on-screen, this movie character satisfies the Romantic racialism and

Negrophobia prongs of the Unholy Trinity generally and satisfies the Menace to Society and Physical Wonder archetypes specifically with his role serving as an outspoken boxer. The final analysis is that this movie fits established patterns of threatening Black men, given the focus on the boxing talents of his body as well as controversy he courted with his public statements emanating from his mind.

Outtakes

• At least three Black Oscar nominations have occurred for films in which the actor nominated played a boxer (e.g., *Great White Hope*, *The Hurricane*, *Ali*).

NOMINATION #38, WIN #7—DENZEL WASHINGTON

Backstory

Oscar Details

Best Actor Nomination and Win for Denzel Washington as Alonzo Harris in *Training Day* (2001) for the 74th Academy Awards (Kodak Theater) on March 24, 2002.

Character and Movie Overview

In the movie, Washington plays a crooked cop with a corrupt moral compass. He fought the law and the law won.

Have You Scene It?

The movie's climactic scene culminates with Alonzo shouting publicly, "King Kong ain't got nothing on me!" after being "shot in the ass." If having a bullet discharged from a firearm embedded in his gluteal muscles was not emasculating enough, Alonzo's direct comparison of himself to King Kong was perhaps appropriate in the sense that both he and King Kong represented Black males who were once up on high and were subsequently humbled and brought back down to earth. (The literature is extensive on the symbolic representative nature of race in *King Kong*.)

Black Oscar Angles

Déjà Vu

Washington personally accounts for 10.3 percent of all Black Oscar nominations, with eight.

Gravity of Reality

This movie heavily invokes themes of race given the plot's focus on the world of (mostly Black and Latinx) crime committed on the streets through the lens of a fresh White male recruit. White men are also implicated as committing crimes (the Three Wise Men), but at a higher, hands-off, white-collar level. When Whites are depicted engaging in ground-level, "dirty" crime, it is the Russian mafia, which kills Alonzo on-screen at the end of the movie.

Bottom Line

Final Cut

With respect to traditional images of power and control regarding Black males on-screen, this movie character satisfies the Negrophobia prong of the Unholy Trinity generally and satisfies the Menace to Society and Utopic Reversal archetypes specifically with his role serving as a corrupt police officer. With respect to Utopic Reversal, the "Black male's emasculation becomes indicative of the way Black males are restricted in and controlled by a society built on White male privilege, which is carried over into screen representations."[12] The final analysis is that this movie fits established patterns of threatening Black men, given the focus on his corruption as a peacekeeping officer of the law and his corresponding fall from grace.

Outtakes

• Washington was the second African American to win an Academy Award for Best Actor, following Sidney Poitier for the 1963 film *Lilies of the Field*. Sidney Poitier also received an honorary Oscar that year.

NOMINATION #39, WIN #8—HALLE BERRY

Backstory

Oscar Details

Best Actress Nomination and Win for Halle Berry as Leticia Musgrove in *Monster's Ball* (2001) for the 74th Academy Awards (Kodak Theater) on March 24, 2002.

Character and Movie Overview

In the movie, Berry plays a down-on-her-luck mother whose husband is on death row in a traditionally Southern (read: racist) town. Leticia strikes up an unlikely romance with the man who killed her husband via electrocution.

All the Black men related to Leticia are literally killed off on-screen: Her dark-skinned son is run off the road, but not before being lambasted and condemned by her for being overweight, and her husband (played by rap mogul Sean "P. Diddy" Combs) is graphically executed in the electric chair. Once both Black male figures are out of her life, her romance with Hank (Billy Bob Thornton) begins.

Have You Scene It?

The movie's climactic scene culminates with Leticia moaning Hank, "Make me feel better." The ensuing love scene was the subject of controversy, as some deemed it to be semipornographic in nature, likely to evoke memories of the tragic mulatto role Dorothy Dandridge played half a century earlier.

In addition to this scene, there is the symbology of Leticia's eating chocolate ice cream while Hank most likely performs cunnilingus out of view.

Black Oscar Angles

Gravity of Reality

This movie heavily invokes implicit themes of race, given the plot twist of Leticia falling in love with the prison guard who executed her Black male husband.

Halle Berry, adorned with bandana, in *Monster's Ball*. *Lions Gate Films/Photofest*

Still in the Struggle

The character's financial struggles are paramount.

Bottom Line

Final Cut

With respect to traditional images of power and control regarding Black females on-screen, this movie character satisfies the Romantic racialism and femininity prongs of the Unholy Trinity generally and satisfies the Physical Wonder archetype specifically with her role serving as a widowed, motherless, broken individual in desperate need of repair and the ensuing focus upon her body and sexuality as a result of her unlikely romance. The final analysis is that this movie fits established patterns of embattled Black women.

Outtakes

- Rap musician Mos Def/Yasiin Bey also made an appearance in this movie as a Black musical crossover.

NOMINATION #40—QUEEN LATIFAH

Backstory

Oscar Details

Best Supporting Actress Nomination for Queen Latifah as Matron "Mama" Morton in *Chicago* (2002) for the 75th Academy Awards (Kodak Theater) on March 23, 2003.

Character & Movie Overview

In the movie, Latifah plays a corrupt prison caretaker who introduces herself to the protagonist, Roxie Hart, with the song "When You're Good to Mama."

Have You Scene It?

Mama is introduced as "the Keeper of the Keys, the Countess of the Clink, the Mistress of Murders Row, Matron Mama Morton." This narrative does little to depart from the narrative that Black women have nothing else to do except spend all their time and attention caring for skinnier White women. A possible allusion to her weight and build may be in her opening line about how she looks after the "chickies" in her pen, with herself as the biggest mother hen.

This may also be a false sense of attempted power, as her whole premise is that if one is obedient, then Mama will reciprocate. Mama's threats are unfounded, as she ultimately ends up applauding Roxie in the final scene in recognition of Roxie's triumph in the spotlight.

Black Oscar Angles

Crossover

Latifah started her career as a rapper, not as a classically trained actor.

Bottom Line

Final Cut

With respect to traditional images of power and control regarding Black females on-screen, this movie character satisfies the Romantic racialism and femininity prongs of the Unholy Trinity generally and satisfies the Angel Figure archetype specifically, for despite her initial gruff demeanor, she is there to help the White protagonist. The final analysis is that this movie upholds the pattern of useful Black women.

Outtakes

- Queen Latifah is the rapper's stage name for Dana Owens.
- *Chicago* won Best Picture that year.

NOMINATION #41—DJIMON HOUNSOU

Backstory

Oscar Details

Best Actor Nomination for Djimon Hounsou as Mateo Kuamey in *In America* (2003) for the 76th Academy Awards (Kodak Theater) on February 29, 2004.

Character and Movie Overview

In the movie, Hounsou plays a reclusive Nigerian photographer who befriends two Irish immigrant White girls in his seedy New York apartment building. The girls' father initially warns his daughters to stay away from Mateo because he's Black. The only reason this White family makes contact with Mateo in the first place is that they are poor immigrants, although the father finally lands a job by movie's end.

Have You Scene It?

Mateo turns into a sympathetic character when it is discovered that he is a terminal AIDS patient. The same blood transfusion procedure that was blamed for giving Mateo AIDS miraculously works successfully for Christy when she gives her blood to the baby. The baby's first movements in response to the successful transfusion directly coincide with Mateo's death, as depicted in a visual montage. The baby starts to cry as Mateo, sweating profusely with an oxygen mask over his mouth, is seen with chapped lips, chanting with soothing music in the background. The classic life-for-a-life motif is employed here, with the Black life being the one that was expendable.

Mateo further fulfills the Angel Figure role by paying the hospital bills for a White family he has just met. As an African immigrant himself, it is curious to consider that there are no individuals he knows with whom he could repatriate the funds. In essence, Blacks are celebrated to the extent that they serve and entertain the fantasies of Whites. It is difficult to imagine a reversal of this movie being made.

Black Oscar Angles

Déjà Vu

Hounsou personally accounts for more than one Black Oscar nomination, making him a repeat contender.

Gravity of Reality

This movie heavily invokes themes of race, the premise being that an unlikely friendship is formed between this single Black male and an entire White family.

Still in the Struggle

Mateo for most of the movie appears, based on his living conditions, to struggle with poverty.

Bottom Line

Final Cut

With respect to traditional images of power and control regarding Black males on-screen, this movie character satisfies the Romantic racialism and femininity prongs of the Unholy Trinity generally and satisfies the Angel Figure archetype specifically with his role serving as a terminally ill but generous neighbor of a struggling immigrant family. The final analysis is that this movie fits established patterns of useful Black men, given his sacrificial ability to give to an immigrant White family that he hardly knows. His sacrifice helps them survive while he is unable to survive himself.

Outtakes

- In other Oscar racial news, English actor Sir Ben Kingsley received a Best Actor nomination for his role as an immigrant Iranian father, Colonel Massoud Amir Behrani, in *House of Sand and Fog.*

NOMINATION #42—DON CHEADLE

Backstory

Oscar Details

Best Actor Nomination for Don Cheadle as Paul Rusesabagina in *Hotel Rwanda* (2004) for the 77th Academy Awards (Kodak Theater) on February 27, 2005.

Character and Movie Overview

In the movie, Cheadle plays an empathetic hotel manager who converts a private enterprise into a public humanitarian cause during a period of genocide in Central Africa.

Have You Scene It?

One of the movie's key scenes involve Paul's discovery of a mass grave. But what likely secured Cheadle the nomination was when, during an attempt to maintain his normal routine, his character snaps, rips off his shirt in the middle of putting on his tie, and starts to weep.

Black Oscar Angles

Gravity of Reality

This is a para-realistic film based upon a factual figure.

Still in the Struggle

This character, although a business owner, still struggled with the countrywide ravages of civil war.

Bottom Line

Final Cut

With respect to traditional images of power and control regarding Black males on-screen, this movie character satisfies the Romantic racialism and femininity prongs of the Unholy Trinity generally; given its largely insular-universe status, no clean archetype pattern emerges. The final analysis is that this movie fits established patterns of useful Black men, given his capacity to give and serve others at risk of his own affairs.

NOMINATION #43, WIN #9—JAMIE FOXX

Backstory

Oscar Details

Best Actor Nomination and Win for Jamie Foxx as Ray Charles in *Ray* (2004) for the 77th Academy Awards (Kodak Theater) on February 27, 2005.

Character and Movie Overview

In the movie, Foxx plays a hard-driving, talented Black male musician who also happens to be blind.

Although audiences naturally cultivate sympathy for a physically impaired individual who was able to overcome limitations to achieve extraordinary fame through sheer musical genius, within the visible continuum the movie makes sure to show and share Charles's flaws as a womanizing, often angry and mercurial talent who had difficulty managing both his monetary and his musical affairs.

Have You Scene It?

The movie's climactic scene culminates with Charles singing "Georgia" at the 1996 Olympic Games.

Black Oscar Angles

Crossover

Foxx started his career as a comedian, not as a classically trained actor.

Déjà vu

Foxx personally accounts for more than one Black Oscar nomination, making him a repeat contender.

Gravity of Reality

This movie not only heavily invokes themes of race, but it is also a para-realistic based upon the life of a factual figure.

Still in the Struggle

The Scent of Magnolia is detectable in this example of a contemporary movie that jumps in time to a historically correct time period in which Blacks were undoubtedly subjugated.

Bottom Line

Final Cut

With respect to traditional images of power and control regarding Black males on-screen, this movie character satisfies the Romantic racialism prong of the Unholy Trinity generally and satisfies the Physical Wonder archetype specifically with his role serving as a talented yet troubled musician. The final analysis is that this movie fits established patterns of entertaining Black men given the focus on the musical talents his body can produce.

Outtakes

• Foxx did not necessarily immediately benefit from any Oscar bounce; his next film was *Stealth* (2005), in which his character died early.

NOMINATION #44—JAMIE FOXX

Backstory

Oscar Details

Best Supporting Actor Nomination for Jamie Foxx as Max Durocher in *Collateral* (2004) for the 77th Academy Awards (Kodak Theater) on February 27, 2005.

Character and Movie Overview

In the movie, Foxx plays an unsure cab driver who grows in confidence as he negotiates his relationship with Vincent (Tom Cruise), a hired hit man.

Have You Scene It?

The movie's climactic scene culminates with Vincent dying after a shootout with Max, late at night in the seat of a largely empty Los Angeles Metro train.

While Tom Cruise arguably plays the plot-driving protagonist, Jamie Foxx's character in *Collateral* is one of the rare few Black Oscar–winning examples that successfully complicates the HARM theory. *Dreamworks/Photofest*

Black Oscar Angles

Crossover

Foxx started his career as a comedian, not as a classically trained actor.

Déjà vu

Foxx personally accounts for more than one Black Oscar nomination, making him a repeat contender.

Bottom Line

Final Cut

With respect to traditional images of power and control regarding Black males on-screen, for this movie character no clean archetype pattern emerges, nor does any overarching Unholy Trinity narrative neatly apply. This is a welcome and unique case that does not easily satisfy traditional narratives accorded Black mainstream imagery.

Outtakes

- Foxx had the unusual distinction of being nominated in both male acting categories in the same year.
- While Foxx's character emerges as the hero who saves the day and gets the girl in the end, DreamWorks studio executives shrewdly decided to use the actor's image for marketing only "on bus shelters and billboards in major urban markets," electing to utilize the star power of White male A-list actor Tom Cruise virtually everywhere else.[13]

NOMINATION #45, WIN #10—MORGAN FREEMAN

Backstory

Oscar Details

Best Supporting Actor Nomination and Win for Morgan Freeman as Eddie "Scrap-Iron" Dupris in *Million Dollar Baby* (2004) for the 77th Academy Awards (Kodak Theater) on February 27, 2005.

Character and Movie Overview

In the movie, Freeman plays a devoted and supportive caretaker who dispenses sagacious wisdom to the benefit of Maggie Fitzgerald, a young boxer who wishes to fulfill her dream inside the ring. Scrap is also blind in one eye.

Similar to his role as God in the 2003 film *Bruce Almighty*, Freeman appears with a trashcan in a janitorial role.

Have You Scene It?

When his boss and friend Frankie carries out his plan for euthanasia, Scrap watches from the shadows but does not intervene. In fact, he narrates Frankie's actions: "And he walked out; I don't think he had anything left."

Black Oscar Angles

Déjà Vu

Freeman personally accounts for 6.4 percent of all Black Oscar nominations, with five.

Bottom Line

Final Cut

With respect to traditional images of power and control regarding Black males on-screen, this movie character satisfies the Romantic racialism and femininity prongs of the Unholy Trinity generally and satisfies the Angel Figure archetype specifically with his role serving as an older, genteel, and loyal gym assistant. The final analysis is that this movie fits established patterns of useful Black men, given his devoted service capacity to the main White characters.

Outtakes

• *Million Dollar Baby* received five total Oscar nods and won Best Picture.

NOMINATION #46—SOPHIE OKONEDO

Backstory

Oscar Details

Best Supporting Actress Nomination for Sophie Okonedo as Tatiana Rusesabagina in *Hotel Rwanda* (2004) for the 77th Academy Awards (Kodak Theater) on February 27, 2005.

Character and Movie Overview

In the movie, Okonedo plays the supportive wife of hotel manager Paul Rusesabagina, who provides shelter to evacuees during a period of genocide in Central Africa.

Have You Scene It?

Early in the movie, when Tatiana learns the gruesome truth about her brother's death, her White sister-in-law delivers the news of his passing calmly while Tatiana, distraught with grief, cannot handle the conversation and leaves.

Black Oscar Angles

Black Non-American

Okonedo is a British actor.

Gravity of Reality

This movie is a para-realistic film based upon a factual figure.

Still in the Struggle

This character, although the wife of a hotel manager, still struggled with the countrywide ravages of civil war.

Bottom Line

Final Cut

With respect to traditional images of power and control regarding Black females on-screen, this movie character satisfies the femininity prong of the Unholy Trinity generally; and given its largely insular-universe status, no clean archetype pattern emerges. The final analysis is that this movie fits established patterns of helpful Black women.

Outtakes

- Of note are the differences in phenotype and appearance between the dark-skinned, thicker Tatiana Rusesabagina and the light-skinned, thin actor hired to portray her in the movie. Perhaps due to the movie's release before the rise of social consciousness (i.e., the generational marker of being "woke") and cancel/call-out culture fueled by the increased number of expressive outlets as offered by social media, Okonedo mostly escaped direct, scathing criticisms, unlike Zoë Saldaña who similarly was cast to play a Black woman with a different phenotype and skin complexion in the biopic *Nina* a little more than a decade later in 2016.[14]

NOMINATION #47—TERRENCE HOWARD

Backstory

Oscar Details

Best Actor Nomination for Terrence Howard as DJay in *Hustle & Flow* (2005) for the 78th Academy Awards (Kodak Theater) on March 5, 2006.

Character and Movie Overview

In the movie, Howard plays a pimp who, in his spare time, is also a frustrated executive of a fledgling Memphis, Tennessee, record company.

Have You Scene It?

The movie's climactic scene culminates with DJay coaxing Shug (Taraji P. Henson), one of his "ladies" (read: prostitutes) to sing the chorus for a song he wanted to advance. Shug appears initially hesitant—at least until DJay spanks her on her gluteal muscles, resulting in the proper pitch necessary to record the hit record "It's Hard out Here for a Pimp."

Black Oscar Angles

Gravity of Reality

This movie heavily invokes themes of race, the premise being that DJay is arguably frustrated about his limited choices for economic gain as a Black male; thus he is resigned to pimping.

Fellow Best Supporting Oscar nominees Terrence Howard and Taraji P. Henson performing the anthem "It's Hard out Here for a Pimp" in *Hustle & Flow. MTV Films/ Paramount Classics/Photofest*

Still in the Struggle

DJay's suffering from a lack of resources is a plot device, thereby qualifying as struggle.

Bottom Line

Final Cut

With respect to traditional images of power and control regarding Black males on-screen, this movie character satisfies the Negrophobia prong of the Unholy Trinity generally and satisfies the Menace to Society archetype specifically with his role serving as an aspirational pimp looking to launch his musical career. The final analysis is that this movie fits established patterns of aggressive Black men insofar as a pimp is considered someone who is antagonistic to the shared values of society.

Outtakes

- In other Oscar racial news, *Crash*, a race drama movie written explicitly about race, won Best Picture that year.
- "It's Hard out There for a Pimp" won an Oscar for Best Music, Original Song; it was performed live on-stage during the ceremony by the rap group Three 6 Mafia.

NOMINATION #48—WILL SMITH

Backstory

Oscar Details

Best Actor Nomination for Will Smith as Chris Gardner in *The Pursuit of Happyness* (2006) for the 79th Academy Awards (Kodak Theater) on February 25, 2007.

Character and Movie Overview

In the movie, Smith plays an exasperated, frustrated but nonetheless motivated father who by hook or by crook continues fighting for financial freedom for his family while his wife decides to leave the family.

Have You Scene It?

In the movie's final scene, Gardner and his son cross a San Francisco street and barely notice a bald Black male who crosses their path. This was a cameo by the real Chris Gardner. Yet, unlike many movies featuring White actors who transcend their otherwise humble beginnings, this movie does not spend considerable time within the visible continuum depicting Gardner as enjoying the fruits of his economic labors. The crux of the movie revolves around Gardner's struggle to overcome seemingly insurmountable odds to become financially successful.

Black Oscar Angles

Crossover

Smith started his career as a rap musician before turning his attention to television sitcom acting; he did not start his career as a classically trained actor.

Déjà Vu

Smith personally accounts for more than one Black Oscar nomination, making him a repeat contender.

Gravity of Reality

This movie is a para-realistic film based upon a factual figure.

Still in the Struggle

Gardner and his son are never shown as financially secure; they both are locked in the struggle during the visible continuum.

Bottom Line

Final Cut

With respect to traditional images of power and control regarding Black males on-screen, this movie character satisfies the Romantic racialism and femininity prongs of the Unholy Trinity generally; given its largely insular-universe status with limited contact between Black and White worlds, no clean archetype pattern emerges. The final analysis is that this movie fits established patterns of financially frustrated and impotent Black men.

Outtakes

- Will Smith starred opposite his son Jaden.
- Similar to Sophie Okonedo and her portrayal of Tatiana Rusesabagina, Smith may have escaped direct criticism for this role due to the movie's release before a rise in social consciousness (i.e., the generational marker of being "woke") and cancel/call-out culture fueled by the increased number of expressive outlets as offered by social media. Smith mostly escaped direct, scathing criticisms about his difference in phenotype and appearance from the actual Chris Gardner, even though he is not nearly as dark-skinned and brawny as the real Chris Gardner. This is not as an indictment of Smith's acting ability but more as an indirect and telling commentary of what visual iconography Hollywood is willing to put forward first for the sake of maximum sales in deference to its majority White audience. However, as recently as 2019, Smith found himself the target of sharp Twitter barbs debating a colorism controversy over the choice to cast him as the father of tennis greats Venus and Serena Williams in the movie *King Richard*.[15]

NOMINATION #49, WIN #11—FOREST WHITAKER

Backstory

Oscar Details

Best Actor Nomination for Forest Whitaker as Idi Amin in *The Last King of Scotland* (2006) for the 79th Academy Awards (Kodak Theater) on February 25, 2007.

Character and Movie Overview

In the movie, Whitaker plays a savage and brutal dictator of the African nation Benin. Amin, like most psychopaths, starts off within the visible continuum as being reasonable, but he is, by degrees, clearly revealed to be unstable. Not only is this a general visual referendum against self-sufficient and independent Black power, but this also speaks to Menace to Society images where cold-blooded Africans kill one another without thought.

Have You Scene It?

The movie is told through the narrative voice and gaze of Nicholas Garrigan, a White male. A culture vulture, Garrigan is able to bed a Black woman within minutes of appearing on-screen. Garrigan's sexual energy is apparently so potent that he is not only able to manipulate the existing power structure to get close to the dictator, but he is able to get even closer to Amin's prized possession: a light-skinned female objectified as a target of sexual desire in contrast to the more plentiful dark-skinned "naturally Black" African females. This love interest, Kay Amin, who was played by Kerry Washington, ends up falling for Garrigan, which ends up being a catalytic and cataclysmic event with respect to the final unraveling of dictator Amin. In other words, the final unhinging of this supposedly potent African dictator is the fact that a White boy was able to sexually usurp and conquer the dictator's love interest. This scene is not so much a statement about the White male's virility as much as it is a statement about the Black male's incompetence.

Black Oscar Angles

Gravity of Reality

This movie is a para-realistic film based upon a factual figure.

Still in the Struggle

The country of Uganda appears to be a war-torn, political, and economically impoverished disaster, possibly qualifying as poverty porn à la *Slumdog Millionaire* (2008).

Bottom Line

Final Cut

With respect to traditional images of power and control regarding Black males on-screen, this movie character satisfies the Negrophobia prong of the Unholy Trinity generally and satisfies the Menace to Society archetype specifically with his role serving as an irascible, bloodthirsty dictator. The final analysis is that this movie fits established patterns of threatening Black men; as a bloodthirsty, power-hungry dictator, this character satisfies the Menace to Society archetype.

Outtakes

- Whitaker darkened his skin for this role.[16]

Forest Whitaker in *The Last King of Scotland*. *Fox Searchlight/Photofest*

NOMINATION #50—DJIMON HOUNSOU

Backstory

Oscar Details

Best Supporting Actor Nomination for Djimon Hounsou as Solomon Vandy in *Blood Diamond* (2006) for the 79th Academy Awards (Kodak Theater) on February 25, 2007.

Character and Movie Overview

In the movie, Hounsou plays an African father and fisherman who is desperately looking for opportunities to better his family's financial outlook. He finds a rather large diamond and soon thereafter finds himself surrounded by drama. The movie concludes with Danny Archer (Leonardo DiCaprio) and Maddy Bowen (Jennifer Connelly) exploring the contours of their love relationship on the phone as Archer slowly dies; meanwhile Vandy is in London, reputedly or reportedly with some sort of financial gain.

Djimon Hounsou chases the carats in *Blood Diamond*. *Warner Bros./Photofest*

Have You Scene It?

Likely the most riveting scene for Vandy is when he starts shaking the metal chain-link fence vigorously in protest of his separation from his family. The scene is marked by a lack of dialogue, featuring instead mostly grunting noises and gestures. Yet Hounsou received an Oscar nomination for acting. Also of note is the bombing scene later in the movie, where Vandy has to be directed what to do via cell phone, in contrast to the White alpha male hero, Archer, who instinctively knows what to do.

Black Oscar Angles

Black Non-American

Hounsou is from the West African country of Benin.

Crossover

Hounsou started his career as a model appearing in music videos, not as a classically trained actor.

Déjà vu

Hounsou personally accounts for more than one Black Oscar nomination, making him a repeat contender.

Gravity of Reality

This movie is based around race and is a para-realistic film based upon realistic political events.

Still in the Struggle

In this movie, this character struggles with financial freedom until the very end.

Bottom Line

Final Cut

With respect to traditional images of power and control regarding Black males on-screen, this movie character satisfies the Romantic racialism and femininity prongs of the Unholy Trinity generally and satisfies the Angel Figure archetype specifically with his role serving as a loyal "friend" of the White male protagonist. The final analysis is that this movie fits established patterns of useful Black men, for while Vandy is indeed the primary benefactor of his diamond discovery, in actuality he ultimately helps facilitate the career goals of Maddy, who writes the tell-all exposé that highlights the larger issue of blood diamonds.

Outtakes

* Real child orphan amputees were used during filming as background figures, underscoring the collateral damage of such an unethical trade in which workers were threatened with amputation if they did not labor as directed. However, initial reports were that the studio reneged on their promise to provide prosthetic limbs to participants.[17] The use of the amputees is not in dispute; at issue is whether the studio delayed compensation after production wrapped in June in order to benefit from additional publicity upon the movie's release in December.

NOMINATION #51—EDDIE MURPHY

Backstory

Oscar Details

Best Supporting Actor Nomination for Eddie Murphy as Jimmy "Thunder" Early in *Dreamgirls* (2006) for the 79th Academy Awards (Kodak Theater) on February 25, 2007.

Character and Movie Overview

In the movie, Murphy plays a philandering lover who sinks into depression, drugs, and despair as his former love interest and her singing group become more successful.

Have You Scene It?

In the 1970s, after the golden era of the 1950s and 1960s has faded, Jimmy attempts a comeback during Rainbow Records' televised tenth anniversary special. In exceedingly exuberant fashion, while proclaiming to the audience that "Jimmy got soul!" he apparently wants to lay his feelings bare—and proceeds to drop his pants. The record label promptly drops Jimmy, hastening his downward spiral. He eventually dies from a heroin overdose.

Eddie Murphy as Jimmy Early left the movie early due to heroin addiction in *Dreamgirls*. *DreamWorks SKG/Photofest*

Black Oscar Angles

Crossover

Murphy started his career as a comedian, not as a classically trained actor.

Gravity of Reality

This movie heavily invokes themes of race; the film is also loosely based upon factual figures, roughly tracing the career trajectory of Black Oscar nominee Diana Ross and the Supremes.

Bottom Line

Final Cut

With respect to traditional images of power and control regarding Black males on-screen, this movie character satisfies the Negrophobia prong of the Unholy Trinity generally and satisfies the Utopic Reversal archetype specifically with his role serving as a musical dynamo who loses it all. Initially shown at the top of his game, this character qualifies as a Utopic Reversal based upon his diminished state at the movie's conclusion. The final analysis is that this movie fits established patterns of disempowered Black men.

Outtakes

- Murphy drew attention during the Academy Awards for leaving early after Alan Arkin claimed the top prize for his role in *Little Miss Sunshine*.[18]

NOMINATION #52, WIN #12—JENNIFER HUDSON

Backstory

Oscar Details

Best Supporting Actress Nomination for Jennifer Hudson as Effie White in *Dreamgirls* (2006) for the 79th Academy Awards (Kodak Theater) on February 25, 2007.

Character and Movie Overview

In the movie, Hudson plays a disgruntled singer who wants her former lover to know that she indeed values her self-worth.

Have You Scene It?

Effie's pivotal scene arguably comes toward the end of the movie when she is looking to relaunch her career after placing it on pause to have the baby she conceived with Curtis (Jamie Foxx). At the middling entertainment venue, it is indisputable that Hudson sings her heart out, but there are simply few other scenes worthy of analysis in which she is asked to actually act, as most of her scenes involve perfunctory dialogue before a musical number begins. With respect to the visible continuum, more important is the fact that the audience sees her cast in a mold on-screen that perhaps hearkens back to the more traditional image of a full-figured, bellowing Black woman who can magically sing.

Black Oscar Angles

Crossover

Hudson started her career as a singer, not as a classically trained actor.

Gravity of Reality

This movie heavily invokes themes of race; the film is also loosely based upon factual figures, roughly tracing the career trajectory of Black Oscar nominee Diana Ross and the Supremes.

Bottom Line

Final Cut

With respect to traditional images of power and control regarding Black females on-screen, this movie character satisfies the Romantic racialism prong of the Unholy Trinity generally and satisfies the Physical Wonder archetype specifically with her role serving as a spunky singer. The final analysis is that this movie fits established patterns of useful Black women, given the focus on the musical talents her body can produce.

Outtakes

- Hudson's next speaking film role was of that of a personal assistant in *Sex in the City*.

NOMINATION #53—RUBY DEE

Backstory

Oscar Details

Best Supporting Actress Nomination for Ruby Dee as Mama Lucas in *American Gangster* (2007) for the 80th Academy Awards (Kodak Theater) on February 24, 2008.

Character and Movie Overview

In the movie, Dee plays a matriarchal figure of Frank Lucas, the American gangster responsible for flying in heroin in mass quantities who becomes an independent crime boss in New York City.

Have You Scene It?

After corrupt cops steal his emergency cash supply, Frank sees red and wants immediate revenge, as his dog was killed in the process, tipping the scales toward the inhumane. Mama stops Frank on his way out the door and surprisingly slaps Frank in the face to get his attention, crying, "Don't lie to your mama!" She then warns Frank that if he continues with whatever it is that he is doing to afford them this luxury lifestyle, that she and his paramour, Eva, will leave him. Frank ends up eventually going to jail, doing fifteen years before being paroled; it is unclear according to the visible continuum whether Eva and his mother did in fact leave him or not (although in the closing credits it said that Mama Lucas relocated to North Carolina).

Black Oscar Angles

Gravity of Reality

This movie is a para-realistic film based upon a factual figure.

Still in the Struggle

The lack of finances and resources are a push factor for the Black male protagonist's decision to sell drugs in the first place.

Bottom Line

Final Cut

With respect to traditional images of power and control regarding Black females on-screen, this movie character satisfies the femininity prong of the Unholy Trinity generally and, given her limited screen time and dialogue, fits the Background Figure archetype. The final analysis is that this movie fits established patterns of passively impotent Black women in that mom's advice—even when punctuated with a slap—is not enough to dissuade her son from a life of crime.

Ruby Dee's character tries unsuccessfully to stop her son (Denzel Washington) from engaging in the renumerative but destructive illicit trade of street pharmaceuticals in *American Gangster. Universal Studios/Photofest*

Outtakes

- This is at least the second Black Oscar–nominated role—if Mammy is not included—that has "Mama" in it. Queen Latifah's character in *Chicago* also has "Mama" in it, which speaks to the narrative that Black women are just naturally built for nurturing.
- This Oscar nod may have been a recognition of Dee's seven decades of acting, as even the eighty-three-year-old actor admitted that "the size of the part doesn't have to do with much."[19]

NOMINATION #54—VIOLA DAVIS

Backstory

Oscar Details

Best Supporting Actress Nomination for Viola Davis as Mrs. Miller in *Doubt* (2008) for the 81st Academy Awards (Kodak Theater) on February 22, 2009.

Character and Movie Overview

In the movie, Davis plays an employee at an all-girls Catholic school that is strict on standards but perhaps lenient on discipline when it comes to a possibly philandering priest.

Have You Scene It?

One of the movie's climactic scenes involves Mrs. Miller in a heated exchange during which she makes it plain that she has deep reservations and misgivings—or should we say *doubt*—about the presiding priest's innocence. The scene is marked not only by her riveting dialogue but by the fact that her nose starts running in earnest (apparently a trademark when she cries; see also the 2016 film *Fences*).

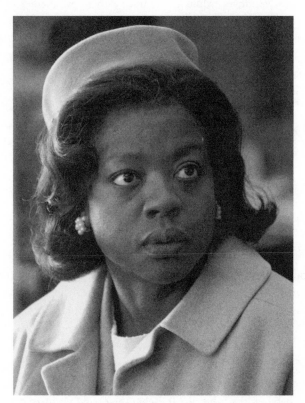

Viola Davis's brief but impactful appearance in *Doubt* left no doubt as to her acting ability. *Miramax/Photofest*

Black Oscar Angles

Déjà Vu

Davis personally accounts for more than one Black Oscar nomination, making her a repeat contender.

Bottom Line

Final Cut

With respect to traditional images of power and control regarding Black females on-screen, given its largely insular-universe status with limited contact between Black and White worlds, no clean archetype pattern emerges. With respect to Unholy Trinity narratives, while it may not neatly apply, themes of femininity are arguably present with respect to Mrs. Miller's having a moral obligation to serve not only the Lord and all of his children at the Catholic school at which she works, but also her direct employers.

Outtakes

• Davis was on-screen for a total of only eleven minutes![20]

NOMINATION #55—TARAJI P. HENSON

Backstory

Oscar Details

Best Supporting Actress Nomination for Taraji P. Henson as Queenie in *The Curious Case of Benjamin Button* (2008) for the 81st Academy Awards (Kodak Theater) on February 22, 2009.

Character and Movie Overview

In the movie, Henson plays a caretaker at a nursing home who discovers an abandoned baby on the front porch. Being the caring nurturer that she is, she keeps the child, calling him Benjamin, and starts raising him as her own. (He calls her "Mama.")

Have You Scene It?

At the beginning of the movie, Queenie and her love interest, Mr. Tizzy (played by Black Oscar winner Mahershala Ali), discover a wrapped baby on the front porch steps. Due to the plot's device of reverse aging that Benjamin Button (Brad Pitt) endures, the baby appears strangely old and disfigured. Queenie's love interest recoils in horror, observing, "We best leave that for the police," before gesturing to leave. Without much deliberation or thought, Queenie picks up the child and takes him downstairs to her room. Looking at the child, she declares, "You sho' is ugly as an old fart, but you still a child of God!"

Queenie conveniently becomes less prominent on-screen as the movie proceeds and Benjamin, taking on his prime body in Brad Pitt, consummates his central and all-important relationship with Daisy (Cate Blanchett). In fact, Queenie and Mr. Tizzy die before the emotional heavy lifting of Benjamin and Daisy's relationship takes full root.

Black Oscar Angles

Still in the Struggle

Queenie's limited financial condition is clear in the beginning of the movie, especially in contrast to the central White female protagonist, Daisy. Additionally, this character dies during the movie.

Bottom Line

Final Cut

With respect to traditional images of power and control regarding Black females on-screen, this movie character satisfies the Romantic racialism and femininity prongs of the Unholy Trinity generally and satisfies the Angel Figure archetype specifically with her role serving as a motherly caretaker. The final analysis is that this movie fits established patterns of useful and servile Black women, although the adjective *servile* adjective may be refuted by the "historically accurate" defense, meaning that whatever is depicted on-screen is consistent with what would have traditionally transpired during that time period.

Blind Faith

Adding to the narrative that Blacks are naturally and devoutly religious, later, when Benjamin is seven, Queenie takes him to a New Orleans religious revival under a tent entitled "Healing through Faith." In what may be an indirect slight to the Black church and faith-based communities, the pastor and congregation laugh off the statement of Benjamin's age as "all of us are children in the eyes of God." The pastor commands Benjamin to rise from his wheelchair and walk, and to the amazement of all present, the "glory of the Lord" allows him to do so, with Queenie right by his side encouraging him every step of the way.

The indirect insult may come from the fact that everyone in the viewing audience outside of the fantasy space of the visible continuum knows even before entering the theater that the film is about a man who experiences reverse aging. Thus, it was only a matter of time before this elderly child would approach prime age and gain strength as he grew younger. In other words, the audience is in on the joke, but the faith-believing Blacks are left to their own, perhaps primitive and childlike, beliefs in the absence of knowledge or the resources to study the problem scientifically (especially if they are blinded by their superior Romantic racialist trait of being super-religious). All they can do is praise the Lord for matters they do not understand or that are above them.

Outtakes

- *Slumdog Millionaire*, which many derided as a prime example of poverty porn, won both Best Picture and Best Director that year.
- In other Oscar racial news, Robert Downey Jr. received a Best Supporting Actor nomination for playing a Black male in actual blackface makeup in the movie *Tropic Thunder* that same year.
- The pastor from the revival scene collapses upon Benjamin's being able to walk. However, it is unknown whether the "glory of the Lord" was able to revive him properly, as it did with Benjamin.

10

OSCARS SO WHITE?
(2010–2019)

This last decade of our analysis features several significant developments. The blockbuster success *Get Out* was released in 2017, with *Black Panther* hitting theaters the following year. *Get Out* is notable for seemingly single-handedly creating a new genre, racial horror, while *Black Panther* broke new ground by featuring a Black superhero who, for once, was actually treated like one. Both movies became virtually required viewing for those wanting to stay current with contemporary African American affairs. Further, despite amassing the highest number of Black Oscar nominations and wins, this decade also is marked by what is likely the most public critique about quality representation of Black filmmakers in Hollywood and the Academy Awards.

As *Black Panther* has no acting wins to speak of, we shall take a brief moment to analyze it here due to its historical significance. Part of the movie's success likely had to do with its distinct departure from most movies that showcase the Black experience in some poverty environment. Backed by the Disney-purchased Marvel Cinematic Universe, it had a significant and sizeable built-in audience, and while part of the movie takes place in the marginalized neighborhoods of Oakland, California, it is refreshing to see Black futurism made tangible. Similar to *Boyz n the Hood* (1991), the movie provides an intimate depiction from an intimate insider perspective rather than through an external White male gaze. (Perhaps the fact that both movies had Black writers and directors was a factor here.) Still, within the movie there are few to no images of Black power being exercised over Whites in any large, sustained capacity. The movie's climactic scene features Blacks fighting other Blacks somewhere in the continent of Africa (i.e., Wakanda).

During this decade, Mahershala Ali also became the first to win Best Supporting Actor twice: first for playing a gangster in *Moonlight* (2016), a movie addressing Black homosexuality, and later for playing a gay pianist in the *Green Book* (2018). The latter movie was met with its own share of controversy surrounding the rights to and the veracity of the story, not to mention the gratuitous use of the n-word at press conferences by the main White actor Viggo Mortensen.[1] *Moonlight* was also notable as the second movie to win Best Picture affiliated with a Black director (Steven McQueen was the first with his win for *12 Years a Slave* in 2013), but there was a bit of controversy there as well, when actor Warren Beatty read *La La Land* as the incorrect Best Picture winner, much to host Jimmy Kimmel's chagrin.[2]

Quantity-wise, 2017 was the record-breaking year of all time for Black Oscar nominees, with a total of six in one year alone. But these numbers did not insulate the Academy from public critique. Following a 2016 ceremony in which all twenty acting category nominees were White, the social media Twitter hashtag #OscarsSoWhite was born.[3] Finally, in 2013, the AMPAS Board of Governors elected African American executive Cheryl Boone Isaacs as the first African American and third woman president, a possible signal of the inclusive direction the organization wished to pursue in the future.

NOMINATION #56—MORGAN FREEMAN

Backstory

Oscar Details

Best Actor Nomination for Morgan Freeman as Nelson Mandela in *Invictus* (2009) for the 82nd Academy Awards (Kodak Theater) on March 7, 2010.

Character and Movie Overview

In the movie, Freeman plays civil rights leader and global icon Nelson Mandela. Not only is this movie based upon a true story, but it is similar to *The Help* in that it features a prominent Black character who does not actually drive the storyline or plot; the movie is instead about François Pienaar (Matt Damon).

If only rugby were introduced as a tool for racial reconciliation earlier, before thousands lost their lives in the diamond mines of South Africa[4] and Mandela spent twenty-seven years in prison. When factoring in a Romantic racialist lens of analysis, a fair question is whether Mandela is deemed worthy of admiration only because he did not come out of jail angry and militant, swearing revenge upon the architects of apartheid that caused him to needlessly suffer for so long.

Have You Scene It?

One of the movie's early scenes features an older, genteel, and gray Mandela lecturing a younger official named Jason about the power of using "forgiveness as a weapon." While this may be true, Americans did not dump tea in Boston Harbor, kicking off the American Revolution, in the name of forgiveness. In other words, messages of forgiveness and patience appeal to the Romantic racialist sensibilities that revenge is never the proper course of action, even after suffering wrongfully from the ravages and savages of racial apartheid.

The young minister Jason, while visibly agitated and frustrated, may not be another "angry Black man" insofar as he simply wants the imbalanced scales to be righted. If the scales were unequal to begin with due to systematic and structural racism, walking away and leaving them untouched does not signify justice. If Mandela were to appear to hold a grudge or seek to even the scales after his decades of imprisonment and the horrors of apartheid, the moviemakers run the risk of alienating part of their audience. As it is, the inclusion of François playing the ultramasculine sport of rugby speaks to multiple audiences and eliminates the challenge of marketing a movie solely about Black people with Mandela as the central character.

Black Oscar Angles

Déjà Vu

Freeman personally accounts for 6.4 percent of all Black Oscar nominations, with five.

Gravity of Reality

The movie is a para-realistic film based upon a factual figure.

Still in the Struggle

Race-based apartheid certainly qualifies as struggle.

Bottom Line

Final Cut

With respect to traditional images of power and control regarding Black males on-screen, this movie character satisfies the Romantic racialism and femininity prongs of the Unholy Trinity generally and satisfies the Angel Figure archetype specifically with his role serving as an older, genteel civil rights leader. The final analysis is that given the amount of quality screen time Freeman's character had relative to Damon's with respect to advancing and developing the plot (with the most riveting and action-involved scenes featuring François), Mandela in this move qualifies as a glorified Background Figure.

Bonus Features

Outtakes

- In contrast to more muted militarism, compare Mandela's character arc with that of Killmonger from *Black Panther*. Killmonger is painted as the movie's antagonist even though all he wants is justice from systematic oppression. He wants to supply his people with weapons and technology to fight back. While logical to some, this is portrayed as the source of lunacy and has to be stopped by any means necessary.
- In other Oscar racial news, in 2010 Sandra Bullock won a Best Actress Oscar for her role as a White mother who takes in a talented but troubled Black male football player in *The Blind Side*. The movie has since been criticized as promoting a White savior narrative.[5]

NOMINATION #57—GABOUREY SIDIBE

Backstory

Oscar Details

Best Actress Nomination for Gabourey Sidibe as Claireece "Precious" Jones in *Precious: Based on the Novel 'Push' by Sapphire* (2009) for the 82nd Academy Awards (Kodak Theater) on March 7, 2010.

Gabourey Sidibe in a powerfully painful performance in *Precious*. *Lionsgate/Photofest*

Character and Movie Overview

In the movie, Sidibe plays a victim of numerous negative social forces that are quite sad, sobering, and stupefying in combination.

Have You Scene It?

One telling scene comes where Precious steals a bucket of fried chicken from a local eatery, Southern Fried Chicken, and runs away from her misdeed, encapsulating a symbolic function and extension of her unfortunate state and status in society. Precious enters the establishment calmly and places her order, surveying the front door carefully. When the bucket of chicken is delivered to her at the countertop where she is waiting, she creates a diversion by asking for a side of potato salad. Once the coast is clear, Precious proceeds to run while placing at least one piece of fried poultry in her mouth. The frustrated waitress is heard off-camera exclaiming, "Get that big b*tch!" as a wide-angle shot shows Precious moving from right to left with the bucket in her right hand, fried chicken in her left, and pink knapsack on her back. The only stable source of help and hope comes in the form of a social worker portrayed by the well-known biracial singer Mariah Carey. Carey's look, aesthetic, appearance, and complexion all serve as stark contrast to the dismal reality Precious shares with her mother (Black Oscar winner Mo'Nique) at home.

Black Oscar Angles

Gravity of Reality

The movie heavily invokes themes of race.

Still in the Struggle

The performativity of pain is abundant here.

Bottom Line

Final Cut

With respect to traditional images of power and control regarding Black females on-screen, this movie character satisfies the Romantic racialism and femininity prongs of the Unholy Trinity generally and satisfies the Menace to Society archetype specifically with her role serving as a social reject. The final analysis is that this movie fits established patterns of embattled and embittered Black women. Moreover, as this character speaks to poverty porn voyeurism, it qualifies as a Menace to Society archetype in that it is one of the greatest fears mainstream America seeks to avoid when building highways around and over the inner city.

Bonus Features

Outtakes

- In terms of Oscar bounce and continued bankability, Sidibe's movie career has not exactly taken off. In contrast, Rebel Wilson, Melissa McCarthy, and Amy Schumer are all White females who have landed starring movie roles despite having nontraditional body types.
- Geoffrey Fletcher won Best Adapted Screenplay for *Precious*, the first African American to win that honor.

NOMINATION #58, WIN #13—MO'NIQUE

Backstory

Oscar Details

Best Supporting Actress Nomination and Win for Mo'Nique as Mary Lee Johnston in *Precious: Based on the Novel 'Push' by Sapphire* (2009) for the 82nd Academy Awards (Kodak Theater) on March 7, 2010.

Character and Movie Overview

In the movie, Mo'Nique plays a neglectful, selfish, and dysfunctional mother whose emotionally volatile antics underscore the pain of being overweight, female, and visibly Black in modern-day America.

To say that this movie showcases poverty and suffering is an understatement; it unfolds almost like a "What else could possibly go wrong?" motif.

Have You Scene It?

Mo'Nique describes her jealousy of Precious in a hard-to-watch scene. Thus, Mo'Nique's nomination and win for a compelling portrayal of a socially problematic character is, if anything, an affirmation of her dexterous acting ability. However, to win for showcasing the worst stereotypes of African American culture is part of a larger, disturbing pattern of poverty porn perpetuated by the power structure. Such Oscar-winning performances contrast markedly from those of White actresses, who are more routinely awarded and rewarded for being smart and attractive (e.g., Sandra Bullock in *The Blind Side*, 2009). In other words, White women are glamorized for being glamorous, while Black women are glamorized for being scandalous, slanderous, and scurrilous.

Mo'Nique as Mary Lee Johnston in *Precious* leaves precious little to the imagination with respect to portraying a problematic parenting model. *Lionsgate/Photofest*

Black Oscar Angles

Crossover

Mo'Nique started her career as a comedian, not as a classically trained actor.

Gravity of Reality

This movie heavily invokes themes of race.

Still in the Struggle

The performativity of pain is abundant here.

Bottom Line

Final Cut

With respect to traditional images of power and control regarding Black females on-screen, this movie character satisfies the Romantic racialism and femininity prongs of the Unholy Trinity generally and satisfies the Menace to Society archetype specifically with her role serving as an abusive maternal figure. The final analysis is that this movie fits established patterns of destructive Black women insofar Mary is clearly not a serious candidate for "Mother of the Year" anytime soon.

Bonus Features

Outtakes

- Geoffrey Fletcher won Best Adapted Screenplay for *Precious*, the first African American to win that honor.
- In her acceptance speech, Mo'Nique specifically referenced Hattie McDaniel by name, thanking McDaniel for her sacrifice; Mo'Nique also intentionally wore White gardenia flowers in her hair, just as McDaniel did upon her historic 1940 win.[6]
- Similar to Oscar winner Louis Gosset Jr., Mo'Nique has publicly complained about the lack of Oscar bounce following her win, stating that producer Lee Daniels communicated to her personally that she has "been blackballed"—meaning that movie studios are deliberately deciding not to work with her for personal, rather than professional reasons.[7]

NOMINATION #59—VIOLA DAVIS

Backstory

Oscar Details

Best Actress Nomination for Viola Davis as Aibileen Clark in *The Help* (2011) for the 84th Academy Awards (Hollywood and Highland Center) on February 26, 2012.

Character and Movie Overview

In the movie, Davis plays a domestic maid in Mississippi during the 1960s.

It is important to note that, like her colleague Minny, Aibileen ends the movie in a maid's uniform. She is optimistic about her desire to become a writer, but within the visible continuum of the film, this aspiration is not made manifest, unlike that of Skeeter (Emma Watson), who faces oppression along gender lines but with the help of a feminist publisher is able to not only find work as a writer in her local community (leveraging Aibileen's sagacity for an advice column in the local paper), but also leverages a publishing deal for a book about the poor Black maids into a writing opportunity in New York. In other words, it is Skeeter who successfully resolves tension with her understanding mother (who, although she employed old Black help in Black Oscar nominee Cicely Tyson, was not actually racist), finds her self-confidence and identity by establishing boundaries in her love life, and pursues her career goals as a woman in a male-dominated profession. The audience sees Skeeter change over time. Meanwhile, while no specific mention is made of the royalty amount, it clearly is not enough for the Black maids to quit their day jobs and move away from the South, like Skeeter did.

Have You Scene It?

One of the movie's more famous scenes features Aibileen in a rocking chair with a little White girl in her lap. Aiblieen has the White girl repeat: "You is smart, you is kind, you is important" before gingerly touching the child's nose while giggling softly. This scene provides fuel for the Romantic racialist fire that is still smoldering. To think that despite her oppression, she still has nothing but love—no resentment—for an innocent child oversimplifies complex racial matters. We do not see any Black woman display similar types of love or affection for a Black child within this visible continuum. Furthermore, we do not see any victims of sexual assault, which was quite common for many defenseless Black women who found themselves compromised in the workplace during this time period.

Black Oscar Angles

Déjà vu

Davis personally accounts for more than one Black Oscar nomination, making her a repeat contender.

Gravity of Reality

The movie is based around race, given the social and economic tensions between well-to-do White women who can afford Black female domestics as "help" around the house.

Still in the Struggle

The Scent of Magnolia is heavy in the air, and not just because the movie takes place in 1960s Mississippi. Political, social, and economic subjugation are indelible parts of the character's identity.

Bottom Line

Final Cut

With respect to traditional images of power and control regarding Black females on-screen, this movie character satisfies the Romantic racialism and femininity prongs of the Unholy Trinity generally and satisfies the Angel Figure archetype specifically with her role serving as a maid, not only to her family but also in serving as a bona fide help to Skeeter as she launches her career. The final analysis is that this movie fits established patterns of servile Black women, as her sole purpose is to aid White characters.

Bonus Features

Out of Focus

While the movie is ostensibly about Aibileen Clark, the movie's protagonist is actually Skeeter, a White female.

This is the latest in a longer tradition of social problem films released beginning in the late 1940s (e.g., *Pinky*) in which "the narrative formula . . . is to deal with racial issues not from a black point of view, but from a white one."[8] Perhaps the concern here is rational, not racist; movie studios must always bear the sensibilities of their significant White audiences in mind if they wish to sell tickets. *Mississippi Burning*, *Driving Miss Daisy*, *The Blind Side*, and *Green Book* are all Oscar-nominated examples of social problem films where the *problem* is that the White perspective and gaze are made primary, thereby marginalizing the experience of the minority characters that the movie is presumably about.

Outtakes

- The movie is based upon the *New York Times* bestselling book by Kathryn Stockett. Stockett models the White female protagonist Skeeter in that she successfully leveraged the stories of Black women for personal pecuniary gain.
- Both Black Oscar nominations for the 84th Academy Awards came from the same movie.
- While her future work status is left open to the imagination, Davis's character is nonetheless in a maid's uniform in her last scene on-screen. Contrast this to Skeeter's condition, which materially changes when she physically leaves the South for a more progressive, urban environment to pursue her writing career.

NOMINATION #60, WIN #14—OCTAVIA SPENCER

Backstory

Oscar Details

Best Supporting Actress Nomination and Win for Octavia Spencer as Minny Jackson in *The Help* (2011) for the 84th Academy Awards (Hollywood and Highland Center) on February 26, 2012.

Character and Movie Overview

In the movie, Spencer plays a dignified domestic maid searching for her place in society. By movie's end, Minny is seen seated at the table smiling (after falsely perceiving the White master of the house's approach as menacing just moments earlier, as an example of the overarching racial tensions in place at the time) eating—of all things—fried chicken with the mistress of the house (Jessica Chastain), who labored to cook a meal for the first time by herself as a means to heal from a miscarriage.

The question is: After the meal, who is going to do the dishes? And then, even if they share in cleaning up, who will do the cooking the next day and the day after that? Is that not the crux of the entire relationship? The final scene portrays a false sense of comity where it appears as if they are peers and friends, when they are not.

Have You Scene It?

In one scene, Minny recounts a story through a confession about how she once served her former employer a taste of her own mean medicine. This scene invokes a couple of techniques simultaneously. First, it conveniently isolates racism to a lone, mean individual. All the White women in the movie benefitted both directly and indirectly from institutional and systemic White privilege and patriarchy, but by featuring one woman as the source of all matters mean and racist (e.g., her refusal to allow Blacks to use her indoor toilet, even when it was raining), the audience is distracted from the seriousness of the subject of Black female subjugation.

Octavia Spencer and Jessica Chastain depict a feel-good friendship in *The Help*. It would be fascinating to see whether audiences would have been as receptive had the power and aesthetic dynamics between the two been reversed. *Dreamworks/Photofest*

But using the distracting veil of comedy—specifically, anal humor—the movie focuses upon the concept of a single mean White woman receiving her come-uppance, but the movie cleverly does not spend time dissecting the exact steps required for the "terrible awful" to occur. In the scene, Minny presents what appears to be an ordinary chocolate pie to her former employer, Hilly (Bryce Dallas Howard). Hilly eats it, while her mother, who also benefits from having a Black maid in the house but is framed as somehow more understanding and benevolent than her daughter, conveniently declines. After she has eaten two slices, Minny informs Hilly that it contains excrement, which later causes Hilly's skin to break out in pimples.

This scene is a source of merriment and delight to the audience: Finally, a mean White racist got what was coming to her! But again, it is not as if a law were passed making it illegal for Black women to serve as maids for White women during this time. Additionally, we now have a situation where a Black woman resorts to literally collecting her excrement in a container somehow. (In full dis-closure, I own a dog—her name is Ms. Puppy—and upon reflection, it is difficult to imagine the collection of human stool after observing the rituals in cleaning up after the dog on a consistent basis—a chore that does not lessen in severity nor stench in its required repetition.) Then she has to mix it with various other ingredients such as butter, sugar, flour, and the like in order to actually create a pie. And we can't overlook the materials required to actually mix together the ingredients. Thus, several questions arise about the collection of fecal material and the use of materials that would likely have to be permanently discarded, and then the baking of the pie. But the pie is perhaps a metaphor for the larger idea that something so shitty can simply be covered up with a bit of sugar in order for it to be digestible and palatable for mainstream audiences.

Black Oscar Angles

Déjà Vu

Spencer personally accounts for more than one Black Oscar nomination, mak-ing her a repeat contender.

Gravity of Reality

The movie is based around race, given the social and economic tensions between well-to-do White women who can afford Black female domestics as "help" around the house.

Still in the Struggle

The Scent of Magnolia is heavy in the air, and not just because the movie takes place in 1960s Mississippi. Political, social, and economic subjugation are indelible parts of the character's identity.

Bottom Line

Final Cut

With respect to traditional images of power and control regarding Black females on-screen, this movie character satisfies the Romantic racialism and femininity prongs of the Unholy Trinity generally and satisfies the Angel Figure archetype specifically with her role serving as a maid and confidante, helping her mistress through a difficult time with her miscarriage. The final analysis is that this movie fits established patterns of servile Black women, as the character's sole purpose is to aid White characters.

Bonus Features

Outtakes

- Both Black Oscar nominations for the 84th Academy Awards came from the same movie.
- The same year, Black Oscar nominee James Earl Jones (*The Great White Hope*) received an Academy Honorary Award.
- It is unknown how much of a royalty was received by the Black women whose testimonies served as the basis of the manuscript Skeeter published in this movie, but chances are it did not rival by much the 20 percent the domestic Delilah received in the 1934 version of *Imitation of Life*. In fact, in real life, Ablene Cooper, the person author Kathryn Stockett based much of the book upon, sued, stating that she received 0 percent royalties from Stockett's intellectual property in crafting the story.[9]
- Spencer's character is seen in a maid's uniform in her last scene on-screen, still employed (happily) as a maid. Contrast this to Skeeter's condition, which materially changes when she physically leaves the South for a more progressive, urban environment to pursue her writing career.

NOMINATION #61—DENZEL WASHINGTON

Backstory

Oscar Details

Best Actor Nomination for Denzel Washington as William "Whip" Whitaker Sr. in *Flight* (2012) for the 85th Academy Awards (Dolby Theater) on February 24, 2013.

Character and Movie Overview

In the movie, Washington plays a drug-addicted, philandering, absentee father and airline pilot who, while skilled at his craft, is saddled with personal demons that interfere with his job performance. Whip opens the movie in the haze and aftermath of a drug-induced sexual orgy with two Latina flight attendants. The audience quickly learns that Whip is not a practicing bigamist when, after snorting his early morning cocaine lines the next morning, Whip is on the phone with his ex-wife discussing scheduling matters related to his son. On the next flight, a weather abnormality occurs, which Whip handles through deft (although risky) maneuvering. Whip successfully lands the plane with minimal casualties, two fatalities being the two Latina flight attendants (indicating, literally, little regard for minority female life).

Have You Scene It?

While Whip does the unimaginable in heroically landing the plane, his heroism is tainted because he was drinking on the flight after having surreptitiously grifted three bottles of alcohol from the beverage cart. Whip is interviewed by investigators who politely inform him that the evidence suggests no one had access to the beverage cart with the exception of the flight crew and flight attendants. Up until this point, Whip is angling to walk away from his drunken offense unscathed, but when attorney Hugh Lang (Don Cheadle) confronts him, stating that he is trying to save his life, Whip angrily retorts, "What f*cking life?!"

Black Oscar Angles

Gravity of Reality

Washington personally accounts for 10.3 percent of all Black Oscar nominations, with eight.

Still in the Struggle

Whip struggles to be an appropriate father figure, struggles to find true love, and struggles with himself and his alcoholism.

Bottom Line

Final Cut

With respect to traditional images of power and control regarding Black males on-screen, this movie character satisfies the Negrophobia prong of the Unholy Trinity generally and satisfies the Menace to Society and Utopic Reversal archetypes specifically. Not only is Whip a threat to public safety, he is a threat to himself, bringing shame to a difficult, respected, and honored profession. Hence, he sees jail time for his transgressions in the end. The final analysis is that this movie fits established patterns of incompetent Black men, given his role serving as a talented yet troubled airline pilot.

Bonus Features

Black in the Hat

The crux of the movie focuses upon Whip's road to rehabilitation and his possible outmaneuvering of consequences even though he was indeed drinking at the time. Harling Mays (John Goodman) comes in as his representative (it appears Whip might benefit from plasticity of White criminality by way of proxy, as Mays properly instructs Whip on what to do to get away with it) and Whip does the right thing by admitting full culpability for his flaws ("know your place"). While Whip's character presents as unconventional and complex, the analysis may be more straightforward. Few movies come to mind that prominently feature Black male airline pilots (and no, Kareem Abdul Jabbar in the 1980 spoof *Airplane!* does not qualify). The one movie that does feature a Black male pilot of exceptional skill depicts a character who is ultimately damaged goods in his own mind, with a personal life that is literally crashing and burning all around him.

Compare this movie to the 2014 film *Non-Stop*, in which Liam Neeson's protagonist starts off in a similarly morally objectionable state but by movie's end is able to redeem himself as the hero. Specifically, Neeson's character is a federal agent who not only drinks on the job, he violates federal law by using duct tape to intentionally facilitate smoking in the lavatory; the audience forgets these transgressions by movie's end. Here, the most heroic action Whip takes within the visible continuum is simply admitting guilt after relapsing from a successful booze-free stint, to the disappointment of his union representative.

Outtakes

- The film was inspired by the crash of Alaska Airlines Flight 261.
- Hollywood's third rail remains visibly untouched here, although sexual intercourse is intimated after a brief kiss between Whip and the White character Nicole (Kelly Reilly); Nicole, a recovering heroin addict herself, decides to leave Whip after his continued relapses conflict with her personal goal to stay sober.

NOMINATION #62—QUVENZHANÉ WALLIS

Backstory

Oscar Details

Best Actress Nomination for Quvenzhané Wallis as Hushpuppy in *Beasts of the Southern Wild* (2012) for the 85th Academy Awards (Dolby Theater) on February 24, 2013.

Character & Movie Overview

In the movie, Wallis plays a precocious young child seeking answers to large questions as she searches for a better life.

Have You Scene It?

At one point, several people are gathered in a dilapidated dwelling, with bright red boiled crabs spread over a table covered with newspaper. After receiving instruction from a White male about how to use a tool to properly open the crab's back to access the meat inside, Hushpuppy's father, Wink, (who dies in this movie) emphatically jumps up in frustration and breaks open the crab with his hands, sucks the innards dry, and then instructs Hushpuppy, "Beast it!" (while a piece of crab meat hangs suspensefully on his lip). It is unknown what influence or relevance this phraseology has with the movie's title.

Quvenzhané Wallis in *Beasts of the Southern Wild*. Her debut appearance successfully complicates the HARM theory although the film experienced limited box office success. *Fox Searchlight Pictures/Photofest*

After he repeats his command several times, the others in the room gradually join in, chanting, "Beast it!" in a pitched crescendo until Hushpuppy breaks open the crab manually. The group erupts in cheers, and after sucking the crab dry, following her father's example, Hushpuppy then stands on the table and flexes her arms before eliciting a guttural scream (also with crab meat hanging from her lip). Hopefully her father was no longer crabby after this Southern Wild display.

Black Oscar Angles

Still in the Struggle

Impoverished conditions frame the character's existence.

Bottom Line

Final Cut

With respect to traditional images of power and control regarding Black females on-screen, for this movie character no clean archetype pattern emerges, nor does any overarching Unholy Trinity narrative neatly apply. This is a welcome and unique case that does not easily satisfy traditional narratives accorded Black mainstream imagery.

Bonus Features

Outtakes

- At nine years old, Wallis is the youngest Oscar nominee ever!
- Dwight Henry, who played Hushpuppy's father, Wink, had no previous acting experience before this film.[10]
- In other Oscar racial news, Best Picture honors that year went to *Argo*, which featured White male actor Ben Affleck appearing in brownface playing the role of Latino reporter Tony Mendez.
- *Life of Pi* garnered Asian American director Ang Lee a Best Director win the same year.
- Possibly problematic, Christoph Waltz won Best Supporting Actor for his role as Dr. King Schultz in *Django Unchained*—a movie by Quentin Tarantino dealing with the theme of enslavement and problematic due to the one hundred plus times the n-word was used, along with other historic themes that were not accurately represented but were sold under the auspices of entertainment (e.g., "Mandingo fighting").[11]
- The Academy may disagree with the analysis in the previous paragraph, as it awarded Best Original Screenplay to *Django Unchained* the same year.

NOMINATION #63—CHIWETEL EJIOFOR

Backstory

Oscar Details

Best Actor Nomination for Chiwetel Ejiofor as Solomon Northup in *12 Years a Slave* (2013) for the 86th Academy Awards (Dolby Theater) on March 2, 2014.

Character and Movie Overview

In the movie, based on a true story, Ejiofor plays a free Black violinist in the North, who by dastardly device of the Fugitive Slave Act, is sold into slavery even though he is a free man. Northup painstakingly holds out for survival while fighting to keep his will to survive alive in the face of the brutal horrors of slavery.

Have You Scene It?

In one poignant scene, Solomon attempts to literally shake and logically reason Eliza (Adepero Oduye) out of her misery and despair of confronting the horror in being endlessly tortured with no definitive end in sight. Solomon, based upon his background and education, tries to help Eliza by having her focus on the abstract concept of hope. The scene is powerful insofar as it reminds audiences about the emotional and psychological toll exacted on Black bodies in the name of personal profit for Whites. Eliza likely would have had more hope if she were able to befriend Mr. Samuel Bass (Brad Pitt), like Solomon did. Brad Pitt not only served as executive producer, he also makes a cameo in the film and in fact it is through Pitt's character that Northup is able to achieve his freedom. Visually, the late appearance of a bona fide A-list movie star in Pitt signals to the audience that this character has some significance, while associating Pitt's character with the alleviation of the movie's conflict shifts agency away from Northup's character, whose only redeeming quality was to pray his way through intense psychological and physical torture and distress. This larger-than-life White savior idea was confirmed off-screen in the Italian-language poster for the movie, which prominently featured Pitt's face even though the movie is not about him.

Black Oscar Angles

Black Non-American

Ejiofor is a Nigerian British actor.

Gravity of Reality

The movie is based around race and is a para-realistic film based upon the life of a factual figure.

Still in the Struggle

The Scent of Magnolia is strong in this movie about enslavement made in the contemporary era.

Bottom Line

Final Cut

With respect to traditional images of power and control regarding Black females on-screen, this movie character satisfies the Romantic racialism prong of the

Unholy Trinity generally; given its largely insular-universe status with limited contact between Black and White worlds, no clean archetype pattern emerges. The final analysis is that this movie fits established patterns of enslaved Black men.

Bonus Features

Dogg Tired

Martha Stewart's trusted colleague and international hip-hop star Snoop Dogg essentially criticized what an academic would term "slavery porn" by questioning the value of the visual iconography that movies like *12 Years a Slave* offer.

In a series of short videos posted online, Snoop observed, "I'm sick of this. . . . They just going to keep beating that (expletive) into our heads as to how they did us, huh?"[12] While the movie can always be contextualized as being a part of history (although it is not a documentary), this comment speaks to the concept that the bell has already been rung in the symbolic degradation of Black imagery, depicting Blacks when they were maltreated and exploited. Feminist scholar Hortense Spiller would likely classify these gratuitous displays of visual violence as *pornotropic*.[13] For our purposes, we employ the shorthand "slavery porn," in which viewers—as much as they are horrified—are captivated by and become voyeurs of these brute displays of power and control in the form of fictional images featuring subjugated Blacks.

Snoop went on to conjecture, "I don't understand America. They just want to keep showing the abuse that we took hundreds and hundreds of years ago. But guess what? We're taking the same abuse," suggesting a historical link between present struggles and those of the past. In conclusion, Snoop asked rhetorically and exasperatedly, "The only success we have is *Roots* and *12 Years A Slave*?"

Outtakes

- Black British director Steve McQueen was the first Black director to ever be associated with a movie that won Best Picture for his work in *12 Years a Slave*.

NOMINATION #64—BARKHAD ABDI

Backstory

Oscar Details

Best Supporting Actor Nomination for Barkhad Abdi as Abduwali Muse in *Captain Phillips* (2013) for the 86th Academy Awards (Dolby Theater) on March 2, 2014.

Barkhad Abdi makes his successful screen debut as an unsuccessful pirate in *Captain Phillips. Columbia Pictures/Photofest*

Character and Movie Overview

In the movie, Abdi plays a modern-day Somalian pirate. Based upon a true story of the *Maersk Alabama* hijacking, this pirate movie is somehow devoid of the glamour accorded Johnny Depp's Captain Jack Sparrow in *Pirates of the Caribbean.*

Have You Scene It?

Unlike a classic diamond heist movie, the planned takeover of the *Maersk Alabama* by the pirates did not exactly go smoothly. Yelling and shouting, the dark-skinned pirates appear to be in a panic even though they are the ones in control as the holders of the guns. In contrast, the Captain Richard Phillips, depicted by White male A-list actor Tom Hanks, appears cool, calm, and collected. He speaks directly and firmly, initially explaining that the computers are offline and then, realizing the language barrier, simplifies his message for the (childlike) Blacks on-screen, repeating that "the ship is broken," effectively essentializing a complex nautical vehicle costing millions of dollars so that his rabid captors (or savages) can calm down and understand. Muse interrupts, saying, "No one gets hurt if you don't play no games." Phillips protests, knowing that he has more information than he is willing to reveal. Muse then commands the captain to look at him and flatly states, "I'm the captain now."

While the ominous music in the background clues the viewer in to the idea that this statement was indeed one that took power away from Captain Phillips, the truth of the matter is that under the Black in the Hat trend, all will be put in its proper place by movie's end. In fact, upon seeing the title of the movie—*Captain Phillips*—viewers should have a pretty good idea of who is going to come out on top of this power struggle. *Spoiler alert:* The Black pirate loses. As this is based upon a true story and pirates commandeering boats is ethically incorrect, it is true that there is no incentive to portray such pirates in a flattering light; however, the bell hath indeed rung with respect to viewers seeing within the visible continuum disruption, mayhem, violence, and confusion all coming from Black male bodies—bodies that, by movie's end, have provided ample justification for being destroyed, eliminated, and punished as part of the iconography.

Black Oscar Angles

Black Non-American

Abdi is Somali, born in Mogadishu.

Crossover

This was Abdi's first-ever role; he was an employee in a cell phone shop and returned to the shop after filming the movie.

Gravity of Reality

This movie is a para-realistic film based upon a factual figure.

Still in the Struggle

The economic and political background of the pirates pushes them toward crime as a remedy as an explanation, not an excuse.

Bottom Line

Final Cut

With respect to traditional images of power and control regarding Black males on-screen, this movie character satisfies the Negrophobia prongs of the Unholy Trinity generally and satisfies the Background Figure and Menace to Society archetypes specifically with his role serving as a failed pirate with few lines. The Utopic Reversal archetype possibly applies here as well inasmuch Muse is an inept pirate who could not even be evil properly; he watches helplessly on the intercepting *USS Bainbridge* as his fellow pirates fail and die in their mission. The final analysis is that this movie fits established patterns of threatening Black men.

Outtakes

- Abdi subsequently featured in Denis Villeneuve's *Blade Runner 2049* in a minor role of a scientist. He shared one scene with Ryan Gosling, providing him information about where to go next (Angel Figure).

NOMINATION #65, WIN #15—LUPITA NYONG'O

Backstory

Oscar Details

Best Supporting Actress Nomination for Lupita Nyong'o as Patsey in *12 Years a Slave* (2013) for the 86th Academy Awards (Dolby Theater) on March 2, 2014.

Character and Movie Overview

In the movie, Nyong'o plays an enslaved, unmarried Black female who ends up becoming an object of illicit desire by her master, Edwin Epps (Richard Fasbender). Patsey is not only used as an outlet for Epps's sexual proclivities outside of his Christian marriage, but she is also mistreated severely as part of a long-standing, sick, and twisted cycle of abuse.

Have You Scene It?

In the movie's climactic, if not most intense, scene, Epps attempts to discipline Patsey for leaving the plantation to obtain soap. However, the rub is that Epps is commanded to punish Patsey as an act of jealous comeuppance by his Christian wife; he then adds a layer of pathology to the scenario by having Solomon Vandy (the wrongly enslaved free Black male) finish the whipping of a naked Patsey, who is tied to a tree.

Black Oscar Angles

Black Non-American

Born in Mexico City, Mexico, Nyong'o is of Kenyan and Mexican descent.

Neither Michael Fassbender nor Chiwetel Ejiofor were strong enough to protect Lupita Nyong'o from a White woman's wrath in *12 Years a Slave. Fox Searchlight Pictures/Photofest*

Déjà Vu

Nyongo's whipping scene is reminiscent of Denzel Washington's in *Glory* (1989).

Gravity of Reality

This movie is based around race and is a para-realistic film based upon the life of a factual figure.

Still in the Struggle

The Scent of Magnolia is strong in this movie about enslavement made in the contemporary era. Here, historical accuracy may be used as a justifiable defense for the disturbing and problematic content, but this approach fails to observe the detail that this movie is not a documentary made for educational purposes. Lastly, in coming from the vision of a British director (although of the African diaspora), synchronization of sensitivity cannot be assumed. His status as a literal outsider to the United States and its unique history may factor into the reasons Steve McQueen felt comfortable displaying the images he did and using non–African American actors for the two Black leads.

Bottom Line

Final Cut

With respect to traditional images of power and control regarding Black females on-screen, this movie character satisfies the Romantic racialism and femininity prongs of the Unholy Trinity generally and satisfies the Physical Wonder archetype specifically with her role serving as a tool of sexual pleasure. The final analysis is that this movie fits established patterns of abused Black women; as she was sexually exploited for personal gain by the main White character, Patsey's role qualifies as a Physical Wonder.

Bonus Features

Literal Titillation

Similar to Denzel Washington's performance in *Glory*, for which he claimed Best Supporting Actor honors in part due to a riveting scene in which he is publicly whipped, here Patsey is stripped partially naked and is whipped by the protagonist Vandy. This raises the question for our analysis as to whether this is literally a scene of titillation or whether it is high-quality acting. Compare Patsey's treatment with that of Dandrige's Carmen Jones for which she too "received critical acclaim for her performance in a sensationalistic role" in a film that "graphically depicted her being beaten, chased, tied up, and finally murdered."[14] Thus, the question is whether these actresses are merely being rewarded for publicly projecting power dynamics that are possibly pursued privately.

Outtakes

- All three Black Oscar nominations for the 58th Academy Awards came from the same movie.
- Rap artist Common (Lonnie Lynn) and R&B crooner John Legend claimed Best Original Song honors win for their track "Glory" from *Selma*.
- To see whether Nyong'o benefitted from any Oscar bounce, consider the amount of screen time and dialogue she received in her very next film after her Oscar win, *Non-Stop*.
- Black filmmaker Spike Lee won an Honorary Oscar that year as well.

NOMINATION #66—DENZEL WASHINGTON

Backstory

Oscar Details

Best Actor Nomination for Denzel Washington as Troy Maxson in *Fences* (2016) for the 89th Academy Awards (Dolby Theater) on February 26, 2017.

Character and Movie Overview

In the movie, Washington plays the economically frustrated and unfaithful husband of an economically frustrated but faithful wife. Troy is not necessarily an endearing character and appears to have a fractured relationship with his two Black male sons.

While the film explores the nuances of Black drama and trauma, all of which are by-products of a larger institutional and systemic structure, the danger is that audiences walk away from the movie with an unfavorable impression of Black family relationships.

Have You Scene It?

In one scene, Troy spends a good two minutes of screen time explaining to his son Cory (Jovan Adepo) that spending $200 on a television is a foolish idea and that saving the funds for a potential roof repair of $264 would be more prudent. After perhaps processing the brusque tone of the conversation, Cory asks Troy whether he likes him as his son. Troy flatly replies, "I ain't got to like you." Social workers throughout the land likely cringed upon hearing this line.

Black Oscar Angles

Gravity of Reality

This movie heavily invokes themes of race.

Still in the Struggle

This film definitely qualifies as performativity of pain.

Bottom Line

Final Cut

With respect to traditional images of power and control regarding Black males on-screen, this movie character satisfies the femininity prong of the Unholy Trinity generally, given his social emasculation in life; given its largely insular-universe status with limited contact between Black and White worlds, no clean archetype pattern emerges. The final analysis is that this movie fits established patterns of emasculated Black men.

Bonus Features

Outtakes

• This movie is based upon the Pulitzer Prize–winning 1983 August Wilson play bearing the same name.

NOMINATION #67—RUTH NEGGA

Backstory

Oscar Details

Best Actress Nomination for Ruth Negga as Mildred Loving in *Loving* (2016) for the 89th Academy Awards (Dolby Theater) on February 26, 2017.

Character and Movie Overview

In the movie, Negga plays a fair-skinned African American woman whose inter-racial marriage with a White male tests and breaks the now-unconstitutional color barrier against miscegenation in 1960s Virginia.

Have You Scene It?

In one heartwarming scene, Richard and Mildred are out in an open field by themselves and Richard proposes marriage. The scene is well done, with accompanying strings and crisp cinematography to capture the breeze against the crops in the background. While the audience knows better, for those few seconds, the liberating feeling of freedom that love can provide is properly conveyed.

Black Oscar Angles

Black Non-American

Negga is of Ethiopian-Irish ancestry.

Gravity of Reality

The movie is based around race, given the movie's dominant theme of interracial marriage; this para-realistic film is based upon factual figures.

Still in the Struggle

Although set in the late 1960s, the movie still reflects the difficult existence African Americans have to face based upon their complexion.

Bottom Line

Final Cut

With respect to traditional images of power and control regarding Black females on-screen, this movie character satisfies the Romantic racialism and Negrophobia prongs of the Unholy Trinity generally as their mere union posed a threat to White segregationist concepts of normalcy, which also qualifies the character as Menace to Society and Physical Wonder archetypes. The final analysis is that for the movie's sake, this character fulfills established patterns of Black undesirability, since her literal race (or blood composition), not her abstract ability to care for another human, is the subject of controversy.

Bonus Features

Outtakes

- The year 2017 marked the first time in Academy Awards history in which Black actors were nominated in all four main acting categories; in contrast, this has happened *every year* for Whites since the Academy began the awards ceremony.
- Have you ever considered whether the Supreme Court case was successful due to the fact that the property rights of a White male was violated rather than the civil rights of a Black female?[15]

NOMINATION #68, WIN #16—MAHERSHALA ALI

Backstory

Oscar Details

Best Supporting Actor Nomination and Win for Mahershala Ali as Juan in *Moonlight* (2016) for the 89th Academy Awards (Dolby Theater) on February 26, 2017.

Character and Movie Overview

In the movie, Ali plays a drug dealer who helps the main character embrace and discover his true sexual identity. Juan does not have a last name, and it is unclear whether he may be an Afro-Latino.

Have You Scene It?

Juan has a confrontation with the protagonist's mother, Paula (Black Oscar nominee Naomie Harris), in which he convincingly conveys shame for contributing to the problem he wishes to solve; namely, by selling drugs (i.e., crack cocaine)

Mahershala Ali as Juan in *Moonlight*. *A24/Photofest*

out on the streets, Paula is compromised in her ability to provide proper parenting and guidance.

Black Oscar Angles

Gravity of Reality

This movie is based around race and (sexual) identity; this is an insular-universe movie in which more complex Black characters are painted on-screen, but only in the absence of significant White presence.

Still in the Struggle

Juan and most of the characters of color with whom he interacts all are struggling, financially as well as emotionally.

Bottom Line

Final Cut

With respect to traditional images of power and control regarding Black males on-screen, this movie character satisfies the Negrophobia prong of the Unholy Trinity generally and satisfies the Menace to Society archetype specifically with his role serving as the neighborhood drug dealer. The final analysis is that this movie fits established patterns of flawed Black men.

Outtakes

• Ali is the first Black Muslim to ever receive an Oscar nomination.

NOMINATION #69, WIN #17—VIOLA DAVIS

Backstory

Oscar Details

Best Supporting Actress Nomination and Win for Viola Davis as Rose Maxson in *Fences* (2016) for the 89th Academy Awards (Dolby Theater) on February 26, 2017.

Character and Movie Overview

In the movie, Davis plays the economically frustrated but faithful wife of an economically frustrated and unfaithful husband. Despite Troy's affair, Rose resolves to nonetheless stand by her man and attempts to offer counsel to her son.

Have You Scene It?

Later in the movie, after Rose discovers that the less-than-perfect Troy has been having an affair behind her back, he attempts to elicit sympathy for his cursed lot in life. When Troy tries to explain that he's been standing in the same place for eighteen years, Rose abruptly interjects and reminds him, "I've been standing with you! I've got a life, too, Troy!" (Davis's nose is running in this scene, as it was in *Doubt*).

Black Oscar Angles

Déjà Vu

Davis personally accounts for more than one Black Oscar nomination, making her a repeat contender.

Gravity of Reality

This movie heavily invokes themes of race.

Still in the Struggle

This film definitely qualifies as performativity of pain.

Bottom Line

Final Cut

With respect to traditional images of power and control regarding Black females on-screen, this movie character satisfies the femininity prong of the Unholy Trinity generally, given her social emasculation in life; given its largely insular-universe status with limited contact between Black and White worlds, no clean archetype pattern emerges. The final analysis is that this movie fits established patterns of frustrated Black women.

Bonus Features

Outtakes

- This movie is based upon the Pulitzer Prize–winning 1983 August Wilson play bearing the same name.

NOMINATION #70—NAOMIE HARRIS

Backstory

Oscar Details

Best Supporting Actress Nomination for Naomie Harris as Paula in *Moonlight* (2016) for the 89th Academy Awards (Dolby Theater) on February 26, 2017.

Character and Movie Overview

In the movie, Harris plays the mother of a son looking to find himself and his identity.

Have You Scene It?

The drug dealer Juan (Black Oscar winner Mahershala Ali) has a confrontation with Paula in which he convincingly conveys shame for contributing to the problem he wishes to solve; namely, by selling drugs (i.e., crack cocaine) out on the streets, Paula is compromised in her ability to provide proper parenting and guidance.

Black Oscar Angles

Black Non-American

Harris is a British actress.

Déjà Vu

The parenting skills on display here by Harris are reminiscent of Mo'Nique's Oscar-winning performance in *Precious*.

Naomie Harris portrays a potentially problematic parenting model in *Moonlight*.
A24/Photofest

Gravity of Reality

The movie is based around race and sexual identity; this is an insular-universe movie whereby more complex Black characters are painted on-screen, but only in the absence of significant White presence.

Still in the Struggle

Paula and most of the characters of color with whom she interacts all are struggling, financially as well as emotionally.

Bottom Line

Final Cut

With respect to traditional images of power and control regarding Black females on-screen, this movie character satisfies the Negrophobia prong of the Unholy Trinity generally and satisfies the Menace to Society archetype specifically with her role as a crack-addicted mother who neglects her child. The final analysis is that this movie fits established patterns of undesirable Black women.

Bonus Features

Outtakes

- In the previous two years, the Academy Awards had come under scrutiny for the lack of racial diversity among the nominees in major categories; no actors of color were nominated in 2016. A fair question to ask is whether the record-setting six Black Oscar nominations in 2017 was due solely to the acting performances or whether it was a reactionary response to the Oscar whitewashing criticism. (Worth noting, however, is that four of the six nominations came from two movies.)
- Bradford Young became the first African American to be nominated for Best Cinematography, while Joi McMillon became the first African American (and the first woman) to be nominated for Best Film Editing since Hugh A. Robertson for *Midnight Cowboy* (1969).

NOMINATION #71—OCTAVIA SPENCER

Backstory

Oscar Details

Best Supporting Actress Nomination for Octavia Spencer as Dorothy Vaughan *Hidden Figures* (2016) for the 89th Academy Awards (Dolby Theater) on February 26, 2017.

Character and Movie Overview

In the movie, Spencer plays a fiercely determined and resolute NASA employee who calmly challenges both racial and gender barriers in the workplace during the space race of the early 1960s.

Similar to movies like *Green Book*, *The Help*, and *The Blind Side*, this movie speaks to racial reconciliation insofar as by using carefully timed humor, it makes light of situations that were often fraught with tension and pressure. The danger is that a mostly White audience may walk away from the movie falsely believing in a shared sense of racial comity.

Have You Scene It?

Racial comity can be confusing because it appears to be a good thing on the surface, but the danger is eliminating key details that must remain present. For example, in one scene Al Harrison (Kevin Costner) as the director of the Space Task Group physically takes a crowbar and dislodges the "colored" sign from above the restroom. The scene shows that he is fed up and frustrated by the illogic of racial discrimination. But if it only were that simple. There is no indication that Harrison directly opposed racial discrimination; however, there is confirmation that this powerful scene was completely fabricated—arguably to disproportionately highlight "good" White characters and qualities as a means to balance against the backdrop of inexcusable and uncomfortable institutional and systemic racial discrimination.[16] Not only does this run the risk that audience members will falsely believe that dismantling centuries and decades of systemic, institutionalized racial oppression is as simple as removing a sign, but it also centers the White male as the hero responsible for the actions. More agency from African Americans must be emphasized.

Black Oscar Angles

Déjà Vu

Spencer personally accounts for more than one Black Oscar nomination, making her a repeat contender.

Gravity of Reality

The movie is based around the intersecting topics of racial and gender discrimination and is a para-realistic film based upon factual figures.

Still in the Struggle

Dorothy Vaughan had to contend with the unenviable intersectionality of discrimination and disparate treatment based upon both race and gender.

Bottom Line

Final Cut

With respect to traditional images of power and control regarding Black females on-screen, this movie character satisfies the Romantic racialism and femininity prongs of the Unholy Trinity generally and satisfies the Angel Figure archetype specifically with her role serving as a mathematician who ultimately ran the numbers for her White superiors and for her White male colleagues in space. The final analysis is that this movie fits established patterns of servile Black women due to her expected responsibility to produce and perform for her White superiors.

Bonus Features

Outtakes

- The movie is based upon the nonfiction book bearing the same name by the African American author Margot Lee Shetterly.

NOMINATION #72—DANIEL KALUUYA

Backstory

Oscar Details

Best Actor Nomination for Daniel Kaluuya as Chris Washington in *Get Out* (2017) for the 90th Academy Awards (Dolby Theater) on March 4, 2018.

Character and Movie Overview

In the movie, Kaluuya plays a mild-mannered Black male who finds himself in a bizarre and eventually life-threatening interracial relationship.

Daniel Kaluuya as Chris Washington in the groundbreaking movie *Get Out*.
Universal Pictures/Photofest

Have You Scene It?

At the movie's conclusion, Chris's friend comes to the rescue, citing the famous line, "I'm TS motherf*cking A [Transportation Security Administration]!" This may have been a veiled defense of African American workers who are frequently maligned and criticized in the aftermath of the 9/11 terrorist attacks over their ability to maintain airports securely and competently.

Black Oscar Angles

Black Non-American

Kaluuya is a British actor.

Gravity of Reality

The movie is undoubtedly based around and about race.

Still in the Struggle

While perhaps in not as stark terms as earlier movies, part of the tension in this movie revolves around struggles related to class, race, and identity.

Bottom Line

Final Cut

With respect to traditional images of power and control regarding Black males on-screen, this movie character satisfies the Romantic racialism prong of the Unholy Trinity generally and satisfies the Physical Wonder archetype specifically with his role serving as a specimen of desire to be bid upon (like in the enslavement days of old). The final analysis is that this movie fits established patterns of objectified Black men; as he was literally pursued for his body above all else, it qualifies as a Physical Wonder archetype.

Bonus Features

Outtakes

- *Get Out* was novel for creating a storyline within the thriller/horror genre using race as the overarching construct and achieving mainstream success.

NOMINATION #73—DENZEL WASHINGTON

Backstory

Oscar Details

Best Actor Nomination for Denzel Washington as Roman J. Israel in *Roman J. Israel, Esq.* (2017) for the 90th Academy Awards (Dolby Theater) on March 4, 2018.

Character and Movie Overview

In the movie, Washington plays a bright but largely broke lawyer hell-bent on social reform. While touted as a legal maverick who is rumored to be quite formidable as an attorney, within the visible continuum, no evidence of this skill is displayed; it is merely alluded to by other characters.

Have You Scene It?

Early in the movie, when Israel makes an appearance for his partner who passed away from a heart attack, he attempts to negotiate with the prosecuting attorney over the criminal case of young man named Langston Bailey. Israel attempts to contextualize the young man's difficult life, and the rising crescendo of classical music in the background indicates that he will prove persuasive when he finishes with the line, "Each one of us is greater than the worst thing we've ever done." Unmoved, the opposing counsel informs Israel that her conviction rate is 100 percent and Israel walks away. An ominous sign for a brilliant individual who should be able to outthink his opponent. Accordingly, he was unable to outthink himself out of an untimely death.

Black Oscar Angles

Déjà Vu

Washington personally accounts for 10.3 percent of all Black Oscar nominations, with eight.

Gravity of Reality

The movie is based around race and social justice.

Still in the Struggle

Israel appears to be invigorated by fighting—perhaps just not effectively—for those who are disaffected and marginalized.

Bottom Line

Final Cut

With respect to traditional images of power and control regarding Black females on-screen, this movie character satisfies the femininity prong of the Unholy Trinity generally and satisfies the Utopic Reversal archetype specifically with his role in bumbling an informant's status, resulting in the informant's (and his own) death. The final analysis is that this movie fits established patterns of incompetent Black men, given the fact that despite his reputed intellectual skill, Israel's error of judgment directly leads to murder.

Bonus Features

Outtakes

- This Oscar nomination represents Washington's eighth, the most of any African American performer. (Jack Nicholson is the most nominated male performer, with twelve total.)
- Washington as an older, disheveled, unkempt, and scatterbrained attorney who dies a murderous death receives an Oscar nomination, while his performance in *Philadelphia* (1993) as a bright young upstart attorney who fought for another's life did not receive a nomination.

NOMINATION #74—MARY J. BLIGE

Backstory

Oscar Details

Best Supporting Actress Nomination for Mary J. Blige as Florence Jackson in *Mudbound* (2017) for the 90th Academy Awards (Dolby Theater) on March 4, 2018.

Character and Movie Overview

In the movie, Blige plays the wife of a poor tenant farmer. While there is nothing inherently wrong with a singer playing such a character on-screen, considering the larger spectrum of Black desirability as juxtaposed against consistent reinforcement of the White beauty standard, Blige's character appears rather pedestrian and unglamorous, in stark contrast to the customary exquisite appearances Blige makes as a highly heralded singer. Furthermore, Blige's dressed-down appearance also pales in comparison to the appearance of singer Lady Gaga in the 2018 version of the Academy Award–nominated *A Star Is Born*.

Have You Scene It?

This movie features two Southern families tied together by poverty and war. Sons from both families go off to the war and return with dramatically different results. Blige plays the motherly role of Florence Jackson, and her son Ronsel

(Jason Mitchell) ships off to the war to drive tanks. Before departing, violins play as she takes his face in both of her hands (a supreme sign of affection) and implores him, "Come back—all the way back" after serving his time. She then turns her back to mask her temporal emotions of loss.

Blige's words would prove ominously prophetic, as not only does Ronsel leave a piece of himself in Germany by fathering a child with his German girlfriend, but once a photograph of his girlfriend and mixed-race child was discovered, Ronsel has to pay by having his tongue removed, rendering him mute. Additionally, while the movie does show an illicit consummation of the White pairing Laura McAllen (Carey Mulligan) and her brother-in-law Jamie (Garrett Hedlund), within the visible continuum Hollywood's third rail remains untouched as sexual intercourse between a Black man and a White woman is assumed by the existence of the child, but not displayed.

Black Oscar Angles

Crossover

Blige started her career as an R&B singer, not as a classically trained actor.

Gravity of Reality

This movie is based around race and racial tensions in the South.

Still in the Struggle

The Scent of Magnolia is particularly strong in the air, since not only is it set in late-1930s Mississippi Delta, but also because cotton fields are literally depicted in this film.

Bottom Line

Final Cut

With respect to traditional images of power and control regarding Black females on-screen, this movie character satisfies the femininity prong of the Unholy Trinity generally and satisfies the Angel Figure archetype specifically with her role serving as a housekeeper. The final analysis is that this movie fits established patterns of servile Black women, based upon her aid and assistance rendered to the central White family, not only as their housekeeper but also as a source of comfort to the central White female character Laura after her miscarriage.

Bonus Features

Keeping It Real

Mainstream media made much of Blige's decision to go makeup free during filming.[17] Similar to the reaction to Viola Davis's role as Analisse Keating and her "de-beautification process" in the ABC television series hit *How to Get Away with Murder*,[18] the media reaction raises serious questions about the difference in pressures, expectations, and approachability of beauty standards that are arguably built upon ideals and are difficult if not impossible to reach—even for White women. In other words, tension exists between Black women being free to look how they feel versus mainstream media's sudden praise for the "authenticity" of Black female visual displays when they appear to move in the opposite direction of largely unquestioned but nonetheless observed beauty standards that routinely elevate and benefit White women.

Outtakes

- *Mudbound* is the only Black Oscar–nominated film to be directed by a Black female. To underscore the difficulty non-White females have in obtaining access to power and control over resources on a Hollywood set, note that this movie first achieved buzz with its January 2017 release at the Sundance Film Festival and experienced a limited release in theaters later that year as it was launched through the online platform of Netflix. These nontraditional release channels do not impact the quality of the film in any way; however, they reveal the difficulty in reaching the greatest possible audience in contrast to other widely distributed nationwide releases.

Mary J. Blige au naturel as Florence Jackson in *Mudbound*. *Netflix/Photofest*

- Blige was also nominated for Best Music, Original Song, for "Mighty River" that year, along with Raphael Saadiq and Taura Stinson.

NOMINATION #75—OCTAVIA SPENCER

Backstory

Oscar Details

Best Supporting Actress Nomination for Octavia Spencer as Zelda Deliah Fuller in *The Shape of Water* (2017) for the 90th Academy Awards (Dolby Theater) on March 4, 2018.

Character and Movie Overview

In the movie, Spencer plays a custodian working for a super-secret government laboratory alongside the central White female protagonist, Elisa Esposito (Sally Hawkins).

Have You Scene It?

Zelda upbraids her Black male spouse on-screen for failing to have enough intellectual acuity to discern that an inquiry into their White neighbor's whereabouts is in actuality a menacing threat that should be approached with tact—or at least with more tact that is displayed by him when he initially answers the ominous phone call.

Also important is how Zelda's "help" contrasts in quality and tone with that of Giles (Richard Jenkins), Elisa's closeted neighbor and confidante who facilitates Elisa's intellectual and emotional freedom as he finds his own.

Black Oscar Angles

Déjà Vu

Spencer personally accounts for more than one Black Oscar nomination, making her a repeat contender. Also, this is the second time Spencer has been nominated for a role in which she is a custodian/caretaker/maid.

Still in the Struggle

Although it is a subtle point, it is no less significant that Zelda and her husband live in a modest apartment, presumably off of two incomes. If one of those incomes is that of a custodian, this character does not stray far from traditional narratives of Blacks lacking exorbitant resources.

Bottom Line

Final Cut

With respect to traditional images of power and control regarding Black females on-screen, this movie character satisfies the Romantic racialism and femininity prongs of the Unholy Trinity generally and satisfies the Angel Figure archetype specifically with her role serving as a custodian, translator, and confidante. On-screen, Fuller's character definitely fulfills the Angel Figure archetype insofar as she helps the protagonist by not only forming a mentorship type relationship with Elisa on the job but also attempting to protect her later in the movie when the "bad guys" attempt to detain her and prevent the White romance with the Amphibian Man from blossoming. The final analysis is that this movie fits established patterns of servile Black women for not only serving in her official job as a cleaner/janitor, but also for rendering aid, assistance, and moral support to her mute coworker, Elisa.

Bonus Features

Fluid versus Firm Identity

While quick-thinking readers may quickly retort that the White female protagonist Elisa is also a custodian, there are two points of differentiation that require recognition: (1) While she starts the movie as a custodian, Elisa presumably does not end the movie as a custodian, having acquired "gills" to theoretically swim happily ever after with her amphibious love; and (2) as the whole movie centers around this unusual and unlikely pairing, not all of Elisa's scenes on-screen show her cemented within the custodian role—in fact, in watching the film, one is apt to forget her day job in focusing upon her personal life, thoughts, and feelings outside of her job. In contrast, Zelda is mostly seen on-screen on the job (with the exception of the scene with her husband's incompetence as described above). Additionally, Elisa is indeed the protagonist.

Outtakes

- In other Oscar racial news, Sam Rockwell won Best Supporting Actor for his rendition of a bona fide racist police officer in *Three Billboards outside Ebbing, Missouri.* Similar to arguments floated in defense of *The Birth of a Nation*, Rockwell's win indicates that the overall colorful quality of his performance was worthy of acclaim, while not necessarily supporting the content of his character.
- Black writer and director Jordan Peele won Best Original Screenplay for the surprise smash hit *Get Out.*

NOMINATION #76, WIN #18—MAHERSHALA ALI

Backstory

Oscar Details

Best Supporting Actor Nomination and Win for Mahershala Ali as Don Shirley in *Green Book* (2018) for the 91st Academy Awards (Dolby Theater) on February 24, 2019.

Character and Movie Overview

In the movie, Ali plays an accomplished pianist who, in a reversal of stereotypical roles, hires a White male driver for a two-month concert tour throughout the South. Given the movie's reliance upon the "borderline-racist-redeemed-as-racial-White-savior" trope,[19] it is not difficult to see how, despite an initially modest box office showing, its popularity grew based upon its ability to stimulate the imagination of a majority-White audience. The fantasy employed in this movie that deeprooted institutional and systemic racism can be overcome with chicken bones, love letters, and hugs at Christmas dinners is a powerful one that resonates with many Americans' impatience and desire to usher into a postracial society. A simplistic White savior movie narrative "denies the structures that have continually enabled America's mistreatment of minorities, reinforcing misconceptions that segregation and racism are simply southern, largely lower-class, male phenomena."[20]

Have You Scene It?

While driving, stereotypes are reversed when Tony (Viggo Mortensen) implores Don to try eating fried chicken with his hands. Flummoxed and perplexed, the prim and proper Don inquires whether utensils should be used and complaining that eating with one's hands is unsanitary. (Get it? Apparently not all Black people eat fried chicken.) When asking, "What do we do about the bones?" Tony demonstrates the freedom of the open road and throws the chicken bones out of the window, to which Don also merrily complies. The line is drawn when Tony throws a nonbiodegradable paper cup outside the window; Don, as the employer, exerts his power and has Tony stop and reverse to pick up the litter.

That African Americans received Oscars for racial reconciliation movies in 2019 speaks volumes about Blacks' relatively incremental racial progress within Hollywood's landscape.

Black Oscar Angles

Déjà Vu

Ali personally accounts for more than one Black Oscar nomination, making him a repeat contender.

Gravity of Reality

The movie is based around race and is a para-realistic film based upon a factual figure.

Still in the Struggle

Despite being accomplished and professionally respected, Don is still personally impacted by racial discrimination.

Bottom Line

Final Cut

With respect to traditional images of power and control regarding Black males on-screen, this movie character satisfies the Romantic racialism and femininity prongs of the Unholy Trinity generally and satisfies the Physical Wonder archetypes specifically with his role serving as an accomplished pianist and given the focus on the musical talents his body can produce. Additionally, given the fact that Don Shirley is an eccentric man of refinement, he also assists and aids his rough-around-the-edges driver in composing highly effective love letters to his wife, qualifying him as an Angel Figure. The final analysis is that this movie fits established patterns of useful and entertaining Black men.

Bonus Features

Black in the Hat

One of the movie's final scenes also features another "cute reversal" when Don drives Tony safely home after Tony complains of fatigue. The movie's conclusion cannot be overlooked in terms of the power and control symbology it suggests—namely, that it is Don who leaves *and then returns* to Tony's home after realizing he is alone for the Christmas holiday, with Tony's household now serving as an anchor of stability. While the White male supposedly has worked for the Black male all movie long, at the end it is the Black male who dutifully serves the White male, despite Tony's having specifically been hired by Don to drive, forming the initial context of their relationship.

After Tony briefly defends Don's racial honor one last time, Tony's wife, Dolores (Linda Cardellini), in the movie's final moments whispers in Don's ear and thanks him for helping Tony with the letters, indicating that Don (and Tony) could not quite outsmart her. Even still, rather than celebrating the successful two-month tour's conclusion with his own family, in the Hollywood ending Don is warmly embraced by Tony and Dolores in their home as symbolic verification that Don has now been accepted.

Outtakes

- *Green Book* won Best Picture in 2019.
- The movie obtains its title from the *Negro Motorist Travel Guide*, which published listings of segregated facilities to prepare wary Black visitors attempting to safely navigate the Jim Crow South. The guidebook's creator, Victor H. Green, created the book as a way to spare traveling Blacks undue humiliation, having served the nation as a federal employee (a Harlem postal worker) before leaving for more friendly territory in the travel agency business.[21]
- This movie suffered two controversies. The first was when Viggo Mortensen used the n-word at a promotional appearance for the movie, for which he later apologized.[22] The second involved reports surfaced that the surviving members of the Shirley family were scarcely consulted about context and nuance of the actual relationship upon which the movie was based, prompting Mahershala Ali to personally apologize to the family.[23]

NOMINATION #77, WIN #19—REGINA KING

Backstory

Oscar Details

Best Supporting Actress Nomination for Regina King as Sharon Rivers in *If Beale Street Could Talk* (2018) for the 91st Academy Awards (Dolby Theater) on February 24, 2019.

Character and Movie Overview

In the movie, King plays the mother of a son who is falsely accused of a rape he did not commit. She attempts but fails to prove her son's innocence before her grandson is born with her son behind bars.

Have You Scene It?

The movie's climactic scene culminates with Sharon tracking down the "White lady" who has identified her son as her rapist from a police lineup. Victoria Rogers (Emily Rios) is actually Puerto Rican, and Sharon tracks her down in Puerto Rico despite her limited resources. The trip to Puerto Rico comes after a unique scene during which King looks directly into the camera/mirror as she plans to prepare her best appearance but realizes that a wig cannot protect her from what lies ahead, despite her fussy adjustments, and morosely removes it. After Sharon finally confronts Victoria in an alleyway, attempting to appeal to her conscience, Victoria flatly says, "One thing I can tell, lady: you ain't never been raped." It is in this moment where Sharon's hopelessness is sealed. She realizes that the pain of rape is a barrier that she cannot penetrate despite her deep and abiding love for her son.

Black Oscar Angles

Gravity of Reality

The movie is based around race, more specifically a false rape charge by a White woman against a Black male. (This is reminiscent of the Oscar-winning 1962 film *To Kill a Mockingbird*.)

Still in the Struggle

The characters bitterly struggle with the vestiges of poverty and racial discrimination; the performativity of pain is on full display here.

Bottom Line

Final Cut

With respect to traditional images of power and control regarding Black females on-screen, for this movie character no clean archetype pattern emerges, nor does any overarching Unholy Trinity narrative neatly apply. This is a welcome and unique case that does not easily satisfy traditional narratives accorded Black mainstream imagery.

Bonus Features

Outtakes

- King also starred opposite Cuba Gooding Jr. as his foulmouthed, frustrated wife in the Oscar-winning *Jerry Maguire*.
- Cicely Tyson received an Academy Honorary Award this year.
- The movie is based upon a novel by James Baldwin that was first published in 1974.
- *Black Panther* won three Oscars in 2019: Best Original Score, Best Production Design, Best Costume Design (winner Ruth E. Carter was the first African American to win an Academy Award in that category).
- In 2019, Spike Lee won his first competitive Oscar for Best Adapted Screenplay for *BlacKkKlansman*. Perhaps similar to slavery porn critiques, a difficulty and possible by-product of the constant rehashing of images of the Ku Klux Klan is that "many scholars have argued that dismissing segregationists as toxic White trash enables filmmakers to offer a clear culprit for the South's—and therefore the nation's—legacy of racial intolerance and violence."[24]

CONCLUSION

Have We Seen This Movie Before?
A Critical Analysis

SO, WHAT?

Mainstream movies are seen by millions of people and have the potential to make hundreds of millions of dollars. With this in mind, how much can actually be left to chance? Not much. Therefore moviegoers cannot casually dismiss the fleeting presence of a minority on-screen and falsely attribute this minimal exposure to the end-all explanation that the minority character's *role* was simply insignificant. Taking into consideration the practical financial influences and pressures involved with producing and distributing a mainstream movie, hundreds of employees often dedicate thousands of hours toward creating the precise images most likely to contribute to the movie's commercial success. Thus, analyzing the Oscars serves as an excellent litmus test regarding the degree to which our society has truly embraced diversity within the hallowed confines of our sacred imaginations.

In deconstructing more than ninety years of the Academy Awards as an institution, it is not nearly enough to tally how many African Americans received Oscar nominations or wins over the years. Instead, our task here is to critically analyze the value and symbolic meaning of the iconography so recognized. Academy Award wins do not represent definitive evidence of all the social trends that matter in society. Yet, the Oscars represent the most prestigious (sorry, Golden Globes!) award show in movies and arguably across all entertainment genres, and therefore they command an unparalleled audience and influence. Thus, while not dispositive of everything, the Oscars are certainly indicative of something.

Movies reflect and reinforce aspects of life and popular culture. This book's premise has been that studying the history of African Americans at the Academy Awards provides opportunities to analyze the power of the moving image and the visual iconography and corresponding value of Blackness. Hence, to the extent that movies reflect and reinforce existing social structures and strictures in place, this Oscar lens is but one of many that can be applied to the larger picture as a whole. The data amassed here is valuable given AMPAS's global influence, exposure, and widespread cultural significance and acceptance.

QUANTITATIVE ANALYSIS

The suspense is over! Before offering any conclusions about what Black Oscar nominees and winners say about African Americans in society, it is now time to first cull the data. From ninety-one different Academy Award ceremonies spanning nearly a century of moviemaking, out of 1,728 total acting nominees, there are 77 total Black Oscar nominees, representing 57 different actors appearing in 66 different movies, with 19 total competitive wins. The following data points result:

Black Oscar Nominations, 1929–2019

Acting Category	Grand Total # of All Nominees	Total # of Black Nominees	Blacks as % of All Nominees, Acting Category	Blacks as % of All Nominees, Grand Total
Best Actor	447	23	5.1%	1.3%
Best Actress	451	11	2.4%	0.6%
Best Supporting Actor	415	19	4.5%	1%
Best Supporting Actress	415	24	5.7%	1.3%
Grand Total	1728	77	N/A	4.3%

Black Oscar Wins, 1929–2019

Acting Category	Total # of All Winners	Total # of Black Winners	Blacks as % of All Winners, Acting Category	Blacks as % of All Winners, Grand Total
Best Actor	91	4	4.3%	1%
Best Actress	91	1	1%	.2%
Best Supporting Actor	91	6	6.5%	1.6%
Best Supporting Actress	91	8	8.7%	2.1%
Grand Total	**364**	**19**	**N/A**	**5.2%**

Overall, 5.2 percent (19/364) of all total acting awards throughout the entire history of the Academy Awards have resulted in Black Oscar wins. Additionally, of the ninety-one Academy Awards ceremonies, there were no Black Oscar nominations for award cycle in fifty separate years, with 2016 being the last year this occurred. These numbers illustrate that at least within this institution, Black contributions are limited.

Although the Academy in 2013 elected an African American woman, Cheryl Boone Isaacs, as president, a fair question is whether the timing was at all influenced by stinging criticism from recent years prior. The data amassed here for Black Academy Award nominees and winners certainly indicates a lack of consistent inclusion, regardless of good intentions. Racism, especially when institutionalized at the onset of an organization's structural operation, can be long lasting regardless of individual intent. Thus, analyzing the visual iconography for consistent patterns allows us to see that which is hidden in plain view.

What is plain to see is that AMPAS shows no signs of slowing growth, with its own museum slated to complete construction in 2020.[1] Millions of viewers continue to develop intimate relationships with the ceremony, its history, and its winners, even though the overwhelming majority of the audience simply accepts the results as decreed without any potential for influence. For example, *Titanic* was deemed the Best Picture of 1997 *for all of us*, even though a small, elite, largely obscure group of people made this selection.[2] In other words, the Academy Awards is a private party with private invitations where privately selected winners are publicly announced, publicly celebrated, and publicly venerated.

Hidden Figures

As AMPAS is a private body, we must acknowledge that its methods and rationales for selection are relatively unknown; thus an award is not dispositive of definitive proof that the Best Picture Oscar winner was necessarily the most perfectly crafted film made that year. Due to a lack of transparency, it is unknown to what degree AMPAS voters are influenced or swayed by either heavy campaigning—a technique popularized by the infamous Harvey Weinstein of the #MeToo social media campaign—or heavy compassion after viewing a movie.

What we do know, however, from looking at the numbers is that the odds magically increase when more diversity is present both in front of and behind the camera. With 57.1 percent (44/77) of all Black Oscar nominations coming after the year 2000, we see that 68.4 percent (13/19) of all Black Oscar winners also come during that same time frame. In other words, the more that members of Hollywood—whether they be directors, writers, or producers—sincerely invest in Black imagery, the more movies there are to select from that may feature more performances worthy of both nomination and award.

QUALITATIVE ANALYSIS

Black Oscar Angles, the Sequel

Granted, movies are a private affair. There is neither a public nor a fiduciary obligation for movies to serve as revolutionary spaces for radical thought. Further, as AMPAS is not an official governing body that determines social standards, this quantitative data simply cannot encompass the full impact that all Black images have collectively made on our society's movie screens. However, AMPAS is the biggest game in town when it comes to evaluating and recognizing movies when compared to other entities that perform similar functions with considerably less fanfare and advertising dollars (e.g., the Golden Globe Awards). Thus, to be consistent and systematic, we shall now revisit the five different Black Oscar Angles for qualitative analysis as referenced throughout the text.

Black Non-American

Of the seventy-seven Black Oscar nominations, roughly one out of every five actors is not fully African American (19.2 percent).[3] Again, congratulations and kudos are well-deserved for these individuals who found success with their talents, as this categorization is not designed to impugn or question anyone's identity. At issue here are the larger structural and institutional barriers within both society generally and Hollywood specifically that allow for only such a small fraction of potential talent within the African American community to even pursue acting as a full-time passion and profession. Perhaps the overarching shadow of the Unholy Trinity is so strong off-screen that a disproportionate number of African Americans cannot even afford to consider an abstract career such as acting if they have to secure their survival by other, more practical means. This does not mean that individuals coming from outside the United States cannot appreciate and acknowledge the continuing effects of racial discrimination, but being raised in a different country and culture may allow or provide for a different experience and relationship with American racial discrimination.

Crossover

Additionally, of the seventy-seven Black Oscar nominations, one-third of all Black characters are portrayed by individuals who did not start their careers in Hollywood (35 percent).[4] As with the category Black Non-American, this designation is not to shame or cast aspersions on those who did not grow up performing Shakespeare in a classical setting; rather, this category is designed to illustrate how difficult it seems to be for Hollywood to invest in regular, ordinary Blackness. As previously discussed, mainstream movie products are expensive propositions, so Hollywood seeks to hedge its bets by employing the services of well-known, highly visible Black musicians or comedians rather than develop an unknown Black commodity. But this explanation falls short when considering that virtually every A-list White actor or actress began as an unknown.

Déjà Vu

In nearly a century of recognition, fifty-seven different Black actors have secured a total of seventy-seven nominations, with ten Black actors comprising 40.2 percent of all Black Oscar nominations ever, while four different Black actors account for a quarter of all nods.[5] This percentage is all the more eye-popping considering how many thousands of actors have walked the earth during that time period. While receiving multiple Oscar nominations is an incredible accomplishment that reflects individual skill, for our purposes these data expose the larger structural issue of limited opportunities for African American actors to break into the business and subsequently break out as stars.

Gravity of Reality

Gravity of Reality speaks to the idea that the Black Oscar nominee is cast in a vehicle that specifically deals with race or is based upon a true story. Since all of the nominees analyzed and discussed here classify as Black, the idea that their characters may be concerned with their identity is hardly surprising. At issue here is that the movie's central plot or storyline revolves around race. In contrast, in analyzing the Oscar-winning movie *Gravity*, the race and gender of the protagonist are not central insofar as the overriding quest for survival is paramount. Four out of every five Black Oscar–nominated movies have storylines that explicitly reference and involve the concept of race relations or racial identity as part of the story's narrative (80.3 percent).[6] Thus, in most movies prominently featuring Black Oscar nominees, the crux of the movie hinges upon race and racial tensions specifically, as opposed to other aspects of the human experience generally.

Still in the Struggle

Still in the Struggle refers to the idea that whenever Black Oscar nominees are depicted in full, they are typically couched in scenarios whereby a lack of resources, most especially financial, are simply part of the movie's underlying premise. What this means is that seldom do audiences see Black Oscar nominees traveling freely and making their own choices outside of an all-Black universe and on an even playing field with Whites.

This angle of analysis is telling, as the overarching dark cloud of financial worry (and the associated social, mental, and political problems that can result) is an indirect acknowledgment of the connection to the institutionalized economic handicaps deliberately and consciously wrought upon African Americans through the era of enslavement followed by a failed, too-brief twelve-year Reconstruction period and a legalized apartheid system of Black codes and Supreme Court–sanctioned Jim Crow regulations, followed by neoliberal exultations of a postracial society that therefore eliminates any need for remediation.

This categorization also illustrates how once on-screen, many Black characters have difficulty staying on-screen and establishing a permanent presence in the minds of viewers for the duration of the visible continuum. Thus, it is also not without significance that nearly a quarter of all Black Oscar characters die during the movie's visible continuum (23.3 percent).[7]

Theory of Relativity

For moviegoers born after 1990, many of the concepts discussed so far may not resonate quite so deeply. After all, the only world that youthful moviegoers know is one of purported hope and change. Society has always been diverse. From music videos to sports to the ever-diversifying world of politics, there is a profound and certain belief that many of the racial problems of old are in fact light-years away from our current age (in a galaxy far, far away, perhaps). To bring up historical examples of racial discrimination is to reminisce and to taint the pure euphoria in the air over the ability to change the patterns of yesteryear in the here and now.

Gifted scientist and mathematician Albert Einstein said it was most important to nurture imagination using fairy tales,[8] and thus, the ability to conjure something new based upon that which is familiar is the very definition of innovation and change. Yet Allan G. Johnson notes that of films that won the Oscar for Best Picture from 1965 to 1999, "none set in the United States places people of color at the center of the story without their having to share it with White characters of equal importance."[9] This is a prime example of Hollywood's lack of imagination.

However, it has usually been in hindsight that well-measured statements have been issued about Hollywood's past shortcomings. For instance, the Academy felt pretty proud of itself for breaking new ground with the 1939 awarding of the first-ever Black Oscar. As Hattie McDaniel "made her way to her table, the crowd of almost 1,700 members of the Hollywood film colony broke into a resounding applause." While it sounds quite encouraging and conciliatory that the Academy broke ground by extending the first invitation to an African American in McDaniel, it maintained the status quo by holding the event inside a segregated hotel. McDaniel and her White male sponsor were seated "at their own table, placed at the periphery of the room but near the stage where the awards would be given. Even on this evening of Hollywood firsts, segregation remained the rule."[10] The reaction to McDaniel's Oscar win and the preparation to "accommodate" her at a segregated hotel is a perfect example of merely negotiating, and not fully negating, the existing racial narratives of the time. The fact that McDaniel landed only maid/servant roles for the remainder of her movie career after her Oscar victory is telling of how life stayed the same for McDaniel even though the Academy was able to legitimately say that it was forever changed.

On the other hand, some may argue that McDaniel's Mammy character, image, and role is only now considered racially unflattering and that at the time of *Gone with the Wind*'s release, it was quite revolutionary for McDaniel to even be recognized publicly for her talents. Yet, the fact that she could play a maid with aplomb, and not a free, attractive woman of means relative to her counterpart, Vivien Leigh, means we must critically analyze what exactly there is to celebrate in the grand scheme of things. McDaniel's presence at the 12th Academy Awards undoubtedly represented a new aesthetic change, but perhaps not a substantively significant structural change to a larger system predicated upon the presumption that Black women both on- and off-screen were best suited to exclusively serving as maids within the central White male gaze.

THE BOTTOM LINE: BLACK OSCARS SUFFER FROM PSYCHOLOGICAL SEGREGATION

Currently we have done away with most of the ugly reminders of our formerly legally segregated society. Yet while we presently all have freedom of physical movement, what about the intangible, immeasurable freedom of thought? It appears that while White characters are liberated by the Freedom of Fantasy, Black Oscar nominees and winners have been consistently grounded by the Gravity of Reality, even within the limitless expanses of our collective imagination. Based upon the Black Oscar data amassed within these pages, there is very little to controvert the idea that "the vast majority of Hollywood films have been made and continue to be made by and about White Americans."[11] Although Hollywood is a space and place associated with imagination, freedom, and developing ideas, it ironically disguises its social conservatism like a cleverly hidden zipper on a medieval costume on set.

Rational, Not Racist

An oft-assumed narrative is that since Hollywood is an intensely creative space, it is also unquestionably a liberal space. Not quite. As discussed earlier, Hollywood mainstream movies represent significant investments of time, money, and energy. As a result, the fiscally formulaic nature of Hollywood does not scream change: "Hollywood cinema is an economically conservative medium that tends to rely on proven formulas for storytelling."[12]

When analyzing the track record of mainstream Hollywood movies, the more expensive a movie production is, the more likely it is that the studio will purposely employ patterns of old in order to succinctly connect with mass audiences in the hopes of safely recouping its investment. Studios can safely justify their decisions with an economic argument (i.e., "if it doesn't make dollars, it doesn't make sense"), thereby making decisions professionally rational and not personally racist.

Unfortunately, up until this point, most financially successful formulas involve racial patterns that psychologically segregate or separate Black characters from the true Freedom of Fantasy that White characters more frequently experience. None of this analysis is designed to blame or impugn the Black Oscar nominees and winners, but rather is constructed to illustrate Hollywood's limited imagination in the constant grounding of Blacks by the Gravity of Reality. For it is largely when Blacks are isolated within mostly insular-universe or all-Black movies (e.g, *The Great White Hope*, *If Beale Street Could Talk*) that their characters are more developed and complex and do not fit as easily within the rubrics articulated herein. Yet, when Blacks must make consistent and regular contact with the White world, we see the racial hierarchy emerge, with Whites most always ending up on top or with the last word (e.g., *Green Book*).

Given Hollywood's extensive reach and economic impact, the consistently marginalized Black images in mainstream movies reflect and reinforce messages of racial imbalance worldwide. Further, despite widely available data forecasting the changing demographics in the United States, many studios and marketing firms—whether minority owned or not—have little financial incentive to change current practices that focus almost exclusively on the glamorization of White images. The delicious irony is that a majority-minority audience is still beholden to a small minority of mostly White male producers who naturally are inclined to tailor their efforts to other Whites, with whom they are more comfortable.[13]

From Mammy to Minny

Oscar winner Marlon Brando once quipped, "We supposedly have the technology and the fantasy brains to make anything happen."[14] Yet perfectly playing a maid on-screen is hardly imaginative or groundbreaking for Black female actors. Seeing Black women as subjugated maids was not novel in 1940, when Hattie McDaniel won a Best Supporting Actress Oscar for her role as Mammy in *Gone with the Wind*, nor was it novel in 2012, when Octavia Spencer won a Best Supporting Actress Oscar for her role as Minny in *The Help*. If anything, the underexplored travesty is how so many roles continue to be limited, on-screen and within society, for untold African Americans. This larger issue of equitable representation often goes unchallenged when the focus remains upon individual, incremental movements rather than the lack of movement on a larger, institutionalized scale. In this respect, institutional discrimination is akin to the perpetual villain in a Marvel Comic Universe movie, like Dr. Octopus in *Spider-Man*—they never fully die, in the strictest sense of the word. Every so often these perennial villains rear their ugly heads for an indeterminant amount of time and cause a bit of trouble before being "definitively" put away or shut down by the hero—only to reappear *again* later.

Speaking of the indefinite closure surrounding perpetual villainous threats in our shared world of make believe, "closure is a potent narrative tool in managing ideological conflict, because closure makes it seem as if all problems have been solved. Any actual ideological issues or social strife that may have been raised by a film are allegedly resolved by narrative closure, and thus there is no longer any need for spectators to think about them."[15] In searching for closure of this book, then, what do the Black Oscar wins of Hattie McDaniel for Mammy in *Gone with the Wind* and Octavia Spencer for Minny Jackson in *The Help*, more than seventy years apart, tell us? Perhaps these bookends provide a window of understanding as to what has changed and what has remained consistent with the Black image on-screen if we continue to ask how these two characters are fundamentally different.

A constant visual barrage of disparaging on-screen depictions may classify as what established scholars such as Chester M. Pierce or Derald Wing Sue term *microaggressions*, whereby the African American presence is simply made to be "less than" when juxtaposed against "normal" White imagery.[16] While many symbols and monikers of our previously more racist societies no longer survive within the acceptable mainstream space, ostensibly this does not automatically mean that society is completely free from and rid of their effects.

"In the Hollywood imagination, White heroes are natural-born leaders who continue to deserve the loyalty and admiration of racial others. These images have survived across the twentieth century despite all the changes and the gains made by minority groups."[17] Thus, it is a false debate to quibble about whether Hattie McDaniel or Octavia Spencer played the role of a maid with dignity and aplomb. Performing a subjugated role "with dignity" is perhaps optimistic in some respects, but it is objectively unthreatening to the status quo. This is where Hollywood's collective imagination is limited. A new debate would be that of the moral and ethical choices made by a Black Captain Marvel–type character having dignity and pride saving the world as a superheroine with superpowers instead.

Given the fact that Hollywood has constructed its own rules and has no financial incentive to change them, the current prognosis is that change will continue to occur, but largely in form rather than in substance. By this book's analysis, only two Black Oscar–nominated movies, *Collateral* and *Beasts of the Southern Wild*, steered relatively clear of the common racial patterns delineated by the Unholy Trinity narratives and HARM theory archetypes. Yet readers are free to leverage the analysis contained herein as a starting point for continued debate to see whether more Black movie characters cleanly fit these overarching narratives, merely massage and negotiate them, or challenge, disrupt, and negate them entirely. Regardless, the crux of the time-honored and proven formulas for Hollywood success is steeped in often unchallenged, consistent, and continued racial narratives that appear difficult, if not impossible, to root out entirely.

In the final analysis, the Academy Awards are not racist, per se, but they do indeed play a role in showcasing and rewarding images and patterns that do little to substantively deviate from problematic racist patterns of the past. Viewers and consumers hold movie studios responsible, since the bottom line is that Hollywood mainstream movies are too time-consuming and expensive to leave production up to mere whim, chance, or happenstance. While it is true that there are only a relatively few decision makers manipulating these circumstances, in reality we *all* have a hand in perpetuating this entrenched system of exclusion—even if we only passively participate in a covert culture of consent. Despite our collective agency, the unconscious biases of producers and their limited frames of reference are consistently displayed in movies, even within the creative space of Hollywood.

As *creative* does not mean "enlightened," it is entirely possible for an intensely creative space to maintain a power structure that is ultimately suppressive and oppressive to African Americans, even if it is a power structure based in fantasy and cloaked with good intentions. After all, if after ninety years of rewarding the best of what our limitless imaginations have to offer, as recognized by the Academy of Motion Picture Arts and Sciences, we still end up with the same old story of marginalization when it comes to African Americans, then the idea that the show must go on as presently constituted must continue to be challenged. It appears that in an industry fueled by creativity, a limited spectrum of Black images stubbornly persists. African American characters continue to be collectively typecast.

Ultimately, the solutions to moving Hollywood forward in this illusory postracial era are exceedingly simple. As diverse audiences have faithfully and consistently invested in Hollywood by virtue of steady billion-dollar box office returns, all studios have to do is return the favor by prudently investing in up-and-coming actors, writers, and directors of diverse backgrounds, relinquishing their fears that a non-White production will not be able to recoup its initial financial outlay.

If anything, it is sound business sense for Hollywood producers to make these strategic investments and create movie products that will competently serve rapidly changing audiences. Otherwise, they will stand to lose when another studio is first to market in appealing to diverse consumers with diverse tastes.

David O. Selznick, producer of *Gone with the Wind*, said, "Nothing in Hollywood is permanent. Once photographed, life here is ended. It is almost symbolic of Hollywood. Tara had no rooms inside. It was just a façade. So much of Hollywood is a façade."[18] Perhaps Selznick was referring to the props on set. But film is indeed forever. After all, they say a picture is worth a thousand words. If this is true, and if for nearly a century Hollywood has crafted a visually impactful narrative of the African American experience . . .

. . . and that narrative has mostly vacillated between emasculation and marginalization, while simultaneously oscillating between dehumanizing and disparaging . . .

. . . and this narrative has not only gone largely uninterrupted, save a few exceptional cases, but in actuality has been reinforced and rewarded by the most powerful and influential institution in the self-governed, highly unionized world of moviemaking . . .

. . . then we must say this:

"If a picture is worth 1,000 words, how much is a *moving picture* worth?"

APPENDIX A

Black Oscar Nominations
and Wins Overview, by Decade

Chapter 2	Early Drama behind Early Black Images (1927–1939) *10 years = no nominations*	0 noms/0 wins
Chapter 3	Oscar's Uneasy Breakthrough (1940–1949) *9 years = no nominations*	1 nom/1 win
Chapter 4	New Roles Not Leading Anywhere (1950–1959) *7 years = no nominations*	3 noms/0 wins
Chapter 5	Sidney in the Sixties (1960–1969) *7 years = no nominations*	3 noms/1 win
Chapter 6	The Blaxploitation Effect (1970–1979) *6 years = no nominations*	6 noms/0 wins
Chapter 7	*The Color Purple* through the Bluest Eye (1980–1989) *3 years = no nominations*	10 noms/1 win
Chapter 8	The Denzel Effect (1990–1999) *4 years = no nominations*	11 noms/3 wins

Chapter 9   New Century, New Beginning? (2000–2009)   21 noms/6 wins
1 years = no nominations

Chapter 10   Oscars So White? (2010–2019)   22 noms/7 wins
3 years = no nominations

Black Oscar Nominations by Decade

	1920s/30s	1940s	1950s	1960s	1970s	1980s	1990s	2000s	2010s
Best Actor	0	0	1	1	2	1	4	9	6
Best Actress	0	0	1	0	3	1	1	1	4
Best Supporting Actor	0	0	0	0	1	5	4	5	3
Best Supporting Actress	0	1	1	2	0	3	2	6	9
Grand Total	**0**	**1**	**3**	**3**	**6**	**10**	**11**	**21**	**22**

Black Oscar Wins by Decade

	1920s/30s	1940s	1950s	1960s	1970s	1980s	1990s	2000s	2010s
Best Actor	0	0	0	1	0	0	0	3	0
Best Actress	0	0	0	0	0	0	0	1	0
Best Supporting Actor	0	0	0	0	0	1	2	1	2
Best Supporting Actress	0	1	0	0	0	0	1	1	5
Grand Total	**0**	**1**	**0**	**1**	**0**	**1**	**3**	**6**	**7**

APPENDIX B

List of All Movies with Black Oscar Nominations

Nominations = italics, Wins = bold (number of multiple nominations in parentheses)

1. **Gone with the Wind**
2. *Pinky*
3. *Carmen Jones*
4. *The Defiant Ones*
5. *Imitation of Life*
6. **Lilies of the Field**
7. *Guess Who's Coming to Dinner*
8. *The Reivers*
9. *The Great White Hope*
10. *Sounder (x2)*
11. *Lady Sings the Blues*
12. *Claudine*
13. *Ragtime*
14. **An Officer and a Gentleman**
15. *Cross Creek*
16. *A Soldier's Story*
17. *The Color Purple (x3)*
18. *Round Midnight*
19. *Street Smart*
20. *Cry Freedom*
21. *Driving Miss Daisy*
22. **Glory**
23. **Ghost**
24. *Malcolm X*
25. *The Crying Game*
26. *What's Love Got to Do with It (x2)*
27. *The Shawshank Redemption*
28. *Pulp Fiction*
29. **Jerry Maguire**
30. *Secrets & Lies*
31. *The Hurricane*
32. *The Green Mile*
33. *Ali*
34. **Training Day**
35. **Monster's Ball**
36. *Chicago*
37. *In America*
38. **Ray**
39. *Hotel Rwanda (x2)*
40. **Million Dollar Baby**

41. *Collateral*
42. *Hustle & Flow*
43. ***The Last King of Scotland***
44. *The Pursuit of Happyness*
45. *Blood Diamond*
46. ***Dreamgirls (x2)***
47. *American Gangster*
48. *Doubt*
49. *The Curious Case of Benjamin Button*
50. *Invictus*
51. ***Precious (x2)***
52. ***The Help (x2)***
53. *Flight*
54. *Beasts of the Southern Wild*
55. ***12 Years a Slave (x2)***
56. *Captain Phillips*
57. ***Fences (x2)***
58. *Loving*
59. ***Moonlight (x2)***
60. *Hidden Figures*
61. *Roman J. Israel, Esq.*
62. *Get Out*
63. *Mudbound*
64. *The Shape of Water*
65. ***Green Book***
66. ***If Beale Street Could Talk***

APPENDIX C

List of All Black Oscar Acting Nominees and Wins

Nomination	Win	Name	Category	Film	Year
Nomination #1	Win #1	Hattie McDaniel	Best Supporting Actress	*Gone with the Wind*	1939
Nomination #2		Ethel Waters	Best Supporting Actress	*Pinky*	1949
Nomination #3		Dorothy Dandridge	Best Actress	*Carmen Jones*	1954
Nomination #4		Sidney Poitier	Best Actor	*The Defiant Ones*	1958
Nomination #5		Juanita Moore	Best Supporting Actress	*Imitation of Life*	1959
Nomination #6	Win #2	Sidney Poitier	Best Actor	*Lilies of the Field*	1963
Nomination #7		Beah Richards	Best Supporting Actress	*Guess Who's Coming to Dinner*	1967
Nomination #8		Rupert Crosse	Best Supporting Actor	*The Reivers*	1969
Nomination #9		James Earl Jones	Best Actor	*The Great White Hope*	1970
Nomination #10		Paul Winfield	Best Actor	*Sounder*	1972
Nomination #11		Diana Ross	Best Actress	*Lady Sings the Blues*	1972

Nomination	Win	Name	Category	Film	Year
Nomination #12		Cicely Tyson	Best Actress	*Sounder*	1972
Nomination #13		Diahann Carroll	Best Actress	*Claudine*	1974
Nomination #14		Howard E. Rollins Jr.	Best Supporting Actor	*Ragtime*	1981
Nomination #15	Win #3	Louis Gossett Jr.	Best Supporting Actor	*An Officer and a Gentleman*	1982
Nomination #16		Alfre Woodard	Best Supporting Actress	*Cross Creek*	1983
Nomination #17		Adolph Caesar	Best Supporting Actor	*A Soldier's Story*	1984
Nomination #18		Whoopi Goldberg	Best Actress	*The Color Purple*	1985
Nomination #19		Margaret Avery	Best Supporting Actress	*The Color Purple*	1985
Nomination #20		Oprah Winfrey	Best Supporting Actress	*The Color Purple*	1985
Nomination #21		Dexter Gordon	Best Actor	*Round Midnight*	1986
Nomination #22		Morgan Freeman	Best Supporting Actor	*Street Smart*	1987
Nomination #23		Denzel Washington	Best Supporting Actor	*Cry Freedom*	1987
Nomination #24		Morgan Freeman	Best Actor	*Driving Miss Daisy*	1989
Nomination #25	Win #4	Denzel Washington	Best Supporting Actor	*Glory*	1989
Nomination #26	Win #5	Whoopi Goldberg	Best Supporting Actress	*Ghost*	1990
Nomination #27		Denzel Washington	Best Actor	*Malcolm X*	1992
Nomination #28		Jaye Davidson	Best Supporting Actor	*The Crying Game*	1992
Nomination #29		Laurence Fishburne	Best Actor	*What's Love Got to Do with It*	1993
Nomination #30		Angela Bassett	Best Actress	*What's Love Got to Do with It*	1993
Nomination #31		Morgan Freeman	Best Actor	*The Shawshank Redemption*	1994

Nomination	Win	Name	Category	Film	Year
Nomination #32		Samuel L. Jackson	Best Supporting Actor	*Pulp Fiction*	1994
Nomination #33	Win #6	Cuba Gooding Jr.	Best Supporting Actor	*Jerry Maguire*	1996
Nomination #34		Marianne Jean-Baptiste	Best Supporting Actress	*Secrets & Lies*	1996
Nomination #35		Denzel Washington	Best Actor	*The Hurricane*	1999
Nomination #36		Michael Clarke Duncan	Best Supporting Actor	*The Green Mile*	1999
Nomination #37		Will Smith	Best Actor	*Ali*	2001
Nomination #38	Win #7	Denzel Washington	Best Actor	*Training Day*	2001
Nomination #39	Win #8	Halle Berry	Best Actress	*Monster's Ball*	2001
Nomination #40		Queen Latifah	Best Supporting Actress	*Chicago*	2002
Nomination #41		Djimon Hounsou	Best Actor	*In America*	2003
Nomination #42		Don Cheadle	Best Actor	*Hotel Rwanda*	2004
Nomination #43	Win #9	Jamie Foxx	Best Actor	*Ray*	2004
Nomination #44		Jamie Foxx	Best Supporting Actor	*Collateral*	2004
Nomination #45	Win #10	Morgan Freeman	Best Supporting Actor	*Million Dollar Baby*	2004
Nomination #46		Sophie Okonedo	Best Supporting Actress	*Hotel Rwanda*	2004
Nomination #47		Terrence Howard	Best Actor	*Hustle & Flow*	2005
Nomination #48		Will Smith	Best Actor	*The Pursuit of Happyness*	2006
Nomination #49	Win #11	Forest Whitaker	Best Actor	*The Last King of Scotland*	2006
Nomination #50		Djimon Hounsou	Best Supporting Actor	*Blood Diamond*	2006
Nomination #51		Eddie Murphy	Best Supporting Actor	*Dreamgirls*	2006

Nomination	Win	Name	Category	Film	Year
Nomination #52	Win #12	Jennifer Hudson	Best Supporting Actress	*Dreamgirls*	2006
Nomination #53		Ruby Dee	Best Supporting Actress	*American Gangster*	2007
Nomination #54		Viola Davis	Best Supporting Actress	*Doubt*	2008
Nomination #55		Taraji P. Henson	Best Supporting Actress	*The Curious Case of Benjamin Button*	2008
Nomination #56		Morgan Freeman	Best Actor	*Invictus*	2009
Nomination #57		Gabourey Sidibe	Best Actress	*Precious: Based on the Novel 'Push' by Sapphire*	2009
Nomination #58	Win #13	Mo'Nique	Best Supporting Actress	*Precious: Based on the Novel 'Push' by Sapphire*	2009
Nomination #59		Viola Davis	Best Actress	*The Help*	2011
Nomination #60	Win #14	Octavia Spencer	Best Supporting Actress	*The Help*	2011
Nomination #61		Denzel Washington	Best Actor	*Flight*	2012
Nomination #62		Quvenzhané Wallis	Best Actress	*Beasts of the Southern Wild*	2012
Nomination #63		Chiwetel Ejiofor	Best Actor	*12 Years a Slave*	2013
Nomination #64		Barkhad Abdi	Best Supporting Actor	*Captain Phillips*	2013
Nomination #65	Win #15	Lupita Nyong'o	Best Supporting Actress	*12 Years a Slave*	2013
Nomination #66		Denzel Washington	Best Actor	*Fences*	2016
Nomination #67		Ruth Negga	Best Actress	*Loving*	2016
Nomination #68	Win #16	Mahershala Ali	Best Supporting Actor	*Moonlight*	2016

Nomination	Win	Name	Category	Film	Year
Nomination #69	Win #17	Viola Davis	Best Supporting Actress	*Fences*	2016
Nomination #70		Naomie Harris	Best Supporting Actress	*Moonlight*	2016
Nomination #71		Octavia Spencer	Best Supporting Actress	*Hidden Figures*	2016
Nomination #72		Daniel Kaluuya	Best Actor	*Get Out*	2017
Nomination #73		Denzel Washington	Best Actor	*Roman J. Israel, Esq.*	2017
Nomination #74		Mary J. Blige	Best Supporting Actress	*Mudbound*	2017
Nomination #75		Octavia Spencer	Best Supporting Actress	*The Shape of Water*	2017
Nomination #76	Win #18	Mahershala Ali	Best Supporting Actor	*Green Book*	2018
Nomination #77	Win #19	Regina King	Best Supporting Actress	*If Beale Street Could Talk*	2018

APPENDIX D

List of All Black Nonacting Oscar Winners

Number	Year Awarded	Name	Film	Award
1	1948	James Baskett	*Song of the South*	Academy Special Award: "for his able and heart-warming characterization of Uncle Remus, friend and story teller to the children of the world in Walt Disney's *Song of the South.*"
2	1972	Isaac Hayes	*Shaft*	Best Music, Original Song
3	1984	Irene Cara	*Flashdance*	Best Music, Original Song
4	1985	Stevie Wonder	*The Woman in Red*	Best Music, Original Song
5	1985	Prince	*Purple Rain*	Best Original Song Score
6	1986	Lionel Richie	*White Nights*	Best Music, Original Song
7	1987	Herbie Hancock	*Round Midnight*	Best Music, Original Score
8	1989	Willie D. Burton	*Bird*	Best Sound
9	1990	Russell Williams	*Glory*	Best Sound
10	1991	Russell Williams	*Dances with Wolves*	Best Sound

Number	Year Awarded	Name	Film	Award
11	1995	Quincy Jones	N/A	Jean Hersholt Humanitarian Award
12	2002	Sidney Poitier	N/A	Academy Honorary Award: "in recognition of his remarkable accomplishments as an artist and as a human being."
13	2006	Frayser Boy, Juicy J, DJ Paul	*Hustle & Flow*	Best Music, Original Song
14	2007	Willie D. Burton	*Dreamgirls*	Best Sound Mixing
15	2010	Roger Ross Williams	*Music by Prudence*	Best Documentary Short Subject
16	2010	Geoffrey Fletcher	*Precious: Based on the Novel 'Push' by Sapphire*	Best Writing (Adapted Screenplay)
17	2011	James Earl Jones	N/A	Academy Honorary Award: "for his legacy of consistent excellence and uncommon versatility."
18	2012	Oprah Winfrey	N/A	Jean Hersholt Humanitarian Award
19	2012	TJ Martin	*Undefeated*	Best Documentary Feature
20	2014	Steve McQueen	*12 Years a Slave*	Best Picture
21	2014	John Ridley	*12 Years a Slave*	Best Writing (Adapted Screenplay)
22	2015	Common, John Legend	*Selma*	Best Music, Original Song
23	2016	Spike Lee	N/A	Academy Honorary Award: "filmmaker, educator, motivator, iconoclast, artist."
24	2017	Ezra Edelman	*O.J.: Made in America*	Best Documentary Feature
25	2017	Barry Jenkins, Tarell Alvin McCraney	*Moonlight*	Best Writing (Adapted Screenplay)

Number	Year Awarded	Name	Film	Award
26	2018	Kobe Bryant	*Dear Basketball*	Best Short Film (Animated)
27	2018	Jordan Peele	*Get Out*	Best Writing (Original Screenplay)
28	2018	Charles Burnett	N/A	Academy Honorary Award: "a resolutely independent and influential film pioneer who has chronicled the lives of black Americans with eloquence and insight."
29	2019	Peter Ramsey	*Spider-Man: Into the Spider-Verse*	Best Animated Feature
30	2019	Ruth E. Carter	*Black Panther*	Best Costume Design
31	2019	Hannah Beachler	*Black Panther*	Best Production Design
32	2019	Spike Lee, Kevin Wilmott	*BlacKkKlansman*	Best Writing (Adapted Screenplay)
33	2019	Cicely Tyson	N/A	Academy Honorary Award: "whose unforgettable performances and personal integrity have inspired generations of filmmakers, actors and audiences."

NOTE: As with Black Oscar nominees and winners, most activity for nonacting Black Oscar winners takes place after the year 2000 (22/33 = 66.66 percent).

NOTES

INTRODUCTION: SETTING THE STAGE: WHAT'S SO OSCAR WORTHY?

1. "Movies engage our psychological faculties in profound and unique ways. . . . [T]hey call upon ancient and deep-seated aspects of the mind; and they enjoy significant liaisons with other aspects of our experience of the world." Colin McGinn, *The Power of Movies: How Screen and Mind Interact* (New York: First Vintage Books, 2005), 14.

2. Jamie Wylie, "Oscars 2019 Presenters: Third Round Announced," Oscars, February 19, 2019, https://oscar.go.com/news/oscar-news/oscars-2019-presenters-third-round-announced; Alissa Wilkinson, "The Chaotic Road to the 2019 Oscars Ceremony, Explained," *Vox*, February 16, 2019, https://www.vox.com/culture/2019/2/16/18226372/oscars-ceremony-category-best-song-revolt.

3. Whereas the Academy Awards ceremony is a single award show comprising one evening, the NFL's Super Bowl event is the culmination of four weeks of preseason, seventeen weeks of regular season, and a playoff format from an open competition spanning thirty-two teams from heavily populated cities strategically located throughout the whole country. Suffice it to say that the NFL's viewing structure lends itself to the crescendo of a significant audience. In contrast, the Academy Awards draws its audience by showcasing an affordable and accessible pastime that is a prominent presence in the daily lives of everyday Americans: the movies. Associated Press, "Oscar Ratings up from 2018," *Billboard*, February 26, 2019, https://www.billboard.com/articles/events/oscars/8500124/oscars-ratings-up-from-2018.

4. Arthur Knight, "Star Dances: African American Constructions of Stardom, 1925–1960," in *Classic Hollywood, Classic Whiteness*, ed. Daniel Berardi (Minneapolis: University of Minnesota Press, 2001), 387.

5. Brian Steinberg, "ABC Seeks $2 Million to $3 Million for Oscar Ads (Exclusive)," *Variety*, December 11, 2018, https://variety.com/2018/tv/news/oscars-advertising-abc-commercials-kevin-hart-1203086442/.

6. Hayley C. Cuccinello, "Inside the $148,000 Oscars Gift Bag: From a Luxurious European Cruise to Decadent THC Chocolates," *Forbes*, February 22, 2019, https://www.forbes.com/sites/hayleycuccinello/2019/02/22/inside-the-148000-oscars-gift-bag-from-a-luxurious-european-cruise-to-decadent-thc-chocolates/#678bb8e0735f.

7. Lisa Richwine, "Oscar Nominees Ride Publicity Bounce at Box Office," Reuters, February 27, 2018, https://www.reuters.com/article/us-awards-oscars-boxoffice/oscar-nominees-ride-publicity-bounce-at-box-office-idUSKCN1GB2U1.

8. Tom Stempel and Phillip Dunne; *Framework: A History of Screenwriting in the American Film* (Syracuse, NY: Syracuse University Press, 2000), 70.

9. The participants were studio head Louis B. Mayer, actor Conrad Nagel, director Fred Niblo, and producer Fred Beetson. Debra Ann Pawlak, *Bringing Up Oscar: The Story of the Men and Women Who Founded the Academy* (New York: Pegasus Books, 2011), xiv.

10. Jude Sheerin, "'Fatty' Arbuckle and Hollywood's First Scandal," BBC News, September 4, 2011, https://www.bbc.com/news/magazine-14640719.

11. Petula Dvorak, "The Wrong Oscars Wasn't the First Academy Awards Fiasco. This Was," *Washington Post*, March 4, 2018, https://www.washingtonpost.com/news/retropolis/wp/2018/03/04/the-wrong-oscars-envelope-wasnt-the-first-academy-awards-fiasco-this-was/.

12. Jane Caffrey, "'Envelope, Please': 6 Things You May Not Know about the Oscars Envelope," CNN, February 22, 2015, https://www.cnn.com/2015/02/20/entertainment/oscars-envelope-things-to-know/index.html.

13. Oscars.org, "Oscars Statuette," https://www.oscars.org/oscars/statuette; Hilary Lewis, "Oscars: Who Came Up with the Name 'Oscar' and More about the Statuette's History (Video)," *Hollywood Reporter*, February 18, 2015, https://www.hollywoodreporter.com/news/oscars-who-came-up-name-774775.

14. Oscars.org, "Oscars Statuette."

15. See appendix D, "List of All Black Nonacting Oscar Winners."

16. Barry Jenkins became the second Black director to helm a movie that claimed Best Picture honors with *Moonlight* in 2017. However, Steve McQueen was the first and only Black director to take home a Best Picture Oscar, since he is listed as a producer for the film along with Brad Pitt, Dede Gardner, Jeremy Kleiner, and Anthony Katagas. The winning producers listed for *Moonlight* are Adele Romanski, Dede Gardner, and Jeremy Kleiner.

17. The terms *Black* and *African American* will be used relatively interchangeably throughout the text although they technically refer to two different groups. *Black* refers to the larger, encompassing racial category, while *African American* refers to the more specific ethnic designation. In recognition of complex cultural and conscious racial identity beyond a mere color, the words *Black* and *White* will be capitalized throughout when referring to groups of people.

18. Moving Image Research Center, Library of Congress online, http://www.loc.gov /rr/mopic/.

19. Library of Congress, "About this Collection," https://www.loc.gov/collections /selections-from-the-national-film-registry/about-this-collection/.

20. Eric Greene, *Planet of the Apes as American Myth: Race and Politics in the Films and Television Series* (Jefferson, NC: McFarland, 1996), 11.

21. "We are all familiar with that sense of entrancement that accompanies sitting quietly in the pierced darkness of the movie theatre." McGinn, *The Power of Movies*, 4.

22. Frederick Gooding Jr., *You Mean, There's RACE in My Movie? The Complete Guide to Understanding Race in Mainstream Hollywood* (Silver Spring, MD: On the Reelz Press, 2007), 116.

23. Henry Jenkins, *Wow Climax: Tracing the Emotional Impact of Popular Culture* (New York: New York University Press, 2007), 58.

24. Daniel Frampton, *Filmosophy* (New York: Wallflower Press, 2006), 6; emphasis added.

25. Jean-Anne Sutherland and Kathyrn Feltey, eds., *Cinematic Sociology: Social Life in Film* (Thousand Oaks, CA: SAGE Publications, 2013), 2.

26. However, from 1925 to 1960 Blacks "never earned even two-thirds of the average white income, and they always had a considerably higher—sometimes doubled—rate of unemployment." Knight, "Star Dances," 388.

27. Kathleen M. German, *Promises of Citizenship: Film Recruitment of African Americans in World War II* (Jackson: University Press of Mississippi, 2017), 42.

28. Pamela McClintock, "2018 Box Office Revenue Soars to Record $11.9B in the U.S., Hits $42B Globally," *Hollywood Reporter*, January 2, 2019, https://www.holly woodreporter.com/news/2018-box-office-revenue-soars-record-119m-us-hits-42b -globally-1172215.

29. "Today, U.S. films are shown in more than 150 countries worldwide and American television programs are broadcast in over 125 international markets. The U.S. film industry provides the majority of home entertainment products seen in millions of homes throughout the world." Motion Picture Association of America, "About Us," http://www.mpaa.org/AboutUs.asp.

30. Greene, *Planet of the Apes as American Myth*, 7.

CHAPTER 1: LIGHTS, CAMERA, ANALYSIS!

1. See J. Scott Clark, "What's on Delta's Inflight Entertainment for August 2019," *Points Guy*, August 5, 2019, https://thepointsguy.com/news/whats-on-new-delta-in -flight-entertainment-ife/.

2. Citing the fact that Mammy is "Scarlett's harshest critic," author Riché Richardson posits that "Mammy in effect challenges and unsettles the polarity of their positions within the hierarchy of mistress and slave." Riché Richardson, "Mammy's 'Mules' and

the Rules of Marriage in 'Gone with the Wind,'" in *American Cinema and the Southern Imaginary*, ed. Deborah Barker and Kathyrn B. McKee (Athens: University of Georgia Press, 2011), 73. Others may point out that Mammy is nonetheless enslaved, thereby nullifying any creative interpretation of the character's perceived and temporal shift of power: "The film more or less invented the concept of the sassy Black friend, in Hattie McDaniel as Mammy." Stephen Marche, "The Racism of 'Gone with the Wind' Is Still with Us," *Esquire*, September 24, 2014, https://www.esquire.com/entertainment/movies /a30109/gone-with-the-wind-racism/.

3. Screen Actors Guild–American Federation of Television and Radio Artists, "Performers Bear Brunt of Reality TV and Runaway Production Trends, 2003 Casting Data Shows," October 6, 2004, https://www.sagaftra.org/casting-data-reports.

4. See generally Stacy L. Smith, "Inequality in 1,200 Popular Films: Examining Portrayals of Gender, Race/Ethnicity, LGBTQ & Disability from 2007 to 2018," USC Annenberg Inclusion Initiative, September 2019, 18, https://annenberg.usc.edu/sites /default/files/Dr_Stacy_L_Smith-Inequality_in_900_Popular_Films.pdf.

5. Ibid.

6. Ibid.

7. "Diversity in casting is said to be at 'its peak.'" Anna Majavu, "Race Matters: Hollywood's out of Touch with Audiences, Says Report," *Mail & Guardian*, May 28, 2015, http://mg.co.za/article/2015-05-28-hollywood-out-of-touch-with-audiences-says -diversity-report.

8. *Actor* is a general term that is not gender based. Emma Saunders, "Is It Time to Scrap Gender Specific Awards?" BBC News, May 8, 2017, https://www.bbc.com/news /entertainment-arts-39513543.

9. Christopher D. Shea, "Samuel L. Jackson and Others on Black British Actors in American Roles," *New York Times*, March 9, 2017, https://www.nytimes.com /2017/03/09/movies/samuel-jackson-black-british-african-american-actors.html.

10. Angelica Jade Bastién, "What the Debate around Black American and British Actors Gets Wrong," *Vulture*, April 18, 2017, https://www.vulture.com/2017/04/black -american-and-british-actors-what-the-debate-gets-wrong.html.

11. Charles Stockdale and Evan Comen, "Most Bankable Actors of 2018," MSN, December 20, 2018, https://www.msn.com/en-us/movies/gallery/most-bankable-actors -of-2018/ss-BBReOwm.

12. See generally Donald Bogle, *Toms, Coons, Mulattoes, Mammies and Bucks: An Interpretive History of Blacks in American Films* (New York: Bloomsbury, 2016).

13. Carolyn M. Brown, "10 of the Most Successful Black Producers in Hollywood," *Black Enterprise*, October 24, 2018, https://www.blackenterprise.com/hollywoods -most-bankable-black-producers/.

14. *Gravity* collected the highest number of awards that evening, with seven in the following categories: Best Director, Best Cinematography, Best Visual Effects, Best Film Editing, Best Original Score, Best Sound Editing, and Best Sound Mixing. Carolyn Giardina, "'Gravity' Is First Atmos-Mixed Oscar Winner for Sound Editing, Mixing,"

Hollywood Reporter, March 3, 2014, https://www.hollywoodreporter.com/behind
-screen/gravity-first-atmos-mixed-oscar-685578.

15. Harry Benshoff and Sean Griffin, *America on Film: Representing Race, Class, Gender, and Sexuality at the Movies* (New York: John Wiley & Sons, 2011), 37.

16. Lisa McKenzie, *Getting By: Estates, Class and Culture in Austerity Britain* (Chicago: Policy Press, 2015), 12.

17. Jason Sperb, *Disney's Most Notorious Film: Race, Convergence, and the Hidden Histories of 'Song of the South'* (Austin: University of Texas Press, 2012), 10.

18. David Wharton and Jeremy Grant, *Teaching Analysis of Film Language* (London: British Film Institute, 2005), 25.

19. Ibid.

20. Alexis Clark, "How 'The Birth of a Nation' Revived the Ku Klux Klan," History, August 14, 2018, https://www.history.com/news/kkk-birth-of-a-nation-film.

21. Editor of the New York *Independent,* Theodore Tilton opined during the Civil War that "It is sometimes said . . . that the negro race is the feminine race of the world. This is not only because of his social and affectionate nature, but because he possesses that strange moral, instinctive insight that belongs more to women than men." George Fredrickson, *The Black Image in the White Mind: The Debate on Afro-American Character and Destiny, 1817–1914* (New York: Harper & Row, 1971), 115.

22. "The image of the Negro as natural Christian received its fullest treatment and most influential expression in Harriet Beecher Stowe's *Uncle Tom's Cabin*." Ibid., 110.

23. Harriet Beecher Stowe, *A Key to Uncle Tom's Cabin: Presenting the Original Facts and Documents upon which the Story is Founded together with Corroborative Statements Verifying the Truth of the Work* (Boston: John P. Jewett, 1853), 25.

24. Harriet J. Manning, *Michael Jackson and the Blackface Mask* (New York: Routledge, 2016), 53.

25. Brian Roberts, *Blackface Nation: Race, Reform, and Identity in American Popular Music, 1812–1925* (Chicago: University of Chicago Press, 2017), 101.

26. Ibid.

27. John Strausbaugh, *Black Like You: Blackface, Whiteface, Insult & Imitation in American Popular Culture* (New York: Penguin, 2006), 90.

28. Arthur Knight, "Star Dances: African American Constructions of Stardom, 1925–1960," in *Classic Hollywood, Classic Whiteness*, edited by Daniel Berardi (Minneapolis: University of Minnesota Press, 2001), 389.

29. Fredrickson, *The Black Image in the White Mind*, 102.

30. Scott Jaschik, "Harvard Sued over 19th-Century Biologist's Racism," *Inside Higher Ed*, March 21, 2019, https://www.insidehighered.com/news/2019/03/21/lawsuit -against-harvard-focuses-actions-19th-century-biologist.

31. "De Lawd" is the literal name of the Black protagonist in the movie *Green Pastures,* directed by Mark Connelly and William Keighley (Burbank, CA: Warner Bros., 1936).

32. Robert M. Entman and Andrew Rojecki, *The Black Image in the White Mind: Media and Race in America* (Chicago: University of Chicago Press, 2010), 11–12.

33. Lisa J. Green, *African American English: A Linguistic Introduction* (New York: Cambridge University Press, 2002), 203.

34. Emily Sullivan, "Laura Ingraham Told LeBron James to Shut Up and Dribble; He Went to the Hoop," NPR, February 19, 2018, https://www.npr.org/sections/thetwo-way/2018/02/19/587097707/laura-ingraham-told-lebron-james-to-shutup-and-dribble-he-went-to-the-hoop.

35. UN Women, "Goodwill Ambassadors," https://www.unwomen.org/en/partnerships/goodwill-ambassadors.

36. Douglas Wilson and G. Tyler Fischer, *Omnibus III: Reformation to the Present* (Lancaster, PA: Veritas Press, 2006), 172.

37. Frank J. Wetta and Martin A. Novelli, *The Long Reconstruction: The Post–Civil War South in History, Film, and Memory* (New York: Routledge, 2014), 66.

38. Ibid.

39. Jim Korkis, *Who's Afraid of the Song of the South? And Other Forbidden Disney Stories* (Orlando: Theme Park Press, 2012), 102.

40. Fredrickson, *The Black Image in the White Mind*, 258.

41. United Press International, "Court Lets Stand Workers Comp for Blacks Phobia," June 28, 1991, https://www.upi.com/Archives/1991/06/28/Court-lets-stand-workers-comp-for-Blacks-phobia/7592678081600/.

42. Wade Goodwyn, "Trial Begins in Case of Former Dallas Police Officer Who Killed Unarmed Black Man," KDLG, September 23, 2019, https://www.kdlg.org/post/trial-begins-case-former-dallas-police-officer-who-killed-unarmed-black-man#stream/0. On October 2, 2019, Guyger was sentenced to ten years for her murder conviction, with a possiblity of being eligible for parole after five years. Eliott C. McLaughlin and Steve Almasy, "Amber Guyger Gets 10-Year Murder Sentence for Fatally Shooting Botham Jean," CNN, October 3, 2019, https://www.cnn.com/2019/10/02/us/amber-guyger-trial-sentencing/index.html.

43. "There is room and welcome in this Delta only for the Negro who 'stays in his place.'" James C. Cobb, *The Most Southern Place on Earth: The Mississippi Delta and the Roots of Regional Identity* (New York: Oxford University Press, 1994), 180.

44. Kathleen M. German, *Promises of Citizenship: Film Recruitment of African Americans in World War II* (Jackson: University Press of Mississippi, 2017), 51.

45. Ibid.

46. Ibid., 48.

47. Molly Haskell, *From Reverence to Rape: The Treatment of Women in the Movies* (Chicago: University of Chicago Press, 2016), 163.

48. For an in-depth explanation and analysis of the six minority archetypes, see Frederick W. Gooding Jr., *You Mean, There's RACE in My Movie? The Complete Guide to Understanding Race in Mainstream Hollywood* (Silver Spring, MD: On the Reelz Press, 2007), 56.

49. Talitha L. LeFlouria, *Chained in Silence: Black Women and Convict Labor in the New South* (Chapel Hill: University of North Carolina Press, 2015), 10.

50. "Railroads enabled the white traveler in effect to play master or mistress to black attendants." Kathleen Barry, *Femininity in Flight: A History of Flight Attendants* (Chapel Hill, NC: Duke University Press, 2007), 16.

51. Sonja L. Lanehart, ed., *The Oxford Handbook of African American Language* (New York: Oxford University Press, 2015), 749.

52. See generally Bogle, *Toms, Coons, Mulattoes, Mammies and Bucks*.

53. See generally Rachel A. Feinstein, *When Rape Was Legal: The Untold History of Sexual Violence during Slavery* (New York: Routledge, 2018).

54. Equal Justice Initiative, "Lynching in America: Confronting the Legacy of Racial Terror," https://lynchinginamerica.eji.org/report/.

55. "The first recorded 'hate strike' occurred at the Packard Motor plant in Detroit in the fall of 1941; white workers walked off the job to protest the upgrading of blacks into heretofore 'white' classifications." Robert Asher and Ronald Edsforth, eds., *Autowork* (Albany: State University of New York Press, 1995), 122.

CHAPTER 2: EARLY DRAMA BEHIND EARLY BLACK IMAGES (1927–1939)

1. Recall that *Gone with the Wind*, while released in 1939, was not formally recognized with nominations or awards until the 12th Academy Awards, which took place on February 29, 1940.

2. Matthew Belloni, "Studio Chief Summit: All 7 Top Film Executives, One Room, Nothing Off-Limits (and No Easy Answers)," *Hollywood Reporter*, October 30, 2019, https://www.hollywoodreporter.com/features/hollywood-reporter-executive-roundtable-7-major-studio-chiefs-1250718.

3. Susan Hayward, "Hollywood" in *Cinema Studies: The Key Concepts* (New York: Routledge, 2006), 205.

4. Leah Greenblatt, "The Academy Awards Turn 90 This Year—Here's What the First-Ever Ceremony Was Like," *Entertainment Weekly*, February 23, 2018, https://ew.com/oscars/2018/02/23/academy-awards-first-oscars-ceremony/.

5. Hayward, "Hollywood," 205.

6. Charles E. Pederson, *Thomas Edison* (Edina, MN: ABDO, 2007), 77.

7. BBC News, "Does Subliminal Advertising Actually Work?" January 20, 2015, https://www.bbc.com/news/magazine-30878843.

8. *Business Week*, "A Product-Placement Hall of Fame," June 11, 1998, http://www.businessweek.com/1998/25/b3583062.htm; Associated Press, "Thousands Visit Natural History Museum after Ben Stiller Movie," WIS-TV, January 9, 2007, https://www.wistv.com/story/5916857/thousands-visit-natural-history-museum-after-ben-stiller-movie/.

9. Dale Rutledge, "With 'MIB: International,' Lexus Is Cast as a Blockbuster Car for the Second Straight Year," *Fortune*, June 14, 2019, http://fortune.com/2019/06/13/lexus-men-in-black-international-car-mib-black-panther/.

10. Duncan Campbell, "Hollywood Owns Up," *Guardian*, February 15, 2002, https://www.theguardian.com/film/2002/feb/16/features.weekend1.

11. Stephen Prince, *Classical Film Violence: Designing and Regulating Brutality in Hollywood Cinema, 1930–1968* (New Brunswick, NJ: Rutgers University Press, 2003), 24.

12. Motion Picture Association of America, "Production Code," Production Code Administration Records, Margaret Herrick Library, AMPAS.

13. Ralph Donald, *Hollywood Enlists! Propaganda Films of World War II* (Lanham, MD: Rowman & Littlefield, 2017), xiv.

14. Ibid., 19.

15. Katie Lange, "How & Why the Defense Department Works with Hollywood," *DoDLive*, February 28, 2018, http://www.dodlive.mil/2018/02/28/how-why-the-defense -department-works-with-hollywood/.

16. See César G. Soriano and Ann Oldenburg, "With America at War, Hollywood Follows," *USA Today*, February 8, 2005. The unmanned plane landing was reported in the July 19–25, 2005, issue of the *Hollywood Reporter* on page 16 under the caption "Flying High." See also Mimi Hall, "Hollywood, Pentagon Share Rich Past," *USA Today*, March 7, 2005, http://www.usatoday.com/life/2005-03-07-hollywood-pentagon_x .htm; Scott Bowles, "These Big-Studio Films Won't Fake You Out," *USA Today*, April 13, 2005.

17. César G. Soriano and Ann Oldenburg, "With America at War, Hollywood Follows," *USA Today*, February 8, 2005.

18. Motion Picture Association of America, "Production Code Administration Records," http://digitalcollections.oscars.org/cdm/landingpage/collection/p15759coll30.

19. Errol Hill and James V. Hatch, *A History of African American Theatre* (New York: Cambridge University Press, 2003), 315.

20. Mark E. Benbow, "Birth of a Quotation: Woodrow Wilson and 'Like Writing History with Lightning,'" *Journal of the Gilded Age and Progressive Era* 9, no. 4 (2010): 509.

21. "As was common for the era, both Silas Lynch and Gus were played by white actors in blackface—African Americans were only used as extras in the background scenes." Harr Benshoff and Sean Griffin, *America on Film: Representing Race, Class, Gender, and Sexuality at the Movies* (New York: John Wiley & Sons, 2011), 80.

22. Paul McEwan, *The Birth of a Nation* (New York: Bloomsbury, 2015), 85.

23. Greg Garrett, "When Should a Racist Film Be Required Viewing? Right Now." *Huffington Post*, September 23, 2016, https://www.huffpost.com/entry/when-should-a -racist-film_b_11974684.

24. Recognizing the need to honor achievements that did not fit into fixed categories, the Academy presented two special awards at the very first ceremony in 1929: one to Charlie Chaplin and the other to Warner Bros. for producing the pioneering talking picture *The Jazz Singer*. See Lily Rothman, "What Happened at the First-Ever Oscars," *Time*, February 20, 2015, https://time.com/3711978/first-oscars/.

25. Richard Lamparski, *Whatever Became Of . . . ?* Eighth Series (New York: Crown, 1982), 106–107.

26. Benshoff and Griffin, *America on Film*, 84.

27. James Oliver Horton, *Landmarks of African American History* (New York: Oxford University Press, 2005), 142.

28. See generally George Fredrickson, *The Black Image in the White Mind: The Debate on Afro-American Character and Destiny, 1817–1914* (New York: Harper & Row, 1971).

29. "First impressions tend to be lasting impressions. . . . We may eventually change our impression if enough counterinstances occur." Jeffrey S. Nevid and Spencer A. Rathus, *Psychology and the Challenges of Life* (Hoboken, NJ: John Wiley & Sons, 2012), 214.

30. Kathleen M. German, *Promises of Citizenship: Film Recruitment of African Americans in World War II* (Jackson: University Press of Mississippi, 2017), 50.

31. Stuart Bruchey, *Enterprise: The Dynamic of a Free People* (Cambridge, MA: Harvard University Press, 1990), 239.

32. See generally Edward E. Baptist, *The Half Has Never Been Told: Slavery and the Making of American Capitalism* (New York: Basic Books, 2016).

33. See Monticello, "The Life of Sally Hemmings," https://www.monticello.org /sallyhemings/.

34. Screen Actors Guild–American Federation of Television and Radio Artists, "Performers Bear Brunt of Reality TV and Runaway Production Trends, 2003 Casting Data Shows," October 6, 2004, https://www.sagaftra.org/casting-data-reports; Gregg Mitchell, "WGAW Releases 2016 Hollywood Writers Report," Writers Guild of America West, March 24, 2016, https://www.wga.org/news-events/news/press/2016/wgaw-releases -hollywood-writers-report; Directors Guild of America, "DGA Publishes Inaugural Feature Film Diversity Report: Two-Year Study Reveals Women Account For Only 6.4% of Film Directors—Dropping to Just 3% for Major Box Office Titles," December 9, 2015, https://www.dga.org/News/PressReleases/2015/151209-DGA-Publishes-Inaugural -Feature-Film-Diversity-Report.aspx#fn1.

35. Gwendolyn Audrey Foster, *Performing Whiteness: Postmodern Re/Constructions in the Cinema* (Albany: State University of New York Press, 2003), 30.

36. Directors Guild of America, "DGA Retires D.W. Griffith Award—Guild to Create a New Career Achievement Award," December 14, 1999, https://www.dga.org /News/PressReleases/1999/1214-DGA-Retires-DW-Griffith-Award-Guild-to-Create-a -New-Career-Achievement-Award.aspx.

37. Wil Haygood, "Why Won't Blackface Go Away? It's Part of America's Troubled Cultural Legacy," *New York Times*, February 7, 2019, https://www.nytimes.com /2019/02/07/arts/blackface-american-pop-culture.html.

38. To watch Black actor Rex Ingram play as "De Lawd," see *Green Pastures*, directed by Mark Connelly and William Keighley (Burbank, CA: Warner Bros., 1936).

39. Psyche A. Williams-Forson, *Building Houses Out of Chicken Legs: Black Women, Food, and Power* (Chapel Hill: University of North Carolina Press, 2006), 66.

CHAPTER 3: OSCAR'S UNEASY BREAKTHROUGH (1940–1949)

1. The king in Lewis Carrol's *Alice's Adventures in Wonderland* famously dispensed the following advice to the White Rabbit: "Begin at the beginning . . . and go on till you come to the end: then stop." Lewis Carroll, *Alice's Adventures in Wonderland: And Through the Looking Glass* (New York, NY: The MacMillan Company, 1897), 182.

2. Joseph M. Flora and Lucinda Hardwick, eds., *The Companion to Southern Literature: Themes, Genres, Places, People, Movements, and Motifs* (Baton Rouge: Louisiana State University Press, 2002), 309.

3. The Ernest Dawson poem is entitled "Non sum qualis eram bonae sub regno Cynarae." David Welky, *Everything Was Better in America: Print Culture in the Great Depression* (Urbana: University of Illinois Press, 2008), 197. See also Ellis Amburn, *Olivia de Haviland and the Golden Age of Hollywood* (Lanham, MD: Rowman & Littlefield, 2018), 69.

4. Douglas A. McIntyre, "1939's 'Gone with the Wind' Remains the Top-Grossing Movie of All Time," *24/7 Wall St.*, May 6, 2019, https://247wallst.com /media/2019/05/06/1939s-gone-with-the-wind-remains-the-top-grossing-movie-of-all -time-2/.

5. Axel Nissen, *Actresses of a Certain Character: Forty Familiar Hollywood Faces from the Thirties to the Fifties* (Jefferson, NC: McFarland, 1975), 102.

6. Jim Korkis, *Who's Afraid of the Song of the South? And other Forbidden Disney Stories* (Orlando: Theme Park Press, 2012), 71.

7. Harold H. Kassarjian, "The Negro and American Advertising, 1946–1965," *Journal of Marketing Research* 6, no. 1 (February 1969): 143–44.

8. William Barlow, *Voice Over: The Making of Black Radio* (Philadelphia: Temple University Press, 1999), 38.

9. Ibid.

10. John Strausbaugh, *Black Like You: Blackface, Whiteface, Insult & Imitation in American Popular Culture* (New York: Penguin, 2006), 145.

11. US Bureau of the Census, *Changing Characteristics of the Negro Population* (Washington, DC: Government Printing Office, 1969), 116.

12. Kat Eschner, "What Hattie McDaniel Said about Her Oscar-Winning Career Playing Racial Stereotypes," *Smithsonian*, June 9, 2017, https://www.smithsonianmag .com/smart-news/what-hattie-mcdaniel-said-about-her-oscar-winning-career-playing -racial-stereotypes-180963575/#8k5mDpCA7TPvSBP2.99.

13. McDaniel indeed worked as a domestic. See generally *Baltimore Afro-American*, "This Is Hattie," March 9, 1940, 14.

14. "Although Scarlett is no longer a little girl, Mammy continues to take care of her as if she were." Tatiana Prorokova, "Intergenerational Struggle and Racial Progress in 'The Help' and 'The Butler,'" in *Southern History on Screen: Race and Rights, 1976–2016,* ed. Bryan M. Jack, (Lexington: University of Press Kentucky, 2019), 200.

15. See generally Miriam J. Petty, *Stealing the Show: African American Performers and Audiences in 1930s Hollywood* (Oakland: University of California Press, 2016).

16. Jonathan Yardley, "The Complex Thomas Jefferson in His Place and Time," *Washington Post*, May 12, 2017, https://www.washingtonpost.com/opinions/the-complex-thomas-jefferson-in-his-place-and-time/2017/05/12/969a131a-2e9e-11e7-8674-437ddb6e813e_story.html.

17. Korkis, *Who's Afraid of the Song of the South?*, 112.

18. Aramide A. Tinubu, "Disney's Racist Cartoons Won't Just Stay Hidden in the Vault. But They Could Be Used as a Teachable Moment," NBC News, April 25, 2019, https://www.nbcnews.com/think/opinion/disney-s-racist-cartoons-won-t-just-stay-hidden-vault-ncna998216.

19. Lanre Bakare, "Disney Plus Streaming Site Will Not Offer 'Racist' Song of the South Film," *Guardian*, April 23, 2019, https://www.theguardian.com/media/2019/apr/23/disney-plus-streaming-site-will-not-offer-racist-song-of-the-south-film.

20. Sperb, *Disney's Most Notorious Film*, 12.

21. Oscars.org, "Results," http://awardsdatabase.oscars.org/Search/Nominations?nominationId=2120&view=1-Nominee-Alpha.

22. Sperb, *Disney's Most Notorious Film*, 71.

23. Ibid., 212.

24. Ibid., 183.

25. Nina Martyris, "'Tar Baby': A Folk Tale about Food Rights, Rooted in the Inequalities of Slavery," NPR, May 11, 2017, https://www.npr.org/sections/thesalt/2017/05/11/527459106/tar-baby-a-folktale-about-food-rights-rooted-in-the-inequalities-of-slavery.

26. Sperb, *Disney's Most Notorious Film*, 163.

27. See generally Frederick W. Gooding Jr., *American Dream Deferred: Black Federal Workers in Washington, DC, 1941–1981* (Pittsburgh: University of Pittsburgh Press, 2018).

28. Riché Richardson, "Mammy's 'Mules' and the Rules of Marriage in 'Gone with the Wind,'" in *American Cinema and the Southern Imaginary*, ed. Deborah E. Barker and Kathryn McKee, (Athens: University of Georgia Press, 2011), 54.

29. Jill Watts, *Hattie McDaniel: Black Ambition, White Hollywood* (New York: HarperCollins, 2007), 38.

30. Edward Mapp, *African Americans and the Oscar: Decades of Struggle and Achievement* (Lanham, MD: Scarecrow Press, 2008), 2.

31. Peg A. Lamphier and Rosanne Welch, *Women in American History: A Social, Political, and Cultural Encyclopedia and Document Collection* (Santa Barbara, CA: ABC-CLIO, 2017), 249.

32. Charlene Regester, *African American Actresses: The Struggle for Visibility, 1900–1960* (Bloomington: Indiana University Press, 2010), 250.

33. Ralph Ellison, "What America Would Be without Blacks," in *Black on White: Black Writers on What It Means to Be White*, ed. David R. Roediger (New York: Shocken Books, 1998), 165–66.

34. See generally David R. Roediger, *The Wages of Whiteness: Race and the Making of the American Working Class* (New York: Verso Books, 1999).

35. Harry Benshoff and Sean Griffin, *America on Film: Representing Race, Class, Gender, and Sexuality at the Movies* (New York: John Wiley & Sons, 2011), 227.

36. Perhaps nowhere is this clearer than with Busby Berkeley movies such as *Footlight Parade* and *42nd Street*, in which "an eye-popping display of beautiful show girls cavorted in mind-boggling song and dance routines." Wiley Lee Umphlett, *The Movies Go to College: Hollywood and the World of the College-Life Film* (Cranbury, NJ: Associated University Presses, 1984), 47–48.

37. Annette Lynch and Mitchell D. Strauss, *Ethnic Dress in the United States: A Cultural Encyclopedia* (Lanham, MD: Rowman & Littlefield, 2015), 18.

38. Hernán Vera and Andrew M. Gordon, *Screen Saviors: Hollywood Fictions of Whiteness* (Lanham, MD: Rowman & Littlefield, 2003), 100.

39. Tara McPherson, "Revamping the South: Thoughts on Labor, Relationality, and Southern Representation," in *American Cinema and the Southern Imaginary*, ed. Deborah E. Barker and Kathryn McKee (Athens: University of Georgia Press, 2011), 342.

40. Regester, *African American Actresses*, 142.

41. Marjorie Deen, "It's a Scoop!" *Modern Screen* 22, no 3 (February 1941): 64–65, Hattie and Sam McDaniel papers, Margaret Herrick Library, Academy of Motion Picture Arts and Sciences.

42. *Radio Album*, "Meet 'Beulah'" (October–December 1948): 62–63, Hattie and Sam McDaniel papers, Margaret Herrick Library, Academy of Motion Picture Arts and Sciences.

43. Marjorie Deen, "A Modern Hostess," *Modern Screen* 8, no. 5 (October 1934): 6, Hattie and Sam McDaniel papers, Margaret Herrick Library, Academy of Motion Picture Arts and Sciences.

44. At the movie's premiere at Loew's Grand Theater (decorated to look like the plantation house from the movie), "most of the 2,000 audience members dressed in period costume." Carrie Hagen, "How Gone with the Wind Took the Nation by Storm by Catering to Its Southern Sensibilities," *Smithsonian*, December 15, 2014, https://www.smithsonianmag.com/arts-culture/how-gone-wind-took-nation-storm-feeding-its-southern-sensibilities-180953617/.

45. Ibid.

46. Mapp, *African Americans and the Oscar*, 3.

47. United States Postal Service, "Subject: Black History Month," December 2005, https://about.usps.com/postal-bulletin/2005/html/pb22170/kittxt6.html.

48. Kevin P. Sullivan, "A Guide to December's Best In-Flight Movies, Sorted by Airline," *Vulture*, December 7, 2018, https://www.vulture.com/2018/12/best-plane-flight-movies-airlines-2018.html.

49. Committee for Unity in Motion Pictures, First Annual Motion Picture Unity Award Assembly Program, April 23, 1944, Hattie and Sam McDaniel Papers, Margaret Herrick Library, AMPAS.

50. "Whereas the Negro Actors Guild is dedicated to the purpose of perpetuating the achievements of our people in the profession, BE IT Resolved: That the memory of her will be placed upon our records with her achievements in the field of entertainment and that suitable tribute shall be given at the Annual Memorial Services." Certificate, "In Memory of Our Friend," Hattie and Sam McDaniel Papers, Margaret Herrick Library, AMPAS.

51. Letter, Hattie McDaniel to Hedda Hopper, March 29, 1947, Hedda Hopper Papers, Margaret Herrick Library, AMPAS.

52. Tony Horwitz, "The Mammy Washington Almost Had," *Atlantic*, May 31, 2013, https://www.theatlantic.com/national/archive/2013/05/the-mammy-washington-almost -had/276431/.

53. Andrew F. Smith, ed., *The Oxford Companion to American Food and Drink* (New York: Oxford University Press, 2007), 27.

CHAPTER 4: NEW ROLES NOT LEADING ANYWHERE (1950-1959)

1. *Brown v. Board of Education of Topeka*, 347 U.S. 483 (1954).

2. See generally Angela Aleiss, *Making the White Man's Indian: Native Americans and Hollywood Movies* (Westport, CT: Praeger, 2005).

3. Edward Mapp, *African Americans and the Oscar: Decades of Struggle and Achievement* (Lanham, MD: Scarecrow Press, 2008), 7.

4. Ibid.

5. *Pinky*, directed by Elia Kazan (Hollywood, CA: Columbia Pictures, 1949).

6. Grammy.com, "Grammy Hall of Fame Award," accessed May 15, 2019, http://www2.grammy.com/Recording_Academy/Awards/Hall_Of_Fame/.

7. See *Joseph Burstyn, Inc. v. Wilson* 343 U.S. 495 (1952); see also Laura Wittern-Keller, *Freedom of Screen: Legal Challenges to State Film Censorship, 1915–1981* (Lexington: University Press of Kentucky, 2008), 146.

8. Earl Mills, *Dorothy Dandridge: An Intimate Biography* (New York: Holloway House, 1999), 50. Note: Earl Mills was Dandridge's agent for many years.

9. Eugene P. Moehring and Michael S. Green, *Las Vegas: A Centennial History* (Reno: University of Nevada Press, 2005), 197.

10. Charlene Regester, *African American Actresses: The Struggle for Visibility, 1900–1960* (Bloomington: Indiana University Press, 2010), 282.

11. Ibid., 287.

12. Donald Bogle, *Dorothy Dandridge: A Biography* (New York: HarperCollins, 1999), 180.

13. Marguerite H. Rippy, "Commodity, Tragedy, Desire: Female Sexuality and Blackness in the Iconography of Dorothy Dandridge," in *Classic Hollywood, Classic Whiteness*, ed. Daniel Berardi (Minneapolis: University of Minnesota Press, 2001), 188.

14. "Dandridge's race figured prominently in her sexualization. Unlike [Marilyn] Monroe . . . Dandridge was consistently sexualized in the media discussion of her offstage life, despite her attempts to frame this sexualization as 'performance.'" Rippy further asserts that "celebration of the White sex goddess and the erasure of Dandridge illustrate the contradictory roles of race and gender in the American iconography of miscegenation." Ibid., 185.

15. DeAnn Herringshaw, *Dorothy Dandridge: Singer & Actress* (Edina, MN: ABDO, 2011), 65.

16. Harry Benshoff and Sean Griffin, *America on Film: Representing Race, Class, Gender, and Sexuality at the Movies* (New York: John Wiley & Sons, 2011), 87.

17. Donald Ingram Ulin, "From *Huckleberry Finn* to *The Shawshank Redemption*: Race and the American Imagination in the Biracial Escape Film," *European Journal of American Studies* 8, no. 1 (spring 2013), http://journals.openedition.org/ejas/10026.

18. Internet Movie Database, "'The Defiant Ones': Taglines," https://www.imdb.com/title/tt0051525/taglines.

19. Benshoff and Griffin, *America on Film*, 87.

20. Racial comity occurs when members of different races "act kindly and empathetically enough to see beyond skin color to their own shared interests in a more effective and harmonious society." Robert M. Entman and Andrew Rojecki, *The Black Image in the White Mind: Media and Race in America* (Chicago: University of Chicago Press, 2000), 12.

21. Hernán Vera and Andrew M. Gordon, *Screen Saviors: Hollywood Fictions of Whiteness* (Lanham, MD: Rowman & Littlefield, 2003), 156.

22. "In the final scene, Cullen sits on the ground beneath a tree, holding the wounded Joker in his arms, in a scene critics have compared to a pietà. This pietà image is repeated 31 years later, at the end of *Lethal Weapon 2* (1989) in which Murtaugh (Danny Glover) cradles his wounded White partner Riggs (Mel Gibson)." Ibid., 157. The scene is of course re-created in the 1986 made-for-television version starring Carl Weathers, but the final scene lacks the cigarette gesture and features the interracial couple singing an altered version of Johnny Cash's "The Man Comes Around."

23. AMC Filmsite, "Filmsite Movie Review," https://www.filmsite.org/defi.html.

CHAPTER 5: SIDNEY IN THE SIXTIES (1960–1969)

1. "The film, with its radical-for-its-time interracial romance, marked the first time a White actress and a black actor kissed in a major motion picture." Mark Kennedy, "'Guess Who's Coming to Dinner' Legacy Debated on Anniversary," AP News, April 4, 2017, https://www.apnews.com/b198d2db3ba148a4a9036333cd74cefd.

2. Lisette Voytko, "Universal Announces New Orlando Theme Park, Promises 14,000 New Jobs," *Forbes*, August 1, 2019, https://www.forbes.com/sites/lisette

voytko/2019/08/01/universal-announces-new-orlando-theme-park-promises-14000 -new-jobs/#7c20d73d5498.

3. Steven Handzo, "Intimations of Lifelessness," *Bright Lights Film Journal* (winter 1977): 6.

4. Cedric J. Robinson, *Forgeries of Memory and Meaning: Blacks and the Regimes of Race in American Theater and Film before World War II* (Chapel Hill: University of North Carolina Press, 2012), 356.

5. Harry Benshoff and Sean Griffin, *America on Film: Representing Race, Class, Gender, and Sexuality at the Movies* (New York: John Wiley & Sons, 2011), 274.

6. Edward Mapp, *African Americans and the Oscar: Decades of Struggle and Achievement* (Lanham, MD: Scarecrow Press, 2008), 16.

7. Hernán Vera and Andrew M. Gordon, *Screen Saviors: Hollywood Fictions of Whiteness* (Lanham, MD: Rowman & Littlefield, 2003), 92.

8. Ibid., 93.

9. See generally Fredrick C. Harris, "The Rise of Respectability Politics," *Dissent*, winter 2014, https://www.dissentmagazine.org/article/the-rise-of-respectability-politics.

10. Vera and Gordon, *Screen Saviors*, 90.

11. Ibid., 97.

12. Ibid., 86.

CHAPTER 6: THE BLAXPLOITATION EFFECT (1970–1979)

1. Dan Streible, "Race and the Reception of Jack Johnson Fight Films," in *The Birth of Whiteness: Race and the Emergence of U.S. Cinema*, ed. Daniel Berardi (New Brunswick, NJ: Rutgers University Press, 1996), 173.

2. Ibid., 183.

3. Jim Korkis, *Who's Afraid of the Song of the South? And Other Forbidden Disney Stories* (Orlando: Theme Park Press, 2012), 94–95.

4. See appendix D, "List of All Black Nonacting Oscar Winners."

CHAPTER 7: *THE COLOR PURPLE* THROUGH
THE BLUEST EYE (1980–1989)

1. For example, "For [African American critic Jacqueline] Bobo, Spielberg replaces the strong African American female characters of the novel with negative stereotypes.... Celie (Whoopi Goldberg), the abused Black woman who gains a sense of economic independence and self-worth in the book and is unquestionably its protagonist, loses that role in the film to her abusive husband 'Mister' (Danny Glover), whose moral development becomes the film's major concern." Karen Hollinger, *Feminist Film Studies* (New York: Routledge, 2012), 197.

2. Harry Benshoff and Sean Griffin, *America on Film: Representing Race, Class, Gender, and Sexuality at the Movies* (New York: John Wiley & Sons, 2011), 92.

3. See *Hollywood Shuffle*, directed by Robert Townsend (Los Angeles: Samuel Goldwyn Company, 1987).

4. Erik Pedersen, "John Hurt Dies: 'Elephant Man' Oscar Nominee & 'Harry Potter' Alum was 77," *Deadline*, January 27, 2017, https://deadline.com/2017/01/john -hurt-dead-elephant-man-oscar-nominee-harry-potter-alum-was-77-1201896186/.

5. Jack E. White, "Show Business: Just Another Mississippi Whitewash," *Time*, January 9, 1989, http://content.time.com/time/magazine/article/0,9171,956694,00.html.

6. See generally Noel Ignatiev, *How the Irish became White* (New York: Routledge, 1995).

7. ABC News, "'An Actor and A Gentleman' by Louis Gossett Jr.," May 25, 2010, https://abcnews.go.com/GMA/Books/actor-gentleman-louis-gossett-jr/story ?id=10730213.

8. Ibid.

9. Lester D. Freidman, "Black Like Him: Steven Spielberg's 'The Color Purple,'" in *The Persistence of Whiteness: Race and Contemporary Hollywood Cinema*, ed. Daniel Berardi (New York: Routledge, 2008), 312.

10. Richard Harrington, "'Street Smart,' (R)," *Washington Post*, March 25, 1987, https://www.washingtonpost.com/wp-srv/style/longterm/movies/videos/streetsmart rharrington_a0aa35.htm.

11. Terry Trucco, "Denzel Washington Acclaimed in Biko Role," *Chicago Tribune*, December 30, 1987, https://www.chicagotribune.com/news/ct-xpm-1987-12-30 -8704060865-story.html.

CHAPTER 8: THE DENZEL EFFECT (1990–1999)

1. See *Green Pastures*, directed by Mark Connelly and William Keighley (Burbank, CA: Warner Bros., 1936).

2. *Daily News*, "Kiss Off a Love Scene with Julia? Denzel Did," January 3, 2007, https://www.nydailynews.com/entertainment/gossip/kiss-love-scene-julia-denzel-article -1.261711.

3. Jason Silverstein, "I Don't Feel Your Pain: A Failure of Empathy Perpetuates Racial Disparities," *Slate*, June 27, 2013, https://slate.com/technology/2013/06/racial -empathy-gap-people-dont-perceive-pain-in-other-races.html.

4. Hernán Vera and Andrew M. Gordon, *Screen Saviors: Hollywood Fictions of Whiteness* (Lanham, MD: Rowman & Littlefield, 2003), 278.

5. Ibid., 277.

6. Ibid., 278.

7. Lena Williams, "Spike Lee Says Money from Blacks Saved 'X,'" *New York Times*, May 20, 1992, https://www.nytimes.com/1992/05/20/movies/spike-lee-says-money -from-Blacks-saved-x.html.

CHAPTER 9: NEW CENTURY, NEW BEGINNING? (2000–2009)

1. A. Samuels, "Angela's Fire," *Newsweek*, July 1, 2002, 54.

2. Harry Benshoff and Sean Griffin, *America on Film: Representing Race, Class, Gender, and Sexuality at the Movies* (New York: John Wiley & Sons, 2011), 96–97.

3. In 2007, eight of the twenty Best and Best Supporting Actor/Actress nominees were non-White actors. Adriana Barraza and Rinko Kikuchi were nominated for their supporting roles in *Babel*; Jennifer Hudson claimed Best Supporting Actress for *Dreamgirls*; Djimon Hounsou was nominated for Best Supporting Actor in *Blood Diamond*; Penélope Cruz received a Best Actress nomination for *Volver*; Will Smith received his second Best Actor nomination for *The Pursuit of Happyness*; and Forest Whitaker claimed the Best Actor Oscar for *The Last King of Scotland*.

4. Stephen Rea, "Oscar Hugs and Shrugs: The Academy Award Nominations Show Unusual Diversity this Year and, in the Case of 'Dreamgirls, an Oddity. Oscar Is Doing His Part for Diversity,'" *Philadelphia Inquirer*, January 23, 2007.

5. See generally Gwendolyn Audrey Foster, *Performing Whiteness: Postmodern Re/Constructions in the Cinema* (Albany: State University of New York Press, 2003).

6. "Favorite Oscar® Moment—Adrien Brody Kissing Halle Berry," February 20, 2011, https://www.youtube.com/watch?v=2isqa6BLtkA.

7. Linda Williams, *Playing the Race Card: Melodramas of Black and White from Uncle Tom to O.J. Simpson* (Princeton, NJ: Princeton University Press, 2001), 307.

8. Ibid., 304.

9. Hernán Vera and Andrew M. Gordon, *Screen Saviors: Hollywood Fictions of Whiteness* (Lanham, MD: Rowman & Littlefield, 2003), 180.

10. Said Geisel himself, "*The Cat in the Hat* is a revolt against authority, but it's ameliorated by the fact that the Cat cleans up everything at the end. It's revolutionary in that it goes as far as [Alexander Foyodorvich] Kerensky and then stops. It doesn't go quite as far as Lenin." Jonathan Cott, "The Good Dr. Seuss," in *Of Sneetches and Whos and the Good Dr. Seuss: Essays on the Writings and Life of Theodor Geisel*, ed. Thomas Fensch (Jefferson, NC: McFarland, 1983), 117.

11. Kathleen M. German, *Promises of Citizenship: Film Recruitment of African Americans in World War II* (Jackson: University Press of Mississippi, 2017), 51.

12. Charlene Regester, *African American Actresses: The Struggle for Visibility, 1900–1960* (Bloomington, Indiana University Press, 2010), 294.

13. T. I. Stanley, "The Color of Money: Hollywood Diversifies," *Ad Age*, August 30, 2004, https://adage.com/article/news/color-money-hollywood-diversifies/100260.

14. Adam Howard, "Nina Simone Film Sparks Heated Debate about Colorism in Hollywood," MSNBC, March 4, 2016, http://www.msnbc.com/msnbc/nina-simone-film-sparks-heated-debate-about-colorism-hollywood.

15. Najja Parker, "Will Smith's Possible New Role as Venus and Serena Williams' Dad Sparks Debate about Colorism," *Atlanta Journal-Constitution*, March 6, 2019, https://www.ajc.com/news/world/will-smith-possible-new-role-venus-and-serena-williams-dad-sparks-debate-about-colorism/FXz0Oe5DjsPgA2BXidUFeL/.

16. Teresa Wiltz, "'Mighty Heart'" Casting Stirs Debate over Race," *Seattle Times*, June 27, 2007, https://www.seattletimes.com/entertainment/mighty-heart-casting-stirs-debate-over-race/.

17. *JCK*, "Amputee Victims Reportedly Accuse 'Blood Diamond' Movie Execs of Broken Promises," October 23, 2006, https://www.jckonline.com/editorial-article/amputee-victims-reportedly-accuse-blood-diamond-movie-execs-of-broken-promises/.

18. Kim Masters, "How Much Will Eddie Murphy's Oscar Exit Hurt His Career? Analysis," *Hollywood Reporter*, November 9, 2011, https://www.hollywoodreporter.com/news/eddie-murphy-oscars-career-brett-ratner-259479.

19. S. T. VanAirsdale, "The Oscars: Ruby Dee's Surprise Party," *Vanity Fair*, January 30, 2008, https://www.vanityfair.com/news/2008/01/the-oscars-ruby.

20. Kate Kellaway, "Mother Superior," *Guardian* online, January 3, 2009, https://www.theguardian.com/film/2009/jan/04/doubt-viola-davis.

CHAPTER 10: OSCARS SO WHITE? (2010-2019)

1. Scott Feinberg, "Viggo Mortensen Apologizes for Using N-Word during 'Green Book' Panel," *Hollywood Reporter*, November 8, 2018, https://www.hollywoodreporter.com/race/viggo-mortensen-says-sorry-using-n-word-q-a-1159813.

2. Maria Puente, Andrea Mandell, and Bryan Alexander, "We Were There: How the Worst Flub in Oscar History Went Down," *USA Today*, February 28, 2018, https://www.usatoday.com/story/life/2018/02/28/we-were-there-how-worst-flub-oscar-history-went-down/377305002/.

3. Mashaun D. Simon, "Oscars May Have Black Host, but All White Nominees in Top Categories," NBC News, January 14, 2016, https://www.nbcnews.com/news/nbcblk/oscars-may-have-Black-host-all-White-nominees-top-categories-n496401.

4. See generally J. P. Leger, "Trends and Causes of Fatalities in South African Mines," *Safety Science* 14 (1991): 169–85.

5. Melissa Anderson, "'The Blind Side': What Would Black People Do without Nice White Folks?" *Dallas Observer*, November 19, 2009, https://www.dallasobserver.com/film/the-blind-side-what-would-black-people-do-without-nice-White-folks-6420117.

6. Seth Abramovitch, "Mo'Nique: I Was 'Blackballed' after Winning My Oscar," *Hollywood Reporter*, February 19, 2015, https://www.hollywoodreporter.com/news/monique-i-was-blackballed-winning-774616.

7. Ibid.

8. An excellent example of this dynamic is the 1996 film *A Time to Kill*. Harry Benshoff and Sean Griffin, *America on Film: Representing Race, Class, Gender, and Sexuality at the Movies* (New York: John Wiley & Sons, 2011), 85.

9. Susan Donaldson James, "Black Maid Sues, Says 'The Help' Is Humiliating," ABC News, February 22, 2011, https://abcnews.go.com/Health/lawsuit-Black-maid-ablene-cooper-sues-author-kathryn/story?id=12968562.

10. Gary Baum, "'Beasts of the Southern Wild' Breakout Dwight Henry Expanding Bakery Business," *Hollywood Reporter*, July 18, 2012, https://www.hollywoodreporter.com/news/beasts-of-the-southern-wild-dwight-henry-bakery-350382.

11. Aisha Harris, "Was There Really 'Mandingo Fighting,' Like in *Django Unchained?*" *Slate*, December 24, 2012, https://slate.com/culture/2012/12/django-unchained-mandingo-fighting-were-any-slaves-really-forced-to-fight-each-other-to-the-death.html.

12. Bryan Alexander, "Snoop Dogg Rails against 'Roots' in Expletive-Filled Video," *USA Today*, May 30, 2016, https://www.usatoday.com/story/life/tv/2016/05/30/snoop-dogg-urges-roots-boycott-social-media/85158354/.

13. Ann Heilmann, *Mark Llewellyn, Neo-Victorianism: The Victorians in the Twenty-First Century, 1999–2009* (New York: Palgrave Macmillan, 2010); see the discussion on p. 122.

14. Marguerite H. Rippy, "Commodity, Tragedy, Desire: Female Sexuality and Blackness in the Iconography of Dorothy Dandridge," on *Classic Hollywood, Classic Whiteness*, ed. Daniel Berardi (Minneapolis: University of Minnesota Press, 2001), 189.

15. *Loving v. Virginia*, 388 U.S. 1 (1967).

16. Dexter Thomas, "Oscar-Nominated 'Hidden Figures' Was Whitewashed—but It Didn't Have to Be," *Vice*, January 25, 2017, https://www.vice.com/en_us/article/d3xmja/oscar-nominated-hidden-figures-was-whitewashed-but-it-didnt-have-to-be.

17. Colleen Kratofil, "Mary J. Blige Was Afraid to Go Makeup-Free in *Mudbound*: 'I Was Feeling Super Insecure,'" *People*, November 27, 2017, https://people.com/style/mary-j-blige-no-makeup-mudbound/.

18. Jethro Nededog, "Viola Davis 'Woman-ed Up' for that Unforgettable 'How to Get Away with Murder' Vanity Scene," *Business Insider*, June 23, 2015, https://www.business insider.com/viola-davis-vanity-scene-in-how-to-get-away-with-murders-2015-6.

19. Melanie McFarland, "Hollywood Still Loves a White Savior: 'Green Book' and the Lazy, Feel-Good Take on Race," *Salon*, December 30, 2018, https://www.salon.com/2018/12/30/hollywood-still-loves-a-White-savior-green-book-and-the-lazy-feel-good-take-on-race/.

20. Megan Hunt, "Hollywood's Southern Strategy: Portraying White Christianity in Late Twentieth-Century Civil Rights Melodramas," in *Southern History on Screen: Race and Rights, 1976–2016*, ed. Bryan M. Jack (Lexington: University Press of Kentucky, 2019), 112.

21. Frederick W. Gooding Jr., *American Dream Deferred: Black Federal Workers in Washington, DC, 1941–1981* (Pittsburg: University of Pittsburgh Press, 2018), 41.

22. Matt Donnelly and Meredith Woerner, "Viggo Mortensen Apologizes for Using N-Word at 'Green Book' Panel," *Variety*, November 9, 2018, https://variety.com/2018/film/news/viggo-mortensen-n-word-green-book-1203024519/.

23. Hunter Harris, "Mahershala Ali Apologized to His 'Green Book' Character's Family after Controversy," *Vulture*, December 17, 2018, https://www.vulture.com/amp/2018/12/mahershala-ali-green-book-dr-don-shirley-family-apology.html.

24. Hunt, "Hollywood's Southern Strategy," 171.

CONCLUSION: HAVE WE SEEN THIS MOVIE BEFORE?
A CRITICAL ANALYSIS

1. Scott Feinberg, "Academy Museum Opening Delayed until at Least 2020," *Hollywood Reporter*, June 20, 2019, https://www.hollywoodreporter.com/race/academy -museum-opening-delayed-at-2020-1220122.

2. Jeffrey Jenson Arnett, ed., *Encyclopedia of Children, Adolescents, and the Media* (Thousand Oaks, CA: SAGE Publications, 2006), 639.

3. The eleven names are: Barkhad Abdi, Jaye Davidson, Chiwetel Ejiofor, Naomie Harris, Djimon Hounsou, Marianne Jean-Baptiste, Daniel Kaluuya, Ruth Negga, Lupita Nyong'o, Sophie Okonedo, Sidney Poitier; 11/57 = 19.2 percent.

4. The twenty names are: Barkhad Abdi, Margaret Avery, Mary J. Blige, Adolph Caesar, Diahann Carroll, Dorothy Dandridge, Jaye Davidson, Jamie Foxx, Whoopi Goldberg, Dexter Gordon, Jennifer Hudson, Queen Latifah, Hattie McDaniel, Mo'Nique, Juanita Moore, Eddie Murphy, Diana Ross, Will Smith, Ethel Waters, Oprah Winfrey; 20/57 = 35 percent.

5. The ten names followed by the total number of nominations are: Mahershala Ali, 2; Viola Davis, 3; Jamie Foxx, 2; Morgan Freeman, 5; Whoopi Goldberg, 2; Djimon Hounsou, 2; Sidney Poitier, 2; Will Smith, 2; Octavia Spencer, 3; Denzel Washington, 8; 31/77 = 40.2 percent. The four actors responsible for 27.2% of all Black Oscar nominations are: Denzel Washington, 8; Morgan Freeman, 5; Viola Davis, 3; Octavia Spencer, 3; 21/77 = 27.2 percent.

6. Of the sixty-six movies listed in appendix B, "List of All Movies with Black Oscar Nominations," only thirteen movies do not centrally involve themes of race or identity: *The Reivers, An Officer and a Gentleman, Ghost, The Crying Game, The Shawshank Redemption, Chicago, Million Dollar Baby, Collateral, Doubt, The Curious Case of Benjamin Button, Flight, Beasts of the Southern Wild, The Shape of Water*; 53/66 = 80.3 percent.

7. The eighteen characters, followed by the movie in which they appeared are: Carmen Jones, *Carmen Jones*; Annie Johnson, *Imitation of Life*; Coalhouse Walker Jr., *Ragtime*; Sergeant Vernon Waters, *A Soldier's Story*; Dale Turner, *Round Midnight*; Leo "Fast Black" Smalls Jr., *Street Smart*; Steve Biko, *Cry Freedom*; Private Silas Trip, *Glory*; Malcolm X, *Malcolm X*; John Coffey, *The Green Mile*; Alonzo Harris, *Training Day*; Mateo Kuamey, *In America*; Idi Amin, *The Last King in Scotland*; James "Thunder" Early, *Dreamgirls*; Queenie, *The Curious Case of Benjamin Button*; Troy Maxson, *Fences*; Juan, *Moonlight*; Roman J. Israel, *Roman J. Israel, Esq.*; 18/77 = 23.3 percent.

8. Jerry D. Flack, *TalentEd: Strategies for Developing the Talent in Every Learner* (Englewood, CO: Teacher Ideas Press, 1993), 58.

9. Allan G. Johnson, *Privilege, Power and Difference* (Mountain View, CA: Mayfield, 2001), 108.

10. Jill Watts, *Hattie McDaniel: Black Ambition, White Hollywood* (New York: HarperCollins, 2005), 178.

11. Hernán Vera and Andrew M. Gordon, *Screen Saviors: Hollywood Fictions of Whiteness* (Lanham, MD: Rowman & Littlefield, 2003), 8.

12. Ibid., 279.

13. Alyssa Rosenberg, "How Hollywood Stays White and Male," *Washington Post*, May 14, 2015, https://www.washingtonpost.com/news/act-four/wp/2015/05/14/how-hollywood-stays-White-and-male/?utm_term=.b0ae238bd92f.

14. Letter, Marlon Brando to Lew R. Wasserman of MCA Universal, January 23, 1976, Lisabeth Hush Collection on Sex Discrimination against Women, Margaret Herrick Library, AMPAS.

15. Harry Benshoff and Sean Griffin, *America on Film: Representing Race Class, Gender, and Sexuality at the Movies* (New York: John Wiley & Sons, 2011), 25.

16. See generally Derald Wing Sue, *Microaggressions in Everyday Life: Race, Gender and Sexual Orientation* (Hoboken, NJ: John Wiley & Sons, 2010).

17. Vera and Gordon, *Screen Saviors*, 192.

18. Murray Schumach, "Hollywood Gives Tara to Atlanta," *New York Times*, May 25, 1959.

BIBLIOGRAPHY

ARTICLES

ABC News. "'An Actor and a Gentleman' by Louis Gossett Jr.," May 25, 2010. https://abcnews.go.com/GMA/Books/actor-gentleman-louis-gossett-jr/story?id=10730213.

Abramovitch, Seth. "Mo'Nique: I Was 'Blackballed' after Winning My Oscar." *Hollywood Reporter*, February 19, 2015. https://www.hollywoodreporter.com/news/monique-i-was-blackballed-winning-774616.

Alexander, Bryan. "Snoop Dogg Rails against 'Roots' in Expletive-Filled Video." *USA Today*, May 30, 2016. https://www.usatoday.com/story/life/tv/2016/05/30/snoop-dogg-urges-roots-boycott-social-media/85158354/.

Anderson, Melissa. "'The Blind Side': What Would Black People Do without Nice White Folks?" *Dallas Observer*, November 19, 2009. https://www.dallasobserver.com/film/the-blind-side-what-would-black-people-do-without-White-folks-6420117.

Associated Press. "Oscar Ratings up from 2018." *Billboard*, February 26, 2019. https://www.billboard.com/articles/events/oscars/8500124/oscars-ratings-up-from-2018.

———. "Thousands Visit Natural History Museum after Ben Stiller Movie," WIS-TV, January 9, 2007. https://www.wistv.com/story/5916857/thousands-visit-natural-history-museum-after-ben-stiller-movie/.

Bakare, Lanre. "Disney Plus Streaming Site Will Not Offer 'Racist' Song of the South Film." *Guardian*, April 23, 2019. https://www.theguardian.com/media/2019/apr/23/disney-plus-streaming-site-will-not-offer-racist-song-of-the-south-film.

Baltimore Afro-American. "This Is Hattie," March 9, 1940, 14.

Bastién, Angelica Jade. "What the Debate around Black American and British Actors Gets Wrong." *Vulture*, April 18, 2017. https://www.vulture.com/2017/04/black-american-and-british-actors-what-the-debate-gets-wrong.html.

Baum, Gary. "'Beasts of the Southern Wild' Breakout Dwight Henry Expanding Bakery Business." *Hollywood Reporter*, July 18, 2012. https://www.hollywoodreporter.com/news/beasts-of-the-southern-wild-dwight-henry-bakery-350382.

BBC News. "Does Subliminal Advertising Actually Work?" January 20, 2015. https://www.bbc.com/news/magazine-30878843.

Belloni, Matthew. "Studio Chief Summit: All 7 Top Film Executives, One Room, Nothing Off-Limits (and No Easy Answers)." *Hollywood Reporter*, October 30, 2019. https://www.hollywoodreporter.com/features/hollywood-reporter-executive-round table-7-major-studio-chiefs-1250718.

Bowles, Scott. "These Big-Studio Films Won't Fake You Out." *USA Today*, April 13, 2005.

Brown, Carolyn M. "10 of the Most Successful Black Producers in Hollywood." *Black Enterprise*, October 24, 2018. https://www.blackenterprise.com/hollywoods-most -bankable-black-producers/.

Business Week. "A Product-Placement Hall of Fame," June 11, 1998. http://www .businessweek.com/1998/25/b3583062.htm.

Caffrey, Jane "'Envelope, Please': 6 Things You May Not Know about the Oscars Envelope." CNN, February 22, 2015. https://www.cnn.com/2015/02/20/entertainment /oscars-envelope-things-to-know/index.html.

Campbell, Duncan. "Hollywood Owns Up." *Guardian*, February 15, 2002. https://www.theguardian.com/film/2002/feb/16/features.weekend1.

Clark, Alexis. "How 'The Birth of a Nation' Revived the Ku Klux Klan." History, August 14, 2018. https://www.history.com/news/kkk-birth-of-a-nation-film.

Clark, J. Scott. "What's on Delta's Inflight Entertainment for August 2019." *Points Guy*, August 5, 2019. https://thepointsguy.com/news/whats-on-new-delta-in-flight -entertainment-ife/.

Cuccinello, Hayley C. "Inside the $148,000 Oscars Gift Bag: From a Luxurious European Cruise to Decadent THC Chocolates." *Forbes*, February 22, 2019. https://www.forbes.com/sites/hayleycuccinello/2019/02/22/inside-the-148000-oscars -gift-bag-from-a-luxurious-european-cruise-to-decadent-thc-chocolates/#678bb8e 0735f.

Daily News. "Kiss Off a Love Scene with Julia? Denzel Did," January 3, 2007. https://www.nydailynews.com/entertainment/gossip/kiss-love-scene-julia-denzel -article-1.261711.

Deen, Marjorie. "It's a Scoop!" *Modern Screen* 22, no 3 (February 1941): 64–65. Hattie and Sam McDaniel Papers, Margaret Herrick Library, Academy of Motion Picture Arts and Sciences.

———. "A Modern Hostess." *Modern Screen* 8, no 5 (October 1934): 6. Hattie and Sam McDaniel Papers, Margaret Herrick Library, Academy of Motion Picture Arts and Sciences.

Directors Guild of America. "DGA Retires D.W. Griffith Award—Guild to Create a New Career Achievement Award," December 14, 1999. https://www.dga.org /News/PressReleases/1999/1214-DGA-Retires-DW-Griffith-Award-Guild-to-Create -a-New-Career-Achievement-Award.aspx.

Donnelly, Matt, and Meredith Woerner. "Viggo Mortensen Apologizes for Using N-Word at 'Green Book' Panel." *Variety*, November 9, 2018. https://variety.com/2018 /film/news/viggo-mortensen-n-word-green-book-1203024519/.

Dvorak, Petula. "The Wrong Oscars Wasn't the First Academy Awards Fiasco. This Was." *Washington Post*, March 4, 2018. https://www.washingtonpost.com/news/retro polis/wp/2018/03/04/the-wrong-oscars-envelope-wasnt-the-first-academy-awards -fiasco-this-was/.

Eschner, Kat. "What Hattie McDaniel Said about Her Oscar-Winning Career Playing Racial Stereotypes." *Smithsonian*, June 9, 2017. https://www.smithsonianmag .com/smart-news/what-hattie-mcdaniel-said-about-her-oscar-winning-career-playing -racial-stereotypes-180963575/#8k5mDpCA7TPvSBP2.99.

Feinberg, Scott. "Academy Museum Opening Delayed until at Least 2020." *Hollywood Reporter*, June 20, 2019. https://www.hollywoodreporter.com/race/academy-museum -opening-delayed-at-2020-1220122.

———. "Viggo Mortensen Apologizes for Using N-Word during 'Green Book' Panel." *Hollywood Reporter*, November 8, 2018. https://www.hollywoodreporter.com/race /viggo-mortensen-says-sorry-using-n-word-q-a-1159813.

Foundas, Scott. "'Exodus: Gods and Kings' Director Ridley Scott on Creating His Vision of Moses." *Variety*, November 25, 2014. https://variety.com/2014/film/news /ridley-scott-exodus-gods-and-kings-christian-bale-1201363668/.

Garrett, Greg. "When Should a Racist Film Be Required Viewing? Right Now." *Huffington Post*, September 23, 2016. https://www.huffpost.com/entry/when-should-a -racist-film_b_11974684.

Giardina, Carolyn. "'Gravity' Is First Atmos-Mixed Oscar Winner for Sound Editing, Mixing." *Hollywood Reporter*, March 3, 2014. https://www.hollywoodreporter.com /behind-screen/gravity-first-atmos-mixed-oscar-685578.

Goodwyn, Wade. "Trial Begins in Case of Former Dallas Police Officer Who Killed Unarmed Black Man." *KDLG*, September 23, 2019. https://www.kdlg.org/post/trial -begins-case-former-dallas-police-officer-who-killed-unarmed-black-man#stream/0.

Greenblatt, Leah. "The Academy Awards Turn 90 This Year—Here's What the First-Ever Ceremony Was Like." *Entertainment Weekly*, February 23, 2018. https:// ew.com/oscars/2018/02/23/academy-awards-first-oscars-ceremony/.

Griffin, Nancy "Secrets and Wives." *Sydney Morning Herald*, June 12, 2004. https:// www.smh.com.au/entertainment/movies/secrets-and-wives-20040612-gdj3vg.html.

Hagen, Carrie "How Gone with the Wind Took the Nation by Storm by Catering to Its Southern Sensibilities." *Smithsonian*, December 15, 2014. https://www.smith

sonianmag.com/arts-culture/how-gone-wind-took-nation-storm-feeding-its-southern
-sensibilities-180953617/.

Hall, Mimi. "Hollywood, Pentagon Share Rich Past." *USA Today*, March 7, 2005. http://
www.usatoday.com/life/2005-03-07-hollywood-pentagon_x.htm.

Harrington, Richard. "'Street Smart' (R)." *Washington Post*, March 25, 1987. https://www
.washingtonpost.com/wp-srv/style/longterm/movies/videos/streetsmartrharrington
_a0aa35.htm.

Harris, Aisha. "Was There Really 'Mandingo Fighting,' Like in *Django Unchained*?"
Slate, December 24, 2012. https://slate.com/culture/2012/12/django-unchained
-mandingo-fighting-were-any-slaves-really-forced-to-fight-each-other-to-the-death
.html.

Harris, Fredrick C. "The Rise of Respectability Politics." *Dissent*, winter 2014. https://
www.dissentmagazine.org/article/the-rise-of-respectability-politics.

Harris, Hunter. "Mahershala Ali Apologized to His 'Green Book' Character's Family after Controversy." *Vulture*, December 17, 2018. https://www.vulture.com
/amp/2018/12/mahershala-ali-green-book-dr-don-shirley-family-apology.html.

Haygood, Wil. "Why Won't Blackface Go Away? It's Part of America's Troubled Cultural
Legacy." *New York Times*, February 7, 2019. https://www.nytimes.com/2019/02/07
/arts/blackface-american-pop-culture.html.

Horwitz, Tony. "The Mammy Washington Almost Had." *Atlantic*, May 31, 2013. https://
www.theatlantic.com/national/archive/2013/05/the-mammy-washington-almost-had
/276431/.

Howard, Adam. "Nina Simone Film Sparks Heated Debate about Colorism in Hollywood." MSNBC, March 4, 2016. http://www.msnbc.com/msnbc/nina-simone-film
-sparks-heated-debate-about-colorism-hollywood.

James, Susan Donaldson. "Black Maid Sues, Says 'The Help' Is Humiliating."
ABC News, February 22, 2011, https://abcnews.go.com/Health/lawsuit-black-maid
-ablene-cooper-sues-author-kathryn/story?id=12968562.

Jaschik, Scott. "Harvard Sued over 19th-Century Biologist's Racism." *Inside Higher Ed*,
March 21, 2019. https://www.insidehighered.com/news/2019/03/21/lawsuit-against
-harvard-focuses-actions-19th-century-biologist.

JCK. "Amputee Victims Reportedly Accuse 'Blood Diamond' Movie Execs of Broken
Promises," October 23, 2006. https://www.jckonline.com/editorial-article/amputee
-victims-reportedly-accuse-blood-diamond-movie-execs-of-broken-promises/.

Kellaway, Kate. "Mother Superior." *Guardian*, January 3, 2009. https://www.theguardian
.com/film/2009/jan/04/doubt-viola-davis.

Kennedy, Mark. "'Guess Who's Coming to Dinner' Legacy Debated on Anniversary."
AP News, April 4, 2017. https://www.apnews.com/b198d2db3ba148a4a9036333cd
74cefd.

Kratofil, Colleen. "Mary J. Blige Was Afraid to Go Makeup-Free in *Mudbound*: 'I Was Feeling Super Insecure.'" *People*, November 27, 2017. https://people.com/style/mary -j-blige-no-makeup-mudbound/.

Lange, Katie. "How & Why the Defense Department Works with Hollywood," *DoD-Live*, February 28, 2018. http://www.dodlive.mil/2018/02/28/how-why-the-defense -department-works-with-hollywood/.

Lewis, Hilary. "Oscars: Who Came up with the Name 'Oscar' and More about the Statuette's History (Video)." *Hollywood Reporter*, February 18, 2015. https://www .hollywoodreporter.com/news/oscars-who-came-up-name-774775.

Majavu, Anna. "Race Matters: Hollywood's out of Touch with Audiences, Says Report." *Mail & Guardian*, May 28, 2015. http://mg.co.za/article/2015-05-28-hollywood -out-of-touch-with-audiences-says-diversity-report.

Marche, Stephen. "The Racism of 'Gone with the Wind' Is Still with Us." *Esquire*, September 24, 2014. https://www.esquire.com/entertainment/movies/a30109/gone -with-the-wind-racism/.

Martyris, Nina. "'Tar Baby': A Folk Tale about Food Rights, Rooted in the Inequalities of Slavery." NPR, May 11, 2017. https://www.npr.org/sections/thesalt /2017/05/11/527459106/tar-baby-a-folktale-about-food-rights-rooted-in-the-in equalities-of-slavery.

Masters, Kim. "How Much Will Eddie Murphy's Oscar Exit Hurt His Career? Analysis." *Hollywood Reporter*, November 9, 2011. https://www.hollywoodreporter.com /news/eddie-murphy-oscars-career-brett-ratner-259479.

McClintock, Pamela. "2018 Box Office Revenue Soars to Record $11.9B in the U.S., Hits $42B Globally." *Hollywood Reporter*, January 2, 2019. https://www.holly woodreporter.com/news/2018-box-office-revenue-soars-record-119m-us-hits-42b -globally-1172215.

McFarland, Melanie. "Hollywood Still Loves a White Savior: 'Green Book' and the Lazy, Feel-Good Take on Race." *Salon*, December 30, 2018. https://www.salon .com/2018/12/30/hollywood-still-loves-a-white-savior-green-book-and-the-lazy-feel -good-take-on-race/.

McIntyre, Douglas A. "1939's 'Gone with the Wind' Remains the Top-Grossing Movie of All Time." *24/7 Wall St.*, May 6, 2019. https://247wallst.com/media /2019/05/06/1939s-gone-with-the-wind-remains-the-top-grossing-movie-of-all -time-2/.

McLaughlin, Eliott C., and Steve Almasy. "Amber Guyger Gets 10-Year Murder Sentence for Fatally Shooting Botham Jean." CNN, October 3, 2019. https://www.cnn .com/2019/10/02/us/amber-guyger-trial-sentencing/index.html.

Mullen, Shannon. "Race Remains Hot Topic Despite Obama Presidency." *USA Today*, October 17, 2010. http://usatoday30.usatoday.com/news/nation/2010-10-17-race -obama_N.htm.

Nededog, Jethro. "Viola Davis 'Woman-ed Up' for that Unforgettable 'How to Get Away with Murder' Vanity Scene." *Business Insider*, June 23, 2015. https://www.business insider.com/viola-davis-vanity-scene-in-how-to-get-away-with-murders-2015-6.

Parker, Najja. "Will Smith's Possible New Role as Venus and Serena Williams' Dad Sparks Debate about Colorism." *Atlanta Journal-Constitution*, March 6, 2019. https://www.ajc.com/news/world/will-smith-possible-new-role-venus-and-serena -williams-dad-sparks-debate-about-colorism/FXz0Oe5DjsPgA2BXidUFeL/.

Pedersen, Erik. "John Hurt Dies: 'Elephant Man' Oscar Nominee & 'Harry Potter' Alum was 77." *Deadline*, January 27, 2017. https://deadline.com/2017/01/john-hurt-dead -elephant-man-oscar-nominee-harry-potter-alum-was-77-1201896186/.

Puente, Maria, Andrea Mandell, and Bryan Alexander. "We Were There: How the Worst Flub in Oscar History Went Down." *USA Today*, February 28, 2018. https://www .usatoday.com/story/life/2018/02/28/we-were-there-how-worst-flub-oscar-history -went-down/377305002/.

Radio Album. "Meet 'Beulah'" (October–December 1948): 62–63. Hattie and Sam McDaniel Papers, Margaret Herrick Library, Academy of Motion Picture Arts and Sciences.

Rea, Stephen. "Oscar Hugs and Shrugs: The Academy Award Nominations Show Unusual Diversity This Year and, in the Case of 'Dreamgirls,' an Oddity. Oscar Is Doing His Part for Diversity." *Philadelphia Inquirer*, January 23, 2007.

Richwine, Lisa. "Oscar Nominees Ride Publicity Bounce at Box Office." Reuters, February 27, 2018. https://www.reuters.com/article/us-awards-oscars-boxoffice/oscar -nominees-ride-publicity-bounce-at-box-office-idUSKCN1GB2U1.

Rosenberg, Alyssa. "How Hollywood Stays White and Male." *Washington Post*, May 14, 2015. https://www.washingtonpost.com/news/act-four/wp/2015/05/14/how-holly wood-stays-white-and-male/?utm_term=.b0ae238bd92f.

Rothman, Lily. "What Happened at the First-Ever Oscars." *Time*, February 20, 2015. https://time.com/3711978/first-oscars/.

Rutledge, Dale. "With 'MIB: International,' Lexus Is Cast as a Blockbuster Car for the Second Straight Year." *Fortune*, June 14, 2019. http://fortune.com/2019/06/13/lexus -men-in-black-international-car-mib-black-panther/.

Samuels, A. "Angela's Fire." *Newsweek*, July 1, 2002, 54.

Saunders, Emma. "Is It Time to Scrap Gender Specific Awards?" BBC News, May 8, 2017. https://www.bbc.com/news/entertainment-arts-39513543.

Schumach, Murray. "Hollywood Gives Tara to Atlanta." *New York Times*, May 25, 1959.

Shea, Christopher D. "Samuel L. Jackson and Others on Black British Actors in American Roles." *New York Times*, March 9, 2017. https://www.nytimes.com/2017/03/09 /movies/samuel-jackson-black-british-african-american-actors.html.

Sheerin, Jude. "'Fatty' Arbuckle and Hollywood's First Scandal." BBC News, September 4, 2011. https://www.bbc.com/news/magazine-14640719.

Silverstein, Jason. "I Don't Feel Your Pain: A Failure of Empathy Perpetuates Racial Disparities." *Slate*, June 27, 2013. https://slate.com/technology/2013/06/racial-empathy-gap-people-dont-perceive-pain-in-other-races.html.

Simon, Mashaun D. "Oscars May Have Black Host, but All White Nominees in Top Categories." NBC News, January 14, 2016. https://www.nbcnews.com/news/nbcblk/oscars-may-have-black-host-all-white-nominees-top-categories-n496401.

Soriano, César G., and Ann Oldenburg. "With America at War, Hollywood Follows." *USA Today*, February 8, 2005.

Stanley, T. I. "The Color of Money: Hollywood Diversifies." *Ad Age*, August 30, 2004. https://adage.com/article/news/color-money-hollywood-diversifies/100260.

Steinberg, Brian. "ABC Seeks $2 Million to $3 Million for Oscar Ads (Exclusive)." *Variety*, December 11, 2018. https://variety.com/2018/tv/news/oscars-advertising-abc-commercials-kevin-hart-1203086442/.

Stockdale, Charles, and Evan Comen. "Most Bankable Actors of 2018." MSN, December 20, 2018. https://www.msn.com/en-us/movies/gallery/most-bankable-actors-of-2018/ss-BBReOwm.

Sullivan, Emily. "Laura Ingraham Told LeBron James to Shut Up and Dribble; He Went to the Hoop." NPR, February 19, 2018. https://www.npr.org/sections/thetwo-way/2018/02/19/587097707/laura-ingraham-told-lebron-james-to-shutup-and-dribble-he-went-to-the-hoop.

Sullivan, Kevin P. "A Guide to December's Best In-Flight Movies, Sorted by Airline." *Vulture*, December 7, 2018. https://www.vulture.com/2018/12/best-plane-flight-movies-airlines-2018.html.

Thomas, Dexter. "Oscar-Nominated 'Hidden Figures' Was Whitewashed—but It Didn't Have to Be." *Vice*, January 25, 2017. https://www.vice.com/en_us/article/d3xmja/oscar-nominated-hidden-figures-was-whitewashed-but-it-didnt-have-to-be.

Tinubu, Aramide A. "Disney's Racist Cartoons Won't Just Stay Hidden in the Vault. But They Could Be Used as a Teachable Moment." NBC News, April 25, 2019. https://www.nbcnews.com/think/opinion/disney-s-racist-cartoons-won-t-just-stay-hidden-vault-ncna998216.

Trucco, Terry. "Denzel Washington Acclaimed in Biko Role." *Chicago Tribune*, December 30, 1987. https://www.chicagotribune.com/news/ct-xpm-1987-12-30-8704060865-story.html.

United Press International. "Court Lets Stand Workers Comp for Blacks Phobia," June 28, 1991. https://www.upi.com/Archives/1991/06/28/Court-lets-stand-workers-comp-for-Blacks-phobia/7592678081600/.

United States Census Bureau. "2010 Census Shows America's Diversity," March 24, 2011. https://www.census.gov/newsroom/releases/archives/2010_census/cb11-cn125.html.

VanAirsdale, S. T. "The Oscars: Ruby Dee's Surprise Party." *Vanity Fair*, January 30, 2008. https://www.vanityfair.com/news/2008/01/the-oscars-ruby.

Voytko, Lisette. "Universal Announces New Orlando Theme Park, Promises 14,000 New Jobs." *Forbes*, August 1, 2019. https://www.forbes.com/sites/lisette voytko/2019/08/01/universal-announces-new-orlando-theme-park-promises -14000-new-jobs/#7c20d73d5498.

White, Jack E. "Show Business: Just Another Mississippi Whitewash." *Time*, January 9, 1989. http://content.time.com/time/magazine/article/0,9171,956694,00.html.

Wilkinson, Alissa "The Chaotic Road to the 2019 Oscars Ceremony, Explained." *Vox*, February 16, 2019. https://www.vox.com/culture/2019/2/16/18226372/oscars -ceremony-category-best-song-revolt.

Willens, M. "Box Office Ticket Sales 2014: Revenues Plunge to Lowest in Three Years." *International Business Times*, January 5, 2015. http://www.ibtimes.com/box-office -ticket-sales-2014-revenues-plunge-lowest-three-years-1773368.

Williams, Lena. "Spike Lee Says Money from Blacks Saved 'X.'" *New York Times*, May 20, 1992. https://www.nytimes.com/1992/05/20/movies/spike-lee-says-money-from -blacks-saved-x.html.

Wiltz, Teresa. "'Mighty Heart' Casting Stirs Debate over Race." *Seattle Times*, June 27, 2007. https://www.seattletimes.com/entertainment/mighty-heart-casting-stirs -debate-over-race/.

Wylie, Jamie. "Oscars 2019 Presenters: Third Round Announced." Oscars, February 19, 2019. https://oscar.go.com/news/oscar-news/oscars-2019-presenters-third -round-announced.

Yardley, Jonathan "The Complex Thomas Jefferson in His Place and Time." *Washington Post*, May 12, 2017. https://www.washingtonpost.com/opinions/the-complex -thomas-jefferson-in-his-place-and-time/2017/05/12/969a131a-2e9e-11e7-8674 -437ddb6e813e_story.html.

BOOKS

Aleiss, Angela. *Making the White Man's Indian: Native Americans and Hollywood Movies*. Westport, CT: Praeger, 2005.

Amburn, Ellis. *Olivia de Haviland and the Golden Age of Hollywood*. Lanham, MD: Rowman & Littlefield, 2018.

Arnett, Jeffrey Jenson, ed. *Encyclopedia of Children, Adolescents, and the Media*. Thousand Oaks, CA: SAGE Publications, 2006.

Asher, Robert and Ronald Edsforth, eds. *Autowork*. Albany: State University of New York Press, 1995.

Baptist, Edward E. *The Half Has Never Been Told: Slavery and the Making of American Capitalism*. New York: Basic Books, 2016.

Barlow, William. *Voice Over: The Making of Black Radio*. Philadelphia: Temple University Press, 1999.

Barry, Kathleen. *Femininity in Flight: A History of Flight Attendants*. Chapel Hill, NC: Duke University Press, 2007.

Benshoff, Harry, and Sean Griffin. *America on Film: Representing Race, Class, Gender, and Sexuality at the Movies*. New York: John Wiley & Sons, 2011.

Bogle, Donald. *Dorothy Dandridge: A Biography*. New York: HarperCollins, 1999.

———. *Toms, Coons, Mulattoes, Mammies and Bucks: An Interpretive History of Blacks in American Films*. New York: Bloomsbury, 2016.

Bruchey, Stuart. *Enterprise: The Dynamic of a Free People*. Cambridge, MA: Harvard University Press, 1990.

Carroll, Lewis. *Alice's Adventures in Wonderland: And Through the Looking Glass*. New York: MacMillan, 1897.

Cobb, James C. *The Most Southern Place on Earth: The Mississippi Delta and the Roots of Regional Identity*. New York: Oxford University Press, 1994.

Donald, Ralph. *Hollywood Enlists! Propaganda Films of World War II*. Lanham, MD: Rowman & Littlefield, 2017.

Entman, Robert M., and Andrew Rojecki. *The Black Image in the White Mind: Media and Race in America*. Chicago: University of Chicago Press, 2010.

Feinstein, Rachel A. *When Rape Was Legal: The Untold History of Sexual Violence during Slavery*. New York: Routledge, 2018.

Flack, Jerry D. *TalentEd: Strategies for Developing the Talent in Every Learner*. Englewood, CO: Teacher Ideas Press, 1993.

Flora, Joseph M., and Lucinda Hardwick, eds. *The Companion to Southern Literature: Themes, Genres, Places, People, Movements, and Motifs*. Baton Rouge: Louisiana State University Press, 2002.

Foster, Gwendolyn Audrey. *Performing Whiteness: Postmodern Re/Constructions in the Cinema*. Albany: State University of New York Press, 2003.

Frampton, Daniel. *Filmosophy*. New York: Wallflower Press, 2006.

Fredrickson, George. *The Black Image in the White Mind: The Debate on Afro-American Character and Destiny, 1817–1914*. New York: Harper & Row, 1971.

German, Kathleen M. *Promises of Citizenship: Film Recruitment of African Americans in World War II*. Jackson: University Press of Mississippi, 2017.

Gooding, Frederick W. Jr. *American Dream Deferred: Black Federal Workers in Washington, DC, 1941–1981*. Pittsburgh: University of Pittsburgh Press, 2018.

———. *You Mean, There's RACE in My Movie? The Complete Guide to Understanding Race in Mainstream Hollywood*. Silver Spring, MD: On the Reelz Press, 2007.

Green, Lisa J. *African American English: A Linguistic Introduction*. New York: Cambridge University Press, 2002.

Greene, Eric. *Planet of the Apes as American Myth: Race and Politics in the Films and Television Series*. Jefferson, NC: McFarland, 1996.

Haskell, Molly. *From Reverence to Rape: The Treatment of Women in the Movies*. Chi-cago: University of Chicago Press, 2016.

Heilmann, Ann. *Mark Llewellyn, Neo-Victorianism: The Victorians in the Twenty-First Century, 1999–2009*. New York: Palgrave Macmillan, 2010.

Herringshaw, DeAnn. *Dorothy Dandridge: Singer & Actress*. Edina, MN: ABDO, 2011.

Hill, Errol, and James V. Hatch. *A History of African American Theatre*. New York: Cambridge University Press, 2003.

Hollinger, Karen. *Feminist Film Studies*. New York: Routledge, 2012.

Horton, James Oliver. *Landmarks of African American History*. New York: Oxford University Press, 2005.

Ignatiev, Noel. *How the Irish became White*. New York: Routledge, 1995.

Jenkins, Henry. *Wow Climax: Tracing the Emotional Impact of Popular Culture*. New York: New York University Press, 2007.

Johnson, Allan G. *Privilege, Power and Difference*. Mountain View, CA: Mayfield, 2001.

Korkis, Jim. *Who's Afraid of the Song of the South? And Other Forbidden Disney Stories*. Orlando: Theme Park Press, 2012.

Lamparski, Richard. *Whatever Became Of . . . ?* Eighth Series. New York: Crown, 1982.

Lamphier, Peg A., and Rosanne Welch. *Women in American History: A Social, Political, and Cultural Encyclopedia and Document Collection*. Santa Barbara, CA: ABC-CLIO, 2017.

Lanehart, Sonja L., ed. *The Oxford Handbook of African American Language*. New York: Oxford University Press, 2015.

LeFlouria, Talitha L. *Chained in Silence: Black Women and Convict Labor in the New South*. Chapel Hill: University of North Carolina Press, 2015.

Lynch, Annette, and Mitchell D. Strauss. *Ethnic Dress in the United States: A Cultural Encyclopedia*. Lanham, MD: Rowman & Littlefield, 2015.

Manning, Harriet J. *Michael Jackson and the Blackface Mask*. New York: Routledge, 2016.

Mapp, Edward. *African Americans and the Oscar: Decades of Struggle and Achievement*. Lanham, MD: Scarecrow Press, 2008.

McEwan, Paul. *The Birth of a Nation*. New York: Bloomsbury, 2015.

McGinn, Colin. *The Power of Movies: How Screen and Mind Interact*. New York: First Vintage Books, 2005.

McKenzie, Lisa. *Getting By: Estates, Class and Culture in Austerity Britain*. Chicago: Policy Press, 2015.

Mills, Earl. *Dorothy Dandridge: An Intimate Biography*. New York: Holloway House, 1999.

Moehring, Eugene P., and Michael S. Green. *Las Vegas: A Centennial History*. Reno: University of Nevada Press, 2005.

Mosco, Vincent, and Catherine McKercher. *The Laboring of Communication: Will Knowledge Workers of the World Unite?* Lanham, MD: Rowman & Littlefield, 2009.

Nevid, Jeffrey S., and Spencer A. Rathus. *Psychology and the Challenges of Life*. Hoboken, NJ: John Wiley & Sons, 2012.

Nissen, Axel. *Actresses of a Certain Character: Forty Familiar Hollywood Faces from the Thirties to the Fifties*. Jefferson, NC: McFarland, 1975.

Pawlak, Debra Ann. *Bringing Up Oscar: The Story of the Men and Women Who Founded the Academy*. New York: Pegasus Books, 2011.

Pederson, Charles E. *Thomas Edison*. Edina, MN: ABDO, 2007.

Petty, Miriam J. *Stealing the Show: African American Performers and Audiences in 1930s Hollywood*. Oakland: University of California Press, 2016.

Prince, Stephen. *Classical Film Violence: Designing and Regulating Brutality in Hollywood Cinema, 1930–1968*. New Brunswick, NJ: Rutgers University Press, 2003.

Regester, Charlene. *African American Actresses: The Struggle for Visibility, 1900–1960*. Bloomington: Indiana University Press, 2010.

Roberts, Brian. *Blackface Nation: Race, Reform, and Identity in American Popular Music, 1812–1925*. Chicago: University of Chicago Press, 2017.

Robinson, Cedric J. *Forgeries of Memory and Meaning: Blacks and the Regimes of Race in American Theater and Film before World War II*. Chapel Hill: University of North Carolina Press, 2012.

Roediger, David R. *The Wages of Whiteness: Race and the Making of the American Working Class*. New York: Verso Books, 1999.

Smith, Andrew F., ed. *The Oxford Companion to American Food and Drink*. New York: Oxford University Press, 2007.

Sperb, Jason. *Disney's Most Notorious Film: Race, Convergence, and the Hidden Histories of 'Song of the South'*. Austin: University of Texas Press, 2012.

Stempel, Tom, and Phillip Dunne. *Framework: A History of Screenwriting in the American Film*. Syracuse, NY: Syracuse University Press, 2000.

Stowe, Harriet Beecher. *A Key to Uncle Tom's Cabin: Presenting the Original Facts and Documents upon Which the Story Is Founded together with Corroborative Statements Verifying the Truth of the Work*. Boston: John P. Jewett, 1853.

Strausbaugh, John. *Black Like You: Blackface, Whiteface, Insult & Imitation in American Popular Culture*. New York: Penguin, 2006.

Sue, Derald Wing. *Microaggressions in Everyday Life: Race, Gender and Sexual Orientation*. Hoboken, NJ: John Wiley & Sons, 2010.

Sutherland, Jean-Anne, and Kathyrn Feltey, eds. *Cinematic Sociology: Social Life in Film*. Thousand Oaks, CA: SAGE Publications, 2013.

Umphlett, Wiley Lee. *The Movies Go to College: Hollywood and the World of the College-Life Film*. Cranbury, NJ: Associated University Presses, 1984.

Vera, Hernán, and Andrew M. Gordon. *Screen Saviors: Hollywood Fictions of Whiteness.* Lanham, MD: Rowman & Littlefield, 2003.

Watts, Jill. *Hattie McDaniel: Black Ambition, White Hollywood.* New York: HarperCollins, 2007.

Welky, David. *Everything Was Better in America: Print Culture in the Great Depression.* Urbana: University of Illinois Press, 2008.

Wetta, Frank J., and Martin A. Novelli. *The Long Reconstruction: The Post–Civil War South in History, Film, and Memory.* New York: Routledge, 2014.

Wharton, David, and Jeremy Grant. *Teaching Analysis of Film Language.* London: British Film Institute, 2005.

Williams, Justin A., ed. *The Cambridge Companion to Hip-Hop.* Cambridge: Cambridge University Press, 2015.

Williams, Linda. *Playing the Race Card: Melodramas of Black and White from Uncle Tom to O.J. Simpson.* Princeton, NJ: Princeton University Press, 2001.

Williams-Forson, Psyche A. *Building Houses Out of Chicken Legs: Black Women, Food, and Power.* Chapel Hill: University of North Carolina Press, 2006.

Wilson, Douglas, and G. Tyler Fischer. *Omnibus III: Reformation to the Present.* Lancaster, PA: Veritas Press, 2006.

Wittern-Keller, Laura. *Freedom of Screen: Legal Challenges to State Film Censorship, 1915–1981.* Lexington: University Press of Kentucky, 2008.

FILMS

Green Pastures. Directed by Mark Connelly and William Keighley. Burbank, CA: Warner Bros., 1936.

Hollywood Shuffle. Directed by Robert Townsend. Los Angeles: Samuel Goldwyn Company, 1987.

Pinky. Directed by Elia Kazan. Hollywood, CA: Columbia Pictures, 1949.

JOURNAL ARTICLES/BOOK CHAPTERS

Benbow, Mark E. "Birth of a Quotation: Woodrow Wilson and 'Like Writing History with Lightning.'" *Journal of the Gilded Age and Progressive Era* 9, no. 4, 509–33.

Cott, Jonathan. "The Good Dr. Seuss." In *Of Sneetches and Whos and the Good Dr. Seuss: Essays on the Writings and Life of Theodor Geisel,* edited by Thomas Fensch, 99–123. Jefferson, NC: McFarland, 1983.

Ellison, Ralph. "What America Would Be without Blacks." In *Black on White: Black Writers on What It Means to Be White*, edited by David R. Roediger, 160–71. New York: Shocken Books, 1998.

Freidman, Lester D. "Black Like Him: Steven Spielberg's 'The Color Purple.'" In *The Persistence of Whiteness: Race and Contemporary Hollywood Cinema*, edited by Daniel Berardi, 292–314. New York: Routledge, 2008.

Handzo, Steven. "Intimations of Lifelessness." *Bright Lights Film Journal* (winter 1977): 6.

Hayward, Susan. "Hollywood." In *Cinema Studies: The Key Concepts*. New York: Routledge, 2006.

Hunt, Megan. "Hollywood's Southern Strategy: Portraying White Christianity in Late Twentieth-Century Civil Rights Melodramas." In *Southern History on Screen: Race and Rights, 1976–2016*, edited by Bryan M. Jack, 155–80. Lexington: University Press of Kentucky, 2019.

Kassarjian, Harold H. "The Negro and American Advertising, 1946–1965." *Journal of Marketing Research* 6, no. 1 (February 1969): 143–44.

Knight, Arthur. "Star Dances: African American Constructions of Stardom, 1925–1960." In *Classic Hollywood, Classic Whiteness*, edited by Daniel Berardi, 386–414. Minneapolis: University of Minnesota Press, 2001.

Leger, J. P. "Trends and Causes of Fatalities in South African Mines." *Safety Science* 14 (1991): 169–85.

McPherson, Tara. "Revamping the South: Thoughts on Labor, Relationality, and Southern Representation." In *American Cinema and the Southern Imaginary*, edited by Deborah E. Barker and Kathryn McKee, 336–52. Athens: University of Georgia Press, 2011.

Prorokova, Tatiana. "Intergenerational Struggle and Racial Progress in 'The Help' and 'The Butler.'" In *Southern History on Screen: Race and Rights, 1976–2016*, edited by Bryan M. Jack, 199–210. Lexington: University of Press Kentucky, 2019.

Richardson, Riché. "Mammy's 'Mules' and the Rules of Marriage in 'Gone with the Wind.'" In *American Cinema and the Southern Imaginary*, edited by Deborah E. Barker and Kathryn McKee, 52–78. Athens: University of Georgia Press, 2011.

Rippy, Marguerite H. "Commodity, Tragedy, Desire: Female Sexuality and Blackness in the Iconography of Dorothy Dandridge." In *Classic Hollywood, Classic Whiteness*, edited by Daniel Berardi, 178–209. Minneapolis: University of Minnesota Press, 2001.

Streible, Dan. "Race and the Reception of Jack Johnson Fight Films." In *The Birth of Whiteness: Race and the Emergence of U.S. Cinema*, edited by Daniel Berardi, 170–200. New Brunswick, NJ: Rutgers University Press, 1996.

Ulin, Donald Ingram. "From '*Huckleberry Finn*' to '*The Shawshank Redemption*': Race and the American Imagination in the Biracial Escape Film." *European Journal of American Studies* 8, no. 1 (spring 2013). http://journals.openedition.org/ejas/10026.

LEGAL CASES

Brown v. Board of Education of Topeka. 347 U.S. 483 (1954).
Joseph Burstyn, Inc. v. Wilson. 343 U.S. 495 (1952).
Loving v. Virginia, 388 U.S. 1 (1967).

PAPERS/REPORTS

Certificate, "In Memory of Our Friend." Hattie and Sam McDaniel Papers, Margaret
   Herrick Library, AMPAS.
Committee for Unity in Motion Pictures. First Annual Motion Picture Unity Award As-
   sembly Program, April 23, 1944. Hattie and Sam McDaniel Papers, Margaret Herrick
   Library, AMPAS.
Directors Guild of America. "DGA Publishes Inaugural Feature Film Diversity
   Report: Two-Year Study Reveals Women Account for Only 6.4% of Film Direc-
   tor—Dropping to Just 3% for Major Box Office Titles," December 9, 2015. https://
   www.dga.org/News/PressReleases/2015/151209-DGA-Publishes-Inaugural-Feature
   -Film-Diversity-Report.aspx#fn1.
Equal Justice Initiative. "Lynching in America: Confronting the Legacy of Racial Ter-
   ror," n.d. https://lynchinginamerica.eji.org/report/.
Hunt, Darnell, and Ana-Christina Ramón. *2015 Hollywood Diversity Report: Flipping
   the Script.* Ralph J. Bunche Center for African American Studies at UCLA, Febru-
   ary 2015. https://bunchecenter.pre.ss.ucla.edu/wp-content/uploads/sites/82/2015
   /02/2015-Hollywood-Diversity-Report-2-25-15.pdf.
Letter, Hattie McDaniel to Hedda Hopper, March 29, 1947. Hedda Hopper Papers.
   Margaret Herrick Library, AMPAS.
Letter, Marlon Brando to Lew R. Wasserman of MCA Universal, January 23, 1976.
   Lisabeth Hush Collection on Sex Discrimination against Women. Margaret Herrick
   Library, AMPAS.
Mitchell, Gregg. "WGAW Releases 2016 Hollywood Writers Report." Writers Guild of
   America West, March 24, 2016. https://www.wga.org/news-events/news/press/2016
   /wgaw-releases-hollywood-writers-report.
Screen Actors Guild–American Federation of Television and Radio Artists. "Perform-
   ers Bear Brunt of Reality TV and Runaway Production Trends, 2003 Casting Data
   Shows," October 6, 2004. https://www.sagaftra.org/casting-data-reports.
Smith, Stacy L. "Inequality in 1,200 Popular Films: Examining Portrayals of Gender,
   Race/Ethnicity, LGBTQ & Disability from 2007 to 2018." USC Annenberg Inclu-
   sion Initiative, September 2019, 18. https://annenberg.usc.edu/sites/default/files
   /Dr_Stacy_L_Smith-Inequality_in_900_Popular_Films.pdf.

US Bureau of the Census. *Changing Characteristics of the Negro Population.* Washington, DC: Government Printing Office, 1969.

WEBSITES

AMC Filmsite. "Filmsite Movie Review." https://www.filmsite.org/defi.html.

"Favorite Oscar® Moment – Adrien Brody Kissing Halle Berry." February 20, 2011. https://www.youtube.com/watch?v=2isqa6BLtkA.

Grammy.com. "Grammy Hall of Fame Award." http://www.grammy.com/grammys/awards/hall-of-fame.

Internet Movie Database. "'The Defiant Ones': Taglines." https://www.imdb.com/title/tt0051525/taglines.

Library of Congress. "About this Collection." https://www.loc.gov/collections/selections-from-the-national-film-registry/about-this-collection/.

Monticello. "The Life of Sally Hemmings." https://www.monticello.org/sallyhemings/.

Motion Picture Association of America. "About Us." http://www.mpaa.org/AboutUs.asp.

———. "Production Code Administration Records." http://digitalcollections.oscars.org/cdm/landingpage/collection/p15759coll30.

Moving Image Research Center, Library of Congress online. http://www.loc.gov/rr/mopic/.

Oscars.org. "Oscars Statuette." https://www.oscars.org/oscars/statuette.

———. "Results." http://awardsdatabase.oscars.org/Search/Nominations?nominationId=2120&view=1-Nominee-Alpha.

UN Women. "Goodwill Ambassadors." https://www.unwomen.org/en/partnerships/goodwill-ambassadors.

United States Postal Service. "Subject: Black History Month," December 2005. https://about.usps.com/postal-bulletin/2005/html/pb22170/kittxt6.html.

INDEX

Page references for figures are italicized.

ABOUT THE AUTHOR

Frederick W. Gooding Jr. is an assistant professor of African American studies within the Honors College at Texas Christian University in Fort Worth, Texas. Gooding critically analyzes race within mainstream media, effectively contextualizing contemporary problematic patterns based upon their historical roots.